Raising Your Cat

Raising

Your Cat

A
COMPLETE
ILLUSTRATED
GUIDE

by

ROSANNE
AMBERSON

BONANZA BOOKS, NEW YORK

All photographs by
Rosanne Amberson and Wesley B. McKeown
unless otherwise credited

ACKNOWLEDGMENTS

The author especially wishes to acknowledge the assistance of Frederick
B. Tierney, D.V.M., Head Veterinarian, The Humane Society of New
York, who has not only served as adviser on book content, but has acted
as a close consultant on all health-care and medical material.

Deep appreciation also goes to Mark L. Morris, Jr., D.V.M., of Mark
Morris Associates, whose thoughtful criticisms and extensive comments
on the first draft of the nutrition section were of immeasurable value.

To Ralph W. Jackson, D.V.M., many thanks for a careful reading of
the manuscript and for the use of his clinic—and himself—for some essential photography.

To my brother William R. Amberson, Ph.D., Marine Biological Laboratory, who helped to evaluate and equate human physiology with animal physiology—sincere thanks.

The author is also most grateful for the cooperation and new information on nutrition and health care which has come from the veterinary
colleges and schools at: Clayton Foundation, University of Texas; Con-
naught Medical Research Laboratories, University of Toronto; Washing-
ton State University; University of Pennsylvania; Ohio State University;
University of California; University of Missouri; Cornell University.

Other important scientific data has been made available for inclusion
in this book through: Society for International Veterinary Symposia;
National 4H service; National Academy of Sciences; American Veterinary
Medical Association; American Veterinary Publications, Inc., whose text
Feline Medicine and Surgery brings together research reports from some

thirty-one national and international feline experts; Mark Morris Foundation; *Veterinary Medicine,* a monthly publication for the small-animal clinician.

Commercial organizations interested in feline nutrition and health care have also made available significant findings: B. A. Bernard & Co. Inc.; Roy Goff and Company; Carnation Company; H. J. Heinz Company; Hartz Mountain Products, Inc.; Gaines Research Center; Elanco Products; Fromm Laboratories; Hoffman LaRoche Inc.; Merck, Sharp and Dohme.

And lastly but far from least, my unending thanks to two people who have made this book possible: Jeffry Gorney who prepared most of this manuscript for press, and Ann Purtill who has lived with the book since its inception, and done thousands of chores for it, including preparation, single-handed, of an excellent index.

6

CONTENTS

A WORD BY
Frederick B. Tierney, D.V.M.
Head Veterinarian, The Humane Society of New York

It is with great pleasure that I introduce you to this excellent new book on cat care and management. Over the years, there have been many "cat-care" books. To the best of my knowledge none has incorporated such a wealth of information, especially in the nutritional and medical areas. As it goes to press, this book reports, and in simple language, translates the most important of the recent findings now available in published research and in technical articles. Personal communication with recognized experts in the field has added new data which gives the book a sharp and modern focus.

For the pet owners and their veterinarians, there are some especially interesting chapters. "What to Do Until the Doctor Comes" not only helps the owner develop a keen eye for the detection of health problems, but also details what simple home remedies can be used, and when home treatment should not be attempted under any circumstances. Too little observation or recognition of signs or symptoms often means too late for treatment or cure. Another valuable chapter, "Health and Disease," makes easy reading of normally dull technical material. The author points out many of the amazing similarities between cat and man in body structure, body functioning, and in the diseases and ailments to which cats and people are prone.

Photographically, this book is also unusual. Many of the nearly two hundred illustrations are how-to-do pictures which guide the cat owner in proper methods of care, handling, training, and treatment. In addition, these illustrations capture those delightful and elusive qualities of the cat family which have made it so well loved.

It has been my pleasure to work with the author in determining the scope of health-care and medical information, in checking the new research, and in evaluating its interpretation to meet the needs of the present-day pet owner. For people who have never had a cat, this volume offers solid basic material. For the experienced pet owner, there is significant new information, and for every reader, there are many amusing and telling anecdotes drawn from the author's long and warm relationship with her own pets.

A WORD BY
Ralph W. Jackson, D.V.M.
Clinton, New Jersey

This is a book that every cat owner should read. It answers practically all of the questions asked the veterinarian, and the answers are both simple and sound. The photographs are interesting and helpful. The book should get into the hands of all people, young and old, who are involved in or training for occupations in either veterinary or animal-care fields, for it blends practical information with new and up-to-date research.

I have known the author for more than thirty years, first, during the days when she and her husband ran a diversified farm in my community, and later when she moved to the city with the present members of her cat family. It was a pig—not a cat—that first brought us together, a farrowing sow with a nutritional deficiency. As the years went by, we had many patients: a cow, a calf, a foal—and even chickens. When the snow was too deep for travel we figured things out by phone. I might add that I know most of the cats mentioned in this book, and have given them routine care as well as emergency treatment. Stories and anecdotes about the hundreds of cats the author has raised and loved bring the book alive and make it hard to put down.

The author's close association with all kinds of animals—the big ones as well as the little ones, and some wild ones—during the years she lived in the country is reflected throughout the book.

To both the new and the experienced cat owner, the chapters on nutrition and medical care will be revelations.

Even the busy practicing veterinarian finds it difficult to keep up with the volume of new research on cats that has been pouring in from all over the world in recent years.

There are other chapters I should like to recommend: "Growing Old Gracefully" provides essential information for cat owners who want to keep their old friend young. "There Is No Place Like Home for Cat Accidents" gives practical information for country as well as city families with cat pets. I must admit that I relish the chapter on "Choosing Your Veterinarian." It may seem odd for a veterinarian to suggest the chapter on "ESP and IQ," but although the animal doctor is a trained clinician and must be relative and objective, he cannot fail to recognize the unusual sensitivities of animals. Indeed, if he forgets or fails to recognize the outer limits, he is never a whole doctor.

This book has that strange thing called "heart," and the author has an uncanny knowledge of cats—their personalities, their skills, their intelligence, and their behavior patterns.

9

My great old lady, Pink. It was watching her for more than eighteen years that taught me much of what I know about cats.

1

The Cat Watchers

The society of cat watchers is an ancient and honorable one. Its membership has included kings and pirates, sailors and scientists, sculptors and cartoonists, photographers and poets, to say nothing of millions of just plain everyday folks who get a kick out of watching and watching over cats. No one other animal has brought so much joy and fun into the lives of so many diverse people. Just in the United States alone, the family cat count is placed at roughly twenty million, and guess estimates double and triple this number. The cat is a worker, an actor, a playmate, a companion, and an important factor in our much-vaunted economy, for, to satisfy his needs, vast and thriving industries have come into being, and billions of dollars of TV and radio time promote the products he uses and consumes.

Just what is it about this slightly daffy and endlessly interesting little creature that gives him his greatest appeal? His spirit of independence and love of freedom? His great physical beauty in colorings, markings, and fluid movement? Undoubtedly these are major attractions, but I think the issue goes much deeper. In the middle of a world that has always been a bit mad, the cat walks with confidence. He is natural, normal, adjustable to many environments. He is neat and clean, loving and sensitive. He has few inhibitions and practically no hostilities unless he is attacked. He rarely loses his sense of humor, is not a status seeker, couldn't care less about keeping up with the Joneses. He has no race

11

prejudice and understands the Establishment. By his very presence in a home, a cat provides entertainment, teaches good manners, and releases tensions. Indeed, he knows more about the humanities than most humans, and he even helps you keep the faith. Far from being an overstatement, this is probably an understatement.

It has been my sincere belief for many years that in every home where there are what we now call "senior citizens," there should be a cat, preferably a mother cat who has kittens quite regularly. I remember a charming old Frenchwoman who came to visit us at the farm. She had just had a bad session with a broken hip. This spelled the end to her very active career as a professional artist. As usual, I had a lively kitten litter growing up under the watchful eye of a wise mother cat. As my tired and worried friend watched these gay youngsters run, jump, tussle, go back to mother for a snack and policing, then suddenly drop into the deep sleep of baby animals, that taut, tired look of anxiety drained out of her face. She laughed and talked and visibly lost years.

The protective concern that the cat engenders is a really extraordinary thing indeed. This concern reaches out beyond personal pets to the entire cat family. Recently I stood in line at the supermarket as a well-dressed, pleasant woman next to me unloaded an array of cat foods on the check-out counter. She made it her business, she said, to pick up the strays in Central Park. She had found homes for a hundred or more, or taken the sick ones to one of the city's animal shelter centers. How many of her own did she have? "Just seven," she said, "just seven." Judging from the ratio of people food to the pet food she was buying, those seven were being cared for with intelligence as well as love. "When I die," said she with a smile, "I want to go to whatever heaven has cats. I've made a little contract with God."

A rather astonishing number of veterinarians and animal health experts who write profound papers for technical journals turn out to be cat people. In the many months during which I have been reading scientific literature, I've spotted these people almost instantly. Even in careful and exact reports on surgery and disease control, their warm interest comes through as it does not so often do when the writer is reporting on dogs, cattle, or horses.

As for myself, I am an old-line cat watcher. I have known and enjoyed something more than three hundred of the cat clan who have lived with me on a big country farm and in city apartments. Not all at the same time, I hasten to add, lest you doubt my sanity. To my life they have brought a richness of experience which I have tried to project in this book.

As a veteran cat watcher I nominate this as one of my favorite pictures. The deep and warm relationship between two cats who live together and like it is a lovely thing to see.

2

That Fascinating Family
of Felines

Like all Gaul, the cat family is divided into three parts: the common house cat, who is the product of chance mating and, more often than not, a blend of many breeds; the purebred cat whose breeding has been organized to fix desirable qualities; and show cats, the royalty of the purebred group, outstanding examples of their own special breed, trained and groomed for public show, prime breeding stock rather than pets.

Some people prefer to divide the cat kingdom into longhairs and shorthairs. Some would rather classify according to body structure. Take your choice. Everybody can win accordingly.

Scores of books and thousands of words have been written on breeds and breeding. Cat fancier organizations issue exact specifications for accurate judging. All this body information is available to serious breeders or just interested cat owners, and at a nominal price. So, too, are the rules of show and showing, and the names and addresses of local cat clubs for every known breed. There is no need for this book to repeat what has already been published many times. What I will attempt to do is to give you an overview of the worldwide cat family.

World Citizen. Today's family cat—whether purebred or without pride of ancestry—is a true world citizen. Whether he originally appeared in many widely separated places at exactly the same time, no one really knows. From records found in the Nile Valley we do know surely that cat and man have lived together some 5,000 years. And as we check the languages of the world, we find a word for "cat" in practically all tongues. Obviously, over the centuries he has bred with many of his wild cousins—mates selected by him and not for him. Adjusting to cold climates, he grew long protective hair; and when this warmth was nonessential, nature seems to have clipped his coat short.

Generations of travelers have had a profound influence on the spread and development of the cat family. The caravans of Genghis Khan included cats. The Roman invaders of Egypt fell under the feline spell. Sailors from every part and port of the world imported not just spices and tea, rugs and silks, but delightful and entertaining animals—often cats.

Push back into sailing history and what do we discover? With the kind of spot check true historians detest, we learn that the Manx cat, often tailless, did not originate on the Isle of Man, but was introduced by way of the Spanish Armada, in 1588, and may well have been the first ship's cat. Tracing back still further, we discover that the origin of this husky, water-loving animal was probably Malaya, where he swam from island to island to mate with other cat creatures.

Move forward to the day in 1620 when the Puritans made their voyage into what was then outer space. With them they brought cats, the progenitors of our domestic shorthairs. As prowlers and mousers, the Puritan cats helped to carry the early American Colonists through disaster. They held at bay or destroyed the smaller rodents who threatened to eat up food much needed for human consumption.

Jump two centuries to the 1830's and meet the Maine sailor, a man of a hardy breed. His instinct for acquiring small interesting animals rang loud and clear. From foreign parts his kind brought back not one but dozens of beautiful cats. These world citizens, every color and breed, interbred and produced a fine line of most unusual cats who grew increasingly longer haired as they adjusted to the bitter cold of the Maine climate. Today's magnificent coon cat springs from this mixed-up breeding and not from a mating of cat with coon, as fable would have us believe. Maine folk are fiercely proud of their cats, think their animals the smartest in the world, and have been at the American forefront in establishing local breed associations and clubs.

It is to the English, however, that cat lovers and breeders owe the great debt. As hosts to the Empire dignitaries—who often brought their cats—the English saw the need for breeding standards. Under the patient and careful eye of the British, the first registrations were made and well-defined breeds emerged. A war that almost shattered England almost destroyed the cat-breeding industry. With the sky of England filled with bombers but "not in Hitler's hands," and with a scarcity of food so great that children could not be adequately fed, cat breeders denied themselves to keep some small bit of purebred catdom alive. From England come not only fine cats but some of the best and most exciting findings on feline health, care, and nutrition.

And now, today, American cat breeders along with world breeders are producing beautiful, intelligent animals who have earned an important place in our modern society. It is undoubtedly a pity that more effort is going into the reproduction of exceptional animal strains than is expended on the development of better human beings. However, the intricate study of animal genetics is pointing the way to better human genetics.

Breeding Is a Matter of Degree. Although planned parenthood for cats is controlled by man, the results are not absolute. There are degrees of quality in each and every litter. The basic purpose of breeding is to fix certain characteristics of bone structure, coat and eye colorings, distinctive markings, and length of hair—characteristics that breeders and cat lovers want, like, and demand. Several new breeds are even now in the making, breeds that focus particular attention on new coat colors and new hair textures.

With the most expert of breeding and close attention to genetics, a fair percentage of the kittens comes close to or exactly meets the accepted standards. These top-quality purebreds have great beauty and command high prices.

In a second-class position comes that large number of equally well-bred cats who, though lovely, are lacking in perfection. All these cats justify "papers" showing their bloodlines and are eligible for registration in the books of the cat fancier associations.

Moving down another degree, we find thousands of cats who are sold as Persians or Siamese or any other known breed but who have no papers, cannot be registered, and may not be purebred at all, even if they seem to look the part. Some unscrupulous pet people—and there are a few—will try to unload these cats at bargain prices and will attempt to make arrangements to buy back kittens at even greater bargain prices.

From a breeding standpoint, the lowest level of cat society includes the millions of house pets who have no known bloodlines, delightful cats with attractive markings and colorings. These garden-variety cats occasionally duplicate the top qualities of an established breed. My Big Boy is a fine example. He is a true red tabby with mackerel markings. A soft, glowing

The Siamese, most popu-
lar of breeds, has the foreign or exotic body—not
naturally, but as the re-
sult of breeding to suit
owner tastes. The slim,
sleek body is delicate-look-
ing. The face is pointed
and the ears tipped rather
than rounded. The Sia-
mese is a swaggering buc-
caneer of a cat, but a
royal pirate.

This royal lady is Duch-
ess, and she looks the part.
Purebred Persian, she has
never been shown, for her
owners are only interested
in a house pet.

Calico—one of several tricolor cats whose interesting coats blend black, red, and white. White predominates on face, chest, belly, and legs. The three colors appear as a patched or quilted design with the patches clearly defined, and not running into each other to give an undesirable brindle look. Calicoes appear in both shorthair and longhair breeds.

The classic tabby, probably the original domesticated cat, who traces back to ancient Egypt. The traditional mottled design with well-defined stripings comes in red on lighter red, black on gray, blue on cream, black on brown. The swirling designs appear as bull's-eyes, buttons, goggles. There are well-defined stripes running from base of head to tail. Eye colorings vary with coat colorings.

A second type of tabby, the mackerel tabby, whose design name comes from the bone pattern of the fish of the same name. The true red tabby—my own Big Boy—with glowing red-gold coat, brilliant red-gold eyes and even the hairless parts of the body—lips, nose, mouth, and footpads—red. Necklaces and bracelets on neck and legs, rings on tail. And as with all tabbies, the face of the tiger.

red-gold coat. Well-defined necklaces and bracelets. Golden eyes. A graceful fluffy tail. An almost perfectly proportioned body. And, as in the true red tabby, hairless skin areas—foot pads, lips, rims of eyes, nostrils—all are red. He came from a chance mating of a calico mother and a black father. In eighteen years no other kitten from this calico mother had the same colorings or markings or body conformation. And Big Boy passed along none of his fine qualities to the kittens he sired. Genetically he is a sport.

The Basic Cat—The Tabby. Cat history being as inaccurate as it is, we are often forced to deal with theory rather than fact. When the domesticated cat (domesticated, not domestic) made his appearance, it was presumably in Egypt and he was presumably a tabby. The classic tabby pattern is a mottled pattern, with distinct stripes running from the masked or "M" head design to the base of the tail, and with whirls of concentric patterns—"bull's-eyes," "buttons," and "butterflies"—on the flanks, shoulder blades, and chest. Legs have bracelets, tails are ringed. A second type of tabby design, the mackerel design, takes its name from the skeleton of the fish it resembles. In this pattern, alternate, rather heavy lines of light and dark run down the flanks from the backbone, appear as necklaces and bracelets on legs and neck, and as rings on the tail.

Again and again, in many purebred strains, longhairs and shorthairs, these basic tabby patterns reappear. Sometimes the stripes and whirls are muted, sometimes very sharp. Sometimes flaked, almost shell-like. Always the face of a tabby is a tiger face.

Over years of chance matings, tabby marking often disappeared completely or became so faint that the cat seemed a solid color. Or amusing and attractive markings developed—a tabby design in any color mixed with white. My Pete is an excellent example of the partial tabby. Lemon-colored rather than red or red-gold, he has flaked stripes on his flanks, rings on the end of his tail. A solid-yellow shoulder patch, a duplicate of his mother's shoulder marking, which was in black. A lot of white trimming, including ridiculous white spectacles under his eyes, and solid white on belly and feet. Often it is this mixture of markings that gives the breedless cat his great personality. The irregular characteristics that drive breeders crazy are the very ones that enchant many pet lovers. Irving, out of my line, has a silly nose marking, a gamin blaze. Billy, like all of my "all white" cats, had one tiny tuft of coal-black hair. Blue, once again from my cat family tree, is almost a true English Blue, a deep, rich blue, not the soft lavender kind. He even has the thick plush coat and the foreign body of the true blue.

Every show has a house pet department, and here is where my Pete should be entered. He is that miraculous blend of many breeds.

Coming back to the purebreds, let me give you a very quick rundown on the descriptions of qualified shorthairs and longhairs.

SHORTHAIRS

Two Basic Body Types, Foreign and Domestic. Although structurally the cat's body has not changed in some fifty centuries, some distinct body types have developed. In the shorthairs we find two basic body types, usually described as "domestic," and "foreign" or "oriental." Essentially the domestic cat is a strongly and sturdily built animal, powerful and somewhat blocky. His head is roundish. Eyes, too, are round and well spaced, and the neck is rather short. The nose is well defined but not prominent. Ears erect and rounded at the tip are neither large nor small. Legs show a graceful proportion to the body, neither long nor short. Tail is heavy at the base where it joins the body and usually tapers to the end.

His opposite is the "oriental," often described as "exotic." In general, the oriental cat has slim rather than blocky body lines, slender legs, a pointed and sometimes heart-shaped face, with eyes rather widely spaced, occasionally slanted. The head has a slanted-back look with ears longer and more pointed than in the domestic breeds. The cat with a foreign body looks more delicately made, more fragile, daintier.

The foreign body-structure is not always the original one, but a shape that has been developed by breeding to satisfy a demand for the exotic. The Siamese, for example, originally a big, strong, and powerfully built cat, often with cross-eyes and a kinked tail, has been bred down to structural measurements and body size preferred by owners who have insisted on the slim, sleek, oriental look.

In speaking of feline body types, it must be remembered that a general type can vary from breed to breed. In the human race, we consider Chinese, Japanese, and Indonesians all to be Oriental, but we do not expect different peoples to duplicate each other exactly. So it is with cats.

Shorthairs Preferred. Shorthair enthusiasts are legion, and for the most excellent of reasons. In this great company of cats are many proud breeds.

At the head of the "domestic"-type list is that large family of American Domestics and their equally fine British cousins, who are almost exact counterparts. It has often been said, and rightly, that no one has ever known the full potential of the cat unless he has lived with one of the domestic shorthairs. They are both friendly and fearless, loving and independent, robust and powerful but immensely graceful, well mannered but mischievous—and their intelligence matches their beauty, both of which are great.

Two other breeds, the Manx and the Burmese, have much of the same square-built power of the "domestic" type, with both breeds showing special and distinctive features.

In the "oriental" division we find the Siamese, the so-called Russian Blue, the English Blue, the Abyssinian, the Korat, and among the newer breeds, the Rex and the Havana Brown.

All these breeds have an air of sleek elegance, somewhat more formality and gracious dignity in bearing than the domestics. Perhaps this is a carryover from long-past days, when such slim, distinguished animals were the pets of royalty. To many cat lovers the orientals have a very special appeal. The Siamese, for example, is probably *the* cat in most demand today.

Coat Colorings, Eye Colors, Markings. Very exact standards have been set for both quality of coat, its colorings and markings, and for the shade of eye most desirable. Eye colors that complement or contrast add outstanding appeal. Gold, red-gold, copper, red-orange, and orange eyes characterize many of the shorthair breeds. More rare and highly prized are the breeds with blue and green eyes.

AMERICAN DOMESTICS

To that familiar old question, "Does it come in another color?" the American Domestic has the answer. He not only comes in five solid colors—white, cream, black, blue, and red, but in beautiful two-toned and three-toned patterns blending different combinations of seven basic shades—the five just mentioned plus silver and brown. Patterns may be tabby, both the classic and mackerel varieties. They may be created by tippings or ticking of black on white. Some of the patterns may be patched as in the tricolor breeds. Shaded coats, toning from soft but distinct hues to all-white, add another beauty note to this amazing variety.

Solid Colors must be truly solid, with not one single contrasting hair, not any sign, however faint, of patterns. *White* must be a glistening, snowy white. *Cream*, a rich, soft cream of one color value down to the hair roots. *Black* must be coal black; and *red*, coppery and glowing, with no grayish tinge. In the *blues*, the lighter tones, toward the lavender shades, ·are preferred. The red-orange, orange, gold, and copper eye-tones appear in all the solid-color domestics except the *white*, who can have eyes of either blue or gold, and the *blue*, whose true eye color is green.

Tabbies come in four of the seven basic colors, brown, red, blue, silver. Essentially, these are two-toned cats. Classic or mackerel markings show up as black on a coppery-brown ground color, the same marking in black on a silver base coat, deep blue markings on bluish ivory, and deep red markings on a lighter red coat. Markings are strong, broad, not pencil-line thin. All the tabbies have golden eyes, copper or deep orange, except the Silver Tabby, whose eyes are a clear hazel green.

The mark of "M," the legendary mark of honor, adds to the charm of the tabby face. In many breeds, head marking simulates the "M." This is Nicolino, house pet of Mr. and Mrs. Frederic Tuten.

Photo by Michael Rabb

Patched patterns include the Tortoiseshell, the Calico and the Blue-Cream. Patching must be distinct and clear-cut, with no fade-through or overlap of one patch color into the adjoining one. A brindle or tipped look for the Tortoiseshell or the Blue-Cream is wrong. The orange-black-white coloring of the Tortoiseshell, and the two colors of the Blue-Cream must appear all over the body, including face, as sharply defined tufts or patches. In the Calico, patches are larger, a "quilt" pattern. White dominates on face, chest, legs, and paws. All three breeds of the patched domestics have copper or deep orange eyes.

Chinchilla. An undercoat of pure white with tippings of black scattered liberally over the body, including face and tail. This tipping gives a sparkling silvery effect. Dramatically contrasting eyes of green or blue-green.

Shaded Silver. Pure, unpatterned silver, shading softly from a middle-silver tone on the back ridge to a pure white on chin, chest and belly. And as in the Chinchilla, the eyes green or blue-green.

Smoke. Black and white with touches of silver. A coal-black outer coat, a white undercoat that peeps through the black. Silver frills at the neck, and silver ear tufts. Eyes, brilliant copper or deep orange.

OTHER SHORTHAIRS

Manx. The Manx is certainly not an oriental nor yet a true domestic type, but he comes closer to the domestic, for he has a powerful robust body and the short coupling of the working cat. The flank of the Manx is much deeper than that of any other breed. This water-loving swimmer is sometimes called the "bunny cat," for when he runs, the run is a kind of rabbit hop, due to immensely strong back legs, longer than front legs. Although thought of as a tailless cat, the Manx comes in three styles: tailless, short tail and medium-long tail. His thick double coat repeats all the classic colors, both in solids and patterns. For example, the coat may feature typical tabby markings, trimmings of a second color, such as an under-the-chin locket. Or the Manx may turn up as a Tortoiseshell or Calico. In eye coloring, shades and tones copy the standards for the domestics of similar color and pattern.

Burmese. Again not an oriental and not a typical domestic, but stocky, steerlike, powerfully built. Nothing fragile about this magnificent animal who is rather rare. His glossy satiny coat is a most distinctive seal brown, against which the wide-set orange eyes are startling.

Steerlike Burmese, rich sable brown with remarkable golden eyes. A sturdy body despite the oriental background. This cat is a champion, Ch. Margus' Kayah. Breeder-Owner, Margery S. Hoff.

Siamese. Unquestionably an oriental in modern-day breeding. A slim, swaggering buccaneer of a cat, with many of the qualities of a dog. He walks on leash like a dog, retrieves like a dog—but he jumps and climbs like a monkey, talks as incessantly as a parrot. In ground color he is fawn, although as a kitten his coat may be almost white or cream. His point markings on ears, muzzle, legs, and tail come in seal, chocolate, blue, and lilac. The hair coat is short and snugly fitted to the body, with ear hair paper-thin. Brilliant turquoise-blue eyes add to beauty.

Reputedly he helped to guard the palace walls. Certainly he loves the high places, which in an apartment may be the traverse rod of the draw curtains or the thin top of a door.

Abyssinian. Thought to be the royal Egyptian cat, this fascinating oriental has perhaps the strangest coat of all, for each hair is two- or three-colored—tawny fawn, ruddy brick, black on the tip, giving an allover rusty shade. The elegance of this cat lies not alone in body structure or coat coloring but in the look of proud, regal command. He seems to sense that he is a "biggie." Eyes are golden or copper.

Russian Blue. Like so many things labeled "Russian," the Russian Blue is only Russian to the Russians. Very probably he emerged from a British background, a sport in color, a dimmed black. Like all blue cats, his coat is unusually thick and soft, and the eyes are green or blue-green.

English Blue. Most of the English shorthairs have a domestic body much like the American Domestics, although they are called by their color—English White, English Black, and so on. Strangely, the English Blue has a foreign body type, delicately made with tipped rather than rounded ears, and the slender lines of the oriental. The blue coat is an exotic lavender blue, and the eyes a brilliant green. The fine colorings of the English Blue are not present in the kitten but develop as the cat reaches his second birthday.

Havana Brown. One of the new breeds, a cross of a Domestic shorthair and Siamese. The solid-brown coat of this handsome new cat is not seal brown, like the Burmese, but a rich chocolate brown. Eyes are in the red-orange family.

Rex. Another of the new breeds, this cat is really a mutant who sprang almost spontaneously from the Domestic Shorthairs. His outstanding characteristic is a curly coat. The English Rex maintains this curly quality throughout life. The German Rex shows the curly quality only as a kitten. The Rex can be found in all the seven basic colors—in solids, tabby markings, Tortoiseshell, and Calico. Despite his domestic background, the body type is most usually foreign. Eye colors follow the standard set for the domestics and depend on coat colors.

Old saber-tooth himself. Like many a cat, Chip has this characteristic which has generations behind it; a carryover from the days of tooth and claw.

LONGHAIRS

One Basic Body Type for the Longhairs. In body type, the longhairs are much less diverse than the shorthairs. There is one basic conformation, probably best called the "Persian." The body is cobby. Legs are short. The head has a massive look, with widespread round eyes and a broad, stubby nose. Ears are rather small and rounded. The silky, long-haired coat that covers the body is a sort of camouflage, for under this luxurious exterior lies a strong and sturdy bony skeleton, covered with steel-strong muscles, smooth and lithe.

Because they adhere quite consistently to one body type, there is far less variety in the longhairs. Breed differences depend almost entirely on coat colorings complementing or contrasting eye colors, patterns or markings. As with the American Domestics, the longhairs come in five of the seven basic solid colors—white, cream, black, blue, red. And in marking, we find once again the tabbies, the shaded patterns, the smokes, tipped or ticked designs and tricolors.

To avoid repetition, let me suggest that you turn back a few pages to read the color and marking descriptions for Domestic Shorthairs. The longhair family follows most of these same descriptions and standards. There are a few variations. In the solid or self-color class, purebred white Persians can be odd-eyed, have one blue, one gold eye. Smokes may be blue as well as black. Reds can introduce a Peke face, a dish-shaped face. Tabby patterns are mottled, have a moiré look. And a new color group called "Cameo" brings a new beauty—an ivory base coat with tippings of deeper cream and often red. Also, in the longhairs, the silvers form a special class, a wide range of silver beauties.

Origin of the Longhairs. The origins of the longhair cat are open to discussion. One opinion says that distant ancestors were wildcats with long hair. Another theory suggests that the longhair naturally developed in those parts of the world where cold and bitter climate made a warm coat essential. In years past, there were two well-known breeds of longhairs—Angoras and Persians. The Angora, from Ankara, Turkey, was very probably an all-white cat with a wedge-shaped face, wide-set but rather slanted eyes, medium-sized ears. The Persian, from the area of Afghanistan, had a more stubby look, a more massive head, a broader nose, smaller ears, and wide-set, round eyes. The hair of the Persian was coarser than that of the Angora. Through years of interbreeding, the Angora characteristics have largely been lost as the Persian characteristics have become dominant.

American Domestic, a white one with golden eyes. Blue-eyed white cats are often deaf. Some snowy whites are longhaired and have odd eyes, one blue and one gold. White cats are highly prized and much in demand.

Persian, longhair and luxuriant, seems always dressed for elegant appearance. A strong and sturdy body concealed beneath the silky coat which comes in all the seven basic colors. Broad nose and wide-set almond eyes. This high-bred lady is a Chinchilla Silver, winner of many ribbons, and rightly so. She is Ch. Kohinoor Alyssum of Bean-Ridge. Owner, Mrs. William Bean. Breeder, Mary Kate Carroll.

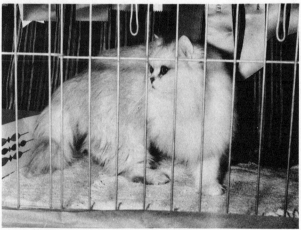

Himalayan, a delicious longhair and one of the newer breeds. Sturdy of body despite the oriental background. A blue-point male, Ch. Jeanine's Lode Star of Shadyhims. Owner, John Lantz. Breeder, Mr. and Mrs. Gray.

A new and most appealing longhair breed is the Himalayan. This lovely cat has a Persian body, Siamese point markings, and the brilliant blue eye of the Siamese, most effective against the snowy white coat. As with the Siamese, the point markings sometimes do not develop until the cat has passed kittenhood.

A consistent and long-running argument exists between shorthair owners and the lovers of the longhairs. Each claims superior beauty, greater intelligence, more gracefulness and charm. Each fan club has, I am sure, complete justification for its claims, for in cats, as with humans, we invest the ones we love with the qualities we admire. Regardless of sex, the longhairs are most assuredly the "dolls" of the feline world. They look elegantly dressed in their formal best, as if headed for a box seat at the opera or a magnificent ball. All the traditional patterns and markings gain a new dimension in this rich, silken coat.

Because of the quality of their coats, longhairs bring special grooming responsibilities to their owners. A daily combing and brushing are essential, not for just cosmetic reasons, but to ensure the comfort and health of the cat. Matted or uncared-for hair makes the cat thoroughly uncomfortable, and can even become pasted down to such a degree that it can interfere with elimination.

SEMILONGHAIRS

The most outstanding example of the semilonghair is the strikingly beautiful Maine coon cat. This cat is a big one, growing up to sixteen or more pounds. He walks tall and proudly. His coat comes in many colors and in most of the traditional marking already described. Many coon cats are black and white, with the white used in attractive designs. The eye varies with the coat color. This is a cat of great personality and charm.

WHEN YOU BUY A PUREBRED

• Within your budget, go to the best breeder of a breed you want. The sincere breeder will be very honest with you as to the bloodlines of the cats that attract you and the good qualities of the animal you finally choose. If you want to go into breeding, even in a small way, the better your cat, the better the price you can command for any kittens. If serious breeding is your objective, remember that this is an expensive and complicated business. You will have to do something much more than read a book. A serious study of genetics is essential, and then long and patient crossing of strains to achieve top animals.

Pet shops may or may not be able to provide you with the purebred that is right for you. A neighbor of mine recently bought a Persian kitten from a local pet shop. Papers were available, she was told, but the price could be cut if she did not insist on papers. What the pet shop owner did not tell my friend was the age and condition of the kitten. In truth, he was barely three weeks old, and not completely weaned. When she brought him to me, he was scrawny and potbellied, crying piteously. His owner, knowing no better, had tried to feed him canned cat foods, which this little one was not ready to handle. I urged her to try baby foods and cottage cheese until she could get the kitten to a veterinarian. A professional checkup indicated that he was basically healthy, and that in time, on a proper diet, he would grow up into a good but not a great cat.

• Make very sure that you get the right papers. Don't walk away without them.

• Find out also from your breed association about recognized stud services. Don't ride on your own decisions for a mate or conveniently select the pet of a friend.

• Keep abreast of the published information on breeds and breeding, nutrition, and health care. Subscription to one or more of the better pet publications is indicated, and if you want to get closer to technical information, a number of the veterinary magazines carry articles that any well-informed layman can understand.

• The world of show is a world in itself. The pride and satisfaction owners get from showing and winning ribbons is psychologically understandable. Remember that show cats live dangerously. Traveling from show to show, exposed as they must be to the stress of travel and that greater danger, exposure to contagious disease, they face health hazards against which you cannot completely protect them. Much as I want to, I rarely go to shows for fear I might bring home some infections.

It may interest you to know that many shows have entry classes for household pets. There are no exact rules for judging, but that uncommon common cat wins lots of applause when he goes onstage.

3

Who Should Have a Cat?

I used to say, somewhat in jest, that if reincarnation existed, I would want to come back as a black cat and live in my own house. This was a fine conversation piece. It drew all kinds of repartee and laughs. But as I have lived with my jest, I realize that it is completely true and meaningful for anyone who takes a cat into his home.

My cats have lived as you and I like to live at our best. They have had freedom to come and go at will, through their own door cut into my door. They have had a sense of safety and security. They were fed, not lavishly but adequately, and their individual preferences were taken into consideration.

Sometimes even the neighbors' cats embarrassingly preferred us to their owners. I remember well one blizzard morning when a half-sick, half-starved white cat dragged herself through the snow to my front door. Of course I took her in, and nursed her back to health. Later I discovered that she came from the next-door farm whose people had gone away for a holiday vacation. Weeks later, when she was well, her owner arrived indignantly to demand his cat. There was nothing I could do but let her go. Three months passed. Then one afternoon, to my astonishment, I found a small white kitten on my living-room couch. As I searched to solve the mystery I saw an amazing thing—my neighbor's white cat across the road with a second kitten in her mouth. Carefully she looked up

There is no age limit for cat owners. Whoever you are, wherever you live, you should have a cat if you will accept him as a member of the family and give him attention and care as you would give your child. This is Hiram, one of my long line of cats which has numbered nearly three hundred.

and down the highway, and when convinced that no danger lurked, she hurried across, dived through the cat hole and deposited kitten number two next to number one. Three more times she repeated this business, then settled down to nurse her five in comfort. She had traveled two miles or more, crossed a swiftly running brook, worked her way through a swampy pasture and finally, five times, crossed and recrossed the highway. This great mother cat wanted to make sure of the better life for her children. Snowy never went back to my neighbor, and for years she gave me beautiful six-toed pure-white youngsters.

Not everyone who takes a cat into his home can give all the things I have mentioned. But to answer the question "Who should have a cat?" I think the pattern is clear. If you can think of cats as members of your family and can give them the love and attention you would give a child, then you should have a cat.

If you want a cat to teach your children good manners—and in my days of placing kittens for adoption I have met mothers like this—don't adopt a cat. Don't expect an animal, even a highly intelligent animal, to do the job you can't do. If you want to experiment with a cat in your home, and then give him away when the experiment does not suit you, don't adopt a cat or any other pet.

A very smart professional woman, a friend of mine, recently acquired a lovely kitten, Buffy by name. She got this cat as a bribe for her grand-daughter, a child she wanted to lure to her home. Buffy scratched furniture, and granddaughter was unkind to cats. So Buffy was given away, or put to sleep, I don't know which, because he did not satisfy a whim.

There are thousands of homes that would be happier and more fun with a cat in residence. Puss is the finest of companions for all kinds of days. He will play instantly with invitation and cooperation, or he will invent hilarious games that he plays all by himself. He will participate in your every activity if you will let him. And contrary to what you may have heard, he will give you intense loyalty and deep affection. The dog's affection is heavily guided by his wish to please you. The cat's affection is more objective and much more sophisticated.

Independently Yours. The cat's image of independence has been vastly distorted. True, in many ways he is delightfully independent, for he has the rare good judgment to accept some people and flatly reject others. I can think of one man who occasionally came to my house, a talkative man with a big, booming voice. He went through the pretense of liking cats, but every time he entered the door, all my animals quietly disappeared and only came out of hiding when he was long gone. It is my guess that many people who secretly or openly don't like cats have been rejected by the wise ones. It is such cat haters who lead the chorus of voices complaining bitterly of kitty's coldness and independence.

People, Not Places. Let no one fool you with the myth that cats prefer places to people. It is true that cats hate change. If they could live in one place for their entire lives, even a place you and I would not choose, they might prefer it. It is nice to know where your bed and plate and playthings are. It is nice to move with confidence. It is nice to have a pattern—but there is no pattern without the people who love puss, and the people whom puss loves.

In a tragic year, when I sold my farm because I had to, a year in which I was forced to be away for long stretches of time, some people lived in my house and promised to care for my kids. They did a very bad job, and if I have any hate in me, I hated them for this. There were five in my cat family at that time—not kittens, grown cats—headed by Pink, the mother of them all. She cased the house situation and then led all five of them into the nearby woods, a place she had barely explored when her folks were at home. Pink taught her brood, all of them, to live off the land and to hide in brush heaps. In the night she led them back to water and what food she could find. I was told that my pets had disappeared. I got home as quickly as humanly possible and went out across my acres calling,

calling. Suddenly I heard a rustle in the brush, and Pink emerged at the head of the family, bringing them back to the person they had loved and trusted for years. They were a bit ragged and had burrs caught in their fur. They were a bit thin, but they came home to eat royally and relax as the owner's flag went up once again.

One of the most beautiful cats I ever had, Jasper, out of a fantastic marbled line who were with me for years, was strongly attached to me. He accepted the fact that I had to earn a living, and that to do so I must leave the farm every Monday in the early dawn. He said good-bye to me gravely and then settled down to wait out the week. He seemed reasonably content, so my farm couple told me, until Friday arrived. Regularly on Friday he posted himself on the front porch and watched up and down the road. He never left the porch—except for a small nibble of food—until I drove up to the front gate. How he knew it was Friday, only he knew. Can cats count? Having watched mother cats count their kittens and go searching for a missing one, I believe they can. But counting days implies a time sense that most humans don't have.

I could tell a dozen stories of how cats come back to people, not just places, about the drive that makes them find their own. When finally I had to bring my cat family to the city, they accepted the move magnificently and adjusted because I was with them.

An interesting experiment was reported recently in one of the veterinarian magazines. Convicts nearing release were allowed to have cats in their cells. Cats, rather than dogs, were chosen for ease of care under confinement. Of the men who loved and cared for their cats, none failed to adjust to society as free men. If cats need people, so do people need cats.

Cat People. It is considered smart and sophisticated to be one of the "cat people." Frankly I think this is a very overworked phrase. It has been my observation that many of the self-styled cat people seek to identify with cat characteristics they admire—independence, beauty, fearlessness, sensuousness. By owning a cat—and no one really *owns* a cat—they hope to imply that some of these traits are reflected in themselves. The true cat people are rather "animal" people who love and enjoy many animals, country and city folk like myself who find great satisfaction in the companionship of barnyard critters, house pets, and the wild ones of the woods and fields that so readily make friends when they can trust.

I must admit that many of the people I have come to like best turn out to like cats. And many I do not like either fear or dislike cats. Selecting your friends on this count is not recommended, but as a small test it may prove interesting and revealing. Many are those who often substitute a cat, a dog, or some other kind of pet for the human companion they do

There is no absolute rule about babies and cats. These two were born on the same day and have always been close friends. Some children are not ready for a cat or any pet until they are much older. And some children are never ready and should never have a pet.

The Christmas cat, a favorite gift. Just make sure it is a welcome one. In her city apartment home, this little lady snuggles under the only tree she will probably ever meet, and under the watchful eye of a proud new owner.

No farm is complete without cats, and in a country setting an alert cat family earns its keep. Squirting the milk from old Bossy's teat into the mouth of an alert kitten used to be a rural pastime. In these days of automatic milking machines a baby's bottle must suffice.

Many living-alone people find a cat a delightful and warm companion. The house never seems empty when an intelligent and loving pet is with you.

Photo by Frank Bear

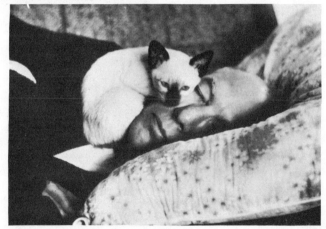

Men who like cats and prefer them to dogs are legion. Frequently men treat a cat with more respect and understanding than the womenfolks.

not have. There is nothing wrong about this, either for you or your pet, as long as you don't get carried overboard. I once met a woman who claimed her three cats as exemptions on federal income tax, because she honestly thought of them as her children. In actual fact you may find a cat easier and more fun to have around than some children, some parents, some husbands, and some wives.

Who Should Not Have a Cat? Many people are borderline pet owners, not too good, not too bad, kind but indifferent, responsible but without warmth. A cat with such an owner will make do physically, probably live well, but he will walk alone. There are, however, a few kinds of people who should not, NOT, have a cat.

The Constant Traveler who must rely on boarding homes. Of course, if such a person happens to be Elizabeth Taylor, the cat will not suffer, but few of this traveling generation fall into the Taylor class.

If some responsible person can replace you while you are gone, all may go well, for a time. Finding responsible people for any job is not always easy, and expecting friends or landladies or kitty sitters to take your place has grave drawbacks.

Your pet may survive dirty dishes and dirty litter boxes, and irregular meals and loneliness, but if he had a health problem, who would recognize it in time? Take my Pete, for example, who has to have a pill a day so that he can live. Who will take over that essential chore? Pete takes his pill like a lamb, from me. He might well hide from a stranger or tear him apart in fear.

Alcoholics and Addicts. If you get your kicks this way, don't have a pet. You may not mean to, but you will forget food, water, litter boxes, medications—and this is unfair to the animal you may love.

People with Allergies. I might add one other kind of person who probably should not have a cat. A cat lover who is allergic to cats, and many people are. I tread lightly in this department, for I know a man, extremely allergic to cats, who has two, has had them for years. He carries a bottle of pills for ready use when he finds breathing difficult. I would never attempt to tell such people that their decision is wrong. For them their decision is right.

Screened for Adoption. Who should have a cat? I think some of the well-known health-care centers have the right answer. They screen for animal adoption as the baby centers screen for child adoption. You must first present yourself at the agency with your credentials. If you pass this round, a home visitor will come to your house or apartment and decide whether it is the right place for a cat or dog. Pass this second test and you will be given a pet in trust.

You must agree to bring the animal back to the adoption center when it needs health care, shots, alteration or spaying, and to return it to the center if you find you cannot keep it any longer.

It is entirely possible to screen yourself. If you pass the tests, honestly pass, then go ahead by all means. There are hundreds of cats waiting for happy homes. Not one of them will care whether you are rich or poor, black or white, president or the lowest man on the totem pole. The cat you pick will adjust to your way of living, your faults, your oddities, if he has you, solidly you, caring for him and loving him.

4

How to Find a Cat

There are really only four ways to acquire a cat. He finds you. You select him. He comes to you as an unasked-for gift. You keep kittens from some of your own litters, either because you plan to, or because you can't find good homes. All these methods can be highly satisfactory, even the last, for sometimes the kitten you don't place for adoption and did not plan to keep turns out to be a sheer delight.

What to Look For in Your Cat. However you acquire your pet, make every effort to determine that he is physically healthy and strong, and, equally important, that he is emotionally well adjusted. I have broken both these rules a number of times and without unfortunate results, but the rules are very valid and most essential for the best kind of pet-family relationship. The sad little stray who looks at you with pleading, weepy eyes and begs for your acceptance can bring serious disease into your home, danger to other cats you may have, even danger to yourself and your children. The overly shy, even fearful animal may or may not adjust. He may live with you, but remain aloof, withdrawn, unhappy, just as you will be unhappy. It may not always be possible to judge accurately physical and emotional health—but certainly you must have a serious go at it.

Kitten or cat, many of the signs of health are obvious. The coat, regardless of breed, longhair or shorthair, is never dull, has a soft, glossy look. This kind of coat is vibrant as you touch it. There should be no thin or bare spots, no sore or scabby areas, no signs of fleas. The eyes of the healthy cat are clear and bright, never sore, sticky, or weepy. At rest or in motion the cat looks comfortable, natural. He moves smoothly, gracefully.

The healthy cat has the right body weight and size for its age, depending on bone structure. At six to eight weeks, the prime adoption age, kittens will average from one and a half to two pounds. They are losing the butterball look of babyhood, leaning out as they build bone. Older cats who have been properly fed will weigh about seven to eight pounds at a year, when most are considered full grown. Don't adhere slavishly to these exact weights, for as with all growing children—animal or man—there are variables from the norm, and occasionally a miniature can appear even in a big family. Body weight plus the look of a well-padded, not fat, frame is usually an indication of the kind of early feeding that is the foundation of health and longevity. Incidentally, females are consistently smaller for their breed than males.

Emotional adjustment is something else again. While good nutrition and intelligent care play a definite part in emotional stability, some cats come into life with emotional problems, often inherited. However you find your cat, look for an outgoing personality. Don't think a kitten "cute" or "funny" if it withdraws from you, tries to hide, or fluffs up its fur and spits. Give it time to smell you, taste you, take your measure, and then if it is still withdrawn or hostile, look over the other availables. On the other hand, don't fall for placid acceptance. You want a bright, alert, intelligent, spunky pet, not a vegetable. Try a gentle scratch under the chin and around the ears. Or at the end of the backbone, near the tail. If your "intended" has a well-functioning nervous system, he will raise his tail aloft as your fingers touch this top-back, near-tail area. See, too, how quickly he responds to a let's-play invitation.

What Breed of Cat? Breed has never meant a thing to me. Nor have the "papers" of the purebred. But to many people breed is not only personally but economically important. This kind of preference has psychological overtones, not to be discounted. In this melting-pot day, when many races and many bloods are intermingled, the human animal still has a high respect for heritage. Many people, fiercely ethnic, boast of their Scottish, English, Polish, or Italian backgrounds, even though far removed. Still others climb the family tree, move heaven and earth to trace themselves back to royalty—the kings of Wales, the czars of Russia, or, failing top brass, a count or countess of something-or-other. In choosing pets, many a man expresses a lot of this same heritage-longing and respect. Instead of saying, "I have a cat," he takes pride in saying, "I have a pure-bred Persian cat," or a Siamese, or an Abyssinian. Of course, as a lover of a particular breed, you may have many other reasons for your prefer-ence. The multiple voice and great agility of the Siamese. The soft luxu-riousness of the long-haired Persian or Angora. The aristocratic and exotic lines of the Abyssinian. Choose a breed, by all means, if this means some-thing to you, but remember that breed and heritage alone will not ensure the pet you want.

What Color of Cat? For thousands of families who want a cat, color is the major determinant. In my long years of placing kittens for adoption, I have found that there are three top-favorite colors—orange (marmalade to the English), jet black, and pure white. Far behind these three are the calico, the blue-gray, and the mixed colors. When I have had that awful decision to make of which kittens to put to sleep and which to place for adoption, I have had to be guided by my knowledge of color preferences that will put a kitten in the high-demand division. Let me hasten to add, however, that color and personality have absolutely no relation. You are simply kidding yourself if you try to associate the traits that intrigue with a color you like.

Male or Female. No one can answer this question for you. I have had many of both sexes and found them equally wonderful. I think that every person who wants a cat should have the experience of watching a mother cat raise a family of kittens. This is something that can never be adequately described, and something that no one should miss—providing homes can be found for the kittens.

People will tell you that the female is more loving than the male, or smarter, or more gentle, or more something else. This is not true. Every cat is individual. They are far less alike than people, who fear to be nonconformists. Desirable and intriguing personality traits have nothing at all to do with sex. Pick the cat you want and the one that wants you. If kittens are a problem, that problem can be solved by a simple and safe operation.

The Older Cat. The charm and beauty and activity of the kitten often blinds the pet owner to the great qualities of the older cat. Cats no longer kittens are a drug on the market. Like older children, they are often passed by for the cooing baby. The older cat who needs and wants a home is one of your best bets if he or she is healthy and well adjusted. This kind of older cat has stored up a fantastic need and a great ability for identification with people who will love him. Most of the strays who have come to me have been older and sometimes quite old cats. I would not have missed any one of them. True, you lose the pleasure of watching them grow up, but they will bring you experience, skills, and sensitive understanding that few kittens have. Let me place a strong vote for the adoption of an older cat.

When Your Cat Finds You. This is a flattering and rewarding experience. The cats who have chosen me have taught me more about the whole family of felines than I could ever have learned from a breeder or pet shop animal. You have already heard the story of my Snowy and her five kittens, and of Pink, who strayed in from the road, an outcast. There have been many more. Tipsy, for one, an automobile-accident victim I am sure. She flopped on my driveway, a completely uncoordinated cat who moved like a human spastic. Had she found another haven, it would have been very temporary. She would have been destroyed. But I kept her, and cured her as far as possible. And she gave me a whole line of healthy, completely delightful animals. The "Jo-Jo" line, we called them. Clown cats, with ridiculous black and white markings—always a well-defined black nose and an eye-mask of black. Talkative cats with multiple voices. A family with an enormous sense of humor. Hid things for the pure joy of watching me hunt. Invented games, not just play games, but purpose games. None of this woud I have had without Tipsy.

Then there was Paint, the ugliest tortoiseshell I have ever seen. My husband named her because she looked like the creation of a mad artist with a splattering brush. We found her one morning crouching under the sheltering bridal wreath, her coat of many colors blended with the background. She was starved, and since no one came unsatisfied to our hill, she was fed, cleaned up, and offered a home. What a great hunter she was. I once watched her catch and kill a weasel, something few cats can do. She gave us magnificent kittens with all the beauty she lacked—jet blacks, golden ones, a true blue. She was gentle and humble, and never demanding. I always thought she knew how ugly she was and tried to compensate. I found her a beautiful cat.

The Old Man drifted in to us when his family died. An unaltered tom, he had already lost one eye in a valiant fight. He, too, was gentle and wise. Had to be invited to eat. And it was the Old Man who showed me how sensitive animal sex could be. When a female in heat did her luring best, he would watch younger and more eager males wear themselves out in approach and rejection. And then, he would move quietly in, reach out a gentle paw, and touch the paw of the queen. Need you ask who won the lady?

Blackbeard came to me in New York, through a jungle of streets, yards, alleyways. He wore a collar. Someone had loved him enough to put their mark on him. I am sure that my Pete is his son. He came first because I had females in heat. I tried to scare him away. Finally he tore apart a strong metal screen, forced his way into my apartment. Not because he wanted to mate, but because he had to have food, warmth, and love. With emphasis on love. I finally let him come and go. Medicated his fight wounds. Fed and, above all else, petted him. The last time he came was in the middle of a great snowstorm. After a rubdown and a snack and a sleep, he slipped away and never came back. He left behind a collar, a son, and my full knowledge that if he had remained alive, he would have come back.

Think carefully when a cat finds you and chooses you. This is an honor not to be treated lightly.

You Select a Cat. You can make the choice in any number of intelligent ways.

Your Friends and Neighbors. The cat population being what it is, you can almost always find someone you know who wants a good home for kittens. Indeed, you will be as welcome as rain. This is an excellent way to find your pet, for you have a chance to meet the mother, to learn her background, and to learn the quality of the family who have loved her and who care about the new home for her kittens. You may even be able to get the breed or color of cat you fancy. Many animals with excellent breeding but without papers will be given gladly to responsible friends and neighbors. Make sure to check your friends on the food your kitten has been getting so that you can continue a diet pattern until your little one is adjusted to his new life.

The Advertised Cat. City and country newspapers usually have a list of pets for adoption, and for free. Investigate these ads, for here again you will be able to evaluate the kind of cat family and the kind of human family that offer you a pet. I have placed scores of kittens by advertising, and placed them well. In New York, ads in sectional city newspapers have brought me people who were right, people who continue to call me three, five years later to report on the joy and satisfaction they and their pets have had, or to ask for information. Not too long ago, I directed a delivery by telephone.

The Pet Shop. This one worries me. There are thousands of pet shops that recruit adoption kittens and cats from anywhere. Some of the shops are clean and well run and sanitary. Some are not. Some cater to people with small incomes who are supposed not to be too particular.

Visit a neighbor who has kittens for adoption—or even an older cat. If you adopt from a friend, you will have the advantage of knowing your new pet's background and personality traits.

Photo by Sue Meyers

If you walk into a pet shop and smell animal, walk out. Your cat is not there.

The Breeder. If you are looking for a special breed and a fine pet with or without papers, the breeder is your target. Make sure that you get the papers if you are paying for a purebred. Question the breeder or the pet shop who offers you a discount on a purebred animal. The bargain purebred may be off only on markings, color, or size, or it may be a sick animal. No good breeder would think of giving you either an undesirable or a pet that did not live up to his standards and your specifications. Just remember that there are good breeders and indifferent ones, just as there are good people and bad ones.

Adoption Centers. Many national and local health and shelter societies maintain adoption centers. The ASPCA is well known and with international scope. Most cities have Humane Society groups who, if they do not include adoption departments, can probably direct you to one. If possible, choose a source that makes a careful screening of your pet and of you. Be watchful of small, privately owned adoption homes run by people who love cats but may have neither the money nor facilities to operate a clean and disease-free group of animals. They may be located in small storefront facilities or keep dozens of cats in big apartments.

Read the want ads in your local news-papers. Often wonderful pets are avail-able free to good homes. Expect to provide credentials which prove your reliability.

You may find your cat in a pet shop. As you look over a litter, suddenly you will know which one is yours. He should be strong, healthy, and outgoing. Remember you are selecting each other for what may well be a lifetime.

If it is a special breed you want, find a good breeder in your com-munity and let him guide you. Unless you plan to be a breeder, just want the cat that suits you, pick the one you want to live with even if he is not best of breed.

Visit the cat shelter groups in your community. Almost all have kittens and older cats for adoption. They will screen you as a prospective owner, often give free medical service to those who cannot afford it.

Get to the cat shows in your vicinity. Here you will have a chance to see cats of many breeds. Decide which kind and color is most appealing to you and note the names of breeders in your locale.

The Kittens You Keep. Every pet owner who encourages or allows her cats to mate is soon completely overrun with an expanding family—unless adoption homes can be located. Cats being cats, the mating is not always scheduled so that kittens will be available in the high-adoption period of the year. Christmas, Easter, early fall, when the summer vacation is over. In summer months, fine kittens go abegging and are almost impossible to place.

In every litter there are special cats. The smart little one who is first to eat and drink, usually a female. Or the one that looks just like his mother. Or the one who knows you and comes to you as soon as he can crawl.

You must be firm and decisive about the size of your cat family, no matter how much it hurts. But occasionally your best planning can go awry. And later you may be thankful. Pete is a shining example. He refused to be adopted. Within six months his grandmother, Pink, and his mother, Little Pink, were gone. Pete is the last of a long line, and he blends many of the qualities of his forebears with very special qualities of his own. This cat is more human than most humans. He has hands, not paws. In an evening, when I work, he finds a place as close to me as possible, and every now and then reaches out a paw just to touch me. He has participated in the work of every page of this book. When he decides it is time for me to stop, he bounces up from nowhere to sit down on my pile of papers or to stop my typewriter. Like some very nice people, he is slightly shy of overt affection. A jealous one, too, loving his brothers, but hurt if he thinks he has been ignored. I certainly did not need another cat when I acquired Pete, but how glad I am that he is with me.

The Unwanted Gift Cat. One morning I found on my lawn a whole basket of cats. There was a note attached. It said, "I cannot afford to keep these. Please take care of them for me. And please watch out specially for the black one." I took the basketful—five in number—to the barn. Fortunately we had plenty of milk and lots of fine table scraps. The new family all came to the house at night for a full-scale meal. And they policed my barns as those barns had never been policed before. Never look a gift cat in the face and walk away. There is, was, or will be some reason why any pet comes into your circle of life. One of those unwanted gift cats saved me from a barn fire. Woke me up in the middle of the night by howling when hot, smoky hay ready for combustion chased him out of a too-warm bed.

5

How to Handle Your Cat

If you were one foot high, how would you like to find yourself in the hands of a six-foot giant? Even a kindly giant is quite capable of swooping you up into the air, dangling you in some undignified position, and talking to you in a voice that makes your eardrums quiver. Well, if you are a cat, that uncomfortable routine can repeat itself many times a day, until you find it possible to sneak away into some safe hidey-hole.

It is my contention, well supported by the hundreds of cats I have known, that kitty likes to meet his or her folks on the same level—eyeball to eyeball, to be exact. Stop and think for a moment of your cat's favorite sleeping and lounging places. Unless you have declared it off bounds, one of those places will be your bed. Here, with both of you on the same level, puss will sleep in utter relaxation. Come morning, he may even have a chance to look down on you as he wakes you with his own special gestures of greatest affection.

As I am typing a page for this book, my Chipper has moved into one of his favorite positions, the top of my file cabinet just a foot away from my typewriter. He will doze there for hours, occasionally opening an eye so that we can look straight at each other. It is this same Chipper who jumps to the top of a table when I come home at night. Now, on the same level, we can touch heads and say hello in proper style.

For real fun, play with your cat on the floor, or the grass, on the table-

This is pure bliss to a cat. The hand of the person he likes best softly scratching that highly sensitive area just under the chin.

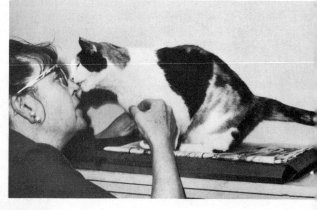

Meet your cat on his own level, eyeball to eyeball, and you will establish a new kind of affectionate and intimate relationship. This is how my fine old lady, Pink, liked best to greet me, with a soft nip on the nose. A cat's version of a kiss.

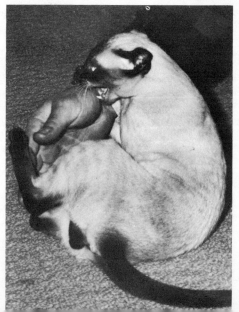

Play that starts as just fun can get rough. When the teeth and claws dig in as you tussle, don't pull your hand away swiftly and invite a scratch. Just hold steady for a moment. Your quiet and confident hand will return the game to a game.

top, if you wish, in case you have reached the point in life where bending and crawling have become chores. When your neighbors catch you at this kind of fun and games—as once mine did while Big Boy and I were playing hide-and-seek in the lily bed—let them cluck and wag their heads. But don't let them make you so self-conscious that you discard this on-the-level sport. Carry the idea a step further and work with your cats. My gang and I plant beans together, pull weeds, clean out closet corners. Try it for yourself. Household and garden tasks may take a bit longer with this technique, but I'll guarantee you won't be bored.

THE LAYING ON OF HANDS

In handling cats, I also firmly believe in the old biblical technique known as the "laying on of hands." When an animal lets you touch him, you and he have made a pact that is very likely to last. Through your fingers you can signal affection, security, firmness of decision, and sometimes something much more.

Years ago my Jo-Jo was hit by a car. The driver, with more decency than some, brought her to me. I could find no broken bones or immediate signs of internal injury, but Jo-Jo was in shock—and shock can kill. I carried her to her favorite sleeping corner, kept her warm, and literally held back disaster with my hands. At one point, when convulsions seemed about to begin, I held her closely and firmly to me, saying her name over and over, almost monotonously. Gradually the shaking slowed down, and finally she slept. Jo-Jo lived happily another four years. She was never quite the same. She would walk as in a dream, sometimes off the edge of a table into space. It was as if a bit of her had been lost in the moment when she almost passed over to the other side. Had I not been able to get my hands on her, I am confident she would have died in minutes.

In far less dramatic ways your laying on of hands can develop a wonderful rapport with your cat. I never pass any of my cat family without touching him, very lightly. I never leave the house in the morning without making the rounds to say that I am going and that I will be back. This touch system pays invaluable dividends when a cat must be handled to examine, to give medicine, to cage for traveling. Rarely will a cat—even a frightened one—attack the hands it trusts.

There are some exceptions to this rule, but they happen only under crisis conditions. I remember an occasion when I was giving away a kitten. The foster family had arrived. They qualified as the right kind of people.

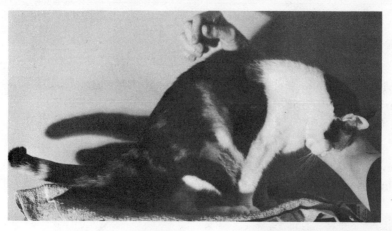

The laying on of hands. With your touch you can give your cat confidence, security, love, or you can communicate stress, fear, anger.

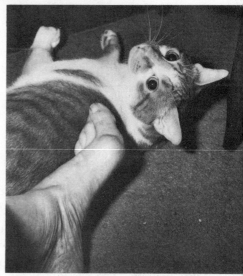

A foot or a hand, it makes no difference. Physical contact with the people they love is the important thing.

The children in the group were enchanted with my little yellow and white tomcat. He held his tail high and gave every evidence of camaraderie.

When I started to carry my kitten to the car, my hands signaled something to him that was negative. Suddenly he turned on me and let go with everything he had. I arrived on the sidewalk with blood streaming down my arm and with a screaming youngster trying to tear its way out of the carrying box. I could see the fear in all the faces around me. Politely the family changed their minds, and in unison. So back to my house I went with my wailing kitten. As soon as he got on home ground, he was himself again, tail in the air, a bubbling purr. Was there a satisfied gleam in his eye? I believe so. He was not deeply frightened. He had found his home and had no intention of leaving it. By putting on a scene, he had settled the whole matter. I might add that I still have this cat.

HOW TO HANDLE
A DISTURBED CAT

A thoroughly angry cat or a tremendously frightened one can be dangerous. Don't try to corner such animals and fight it out. Indoors, try to shut the cat into a room and leave the animal alone until fear or anger is gone. Quietly slip in some food and water and see what a little peace will do. Outdoors, if possible, let the cat run and hide. Usually, as the edge of fear wears thin, he will come out, seeking companionship or food.

I have talked a frightened cat into a carrying case so that I could take him to safety, and medication, if need be. It is even possible to talk a cat down from a tree that proved higher than he dreamed. But keep a pair of lined gloves around so that at some point you can move in swiftly and hang on without danger of severe clawing. If you must grab, do it quickly, gently, and confidently.

There are a few, a very few, badly disturbed cats that cannot be handled under any circumstances. You may have to call professional help for such animals. I knew one such cat, a stray that lurked near my house for two years, snatched food and ran, never could be touched. Our vet finally had to destroy her to take her out of a world of fear.

Sometimes, in play, emotions change and fun turns to fight. This is not very different from what happens in a scrimmage on the football field. Suddenly rules are forgotten and players are clawing at each other. If you have been comfortably rubbing kitty's belly, and abruptly he grabs with tooth and claw, don't snatch away your hand in furious haste, unless you want some fairly bad wounds. Just hold steady for a moment until puss remembers his manners.

TEACHING CHILDREN
HOW TO HANDLE CATS

Many children need no teaching at all. The gentle, sensitive child approaches kitty with careful hands and a soft voice. He completely identifies with the cat who crawls into a paper bag, plays a violent game with a bouncing bead in the bathtub, runs around in mad circles. After all, the child's behavior pattern is much like that of a young or even older animal. Unless given admonitions by an unwise adult, told that kitty may bite or claw him, the child accepts a small scratch or two as part of the game, without a whimper.

Some children instinctively know how to handle animals. Others may be timid, or the reverse—tough.

The common denominator of play is almost sure to bring the two together.

And the relationship is cemented when the cat confidently gives and receives affection.

Incidentally, boys in particular go for the agile Siamese whose shoulder perch is a favorite one.

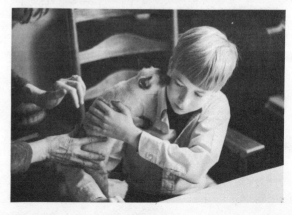

Unfortunately for the cat, some children are cruel, perhaps not intentionally. But they pull tails, chase the cat to see it run, figure out a set of strange tortures similar to those used on younger brothers and sisters. Often this is more the fault of parents than of children. Some parents force a pet—a cat—on their youngsters, in the mistaken belief that every child needs a pet. Some children should have pets, some should not. Some are ready for a pet at an early age. Some are never ready. Some children love to play with a cat, some only want a cat as a plaything. So take a long and very objective look at your child before you bring a cat into your home.

If you decide the combination will work out happily for all concerned, then show your child all the best techniques of handling his pet, and in addition delegate to him some of the daily chores of feeding and care. For the first month, feeding kitty may seem a real delight, but the fun of duties can quickly fade. Suddenly mother finds herself doing the whole bit, including the unattractive job of cleaning the litter box. If this shift in responsibility is allowed to happen, the cause is lost—so don't let it happen. The joy a child can get out of a cat will be magnified many times if he watches over his pet, understands the reasons for routine care, goes along to the doctor when it is time for injections or treatments, becomes involved with his cat both intellectually and emotionally.

HOW TO PICK UP A CAT

If you must pick up your cat, remember his dignity—and comfort, and anatomy. Don't grab him by the middle and haul him up with feet dangling. Get one hand under his feet, so that he has a sense of balance and security. Support his chest with the other hand. Everytime you pick up a cat, stop and figure out whether you would enjoy being handled that way. And be sure to set him down on four feet.

THE SICK CAT —
A SPECIAL HANDLING PROBLEM

Handling a sick animal is something else again. Many sick animals will try to hide. Then you must ferret them out of closets or from under the porch, and this is not always a gentle operation. Your touch signals your own fear and concern. If possible, put the sick cat in a room that can be closed off. A bathroom is one of the best places, for the sick cat cannot always be tidy. Don't let your pet feel that he is being locked away as punishment, but even if he is quite unhappy as a shut-in, remember that rest, lack of exercise, warmth, and freedom from drafts contribute to the recovery of animal as well as man.

When you lift your cat, respect his dignity and comfort. Instead of grabbing him by the middle and lifting him with feet dangling, first support his front feet . . .

. . . then his back feet so that he feels secure.

Now he will trust you to carry him wherever you want to go.

Above all else, learn how to give medicine properly. Full directions for the proper techniques will be given in a later chapter. Awkwardness in giving your pet medicine can make him sicker. For if you fight and fail to get a dose down, you must try until you succeed—a very wearing process.

In general, handle the sick cat exactly as you would a sick child. And if your pet is very sick, be prepared to give endless hours of time. Unless your cat is desperately ill, he will do better at home with you than in a cage at the nearby animal hospital.

LET THE CAT COME TO YOU

Much of the time let your cat come to you. When cats feel a great need of affection, they tell you about it.

When friends and neighbors come to call, urge them to let the cat make the approaches. The cat has a very sure sense of people he likes and trusts and those he does not. If he likes your guests, he will make the advances, in time. If not, he will vanish, never to be seen until the caller is gone.

The best way to handle a cat is not to handle him at all unless he invites it. Many cats are not lap cats, but they long to be close, whatever you are doing. Pete joins me at my desk or typewriter in most of my working hours, always just within reach of my hand.

6

Daily Dialogue

In the art of communication, the cat is an expert. Being less inhibited than you and far better equipped to express fine shades of meaning, he has become a past master at putting across his points. Consistently, puss uses three systems of communication—the sound system, the touch system, and the signal system. And some cats employ a fourth system, which can best be defined as a kind of radar, a strange ability to reach across space with a message to the people they love and trust.

Although the sound system is the most obvious, it is, in my opinion, the least sophisticated. As a tiny newborn, a cat begins to mew within a few minutes after birth, and in many voices he goes on talking for the rest of his life. A very competent set of vocal cords makes this possible. Actually, some people believe that the cat has a dual set of cords, one false and one true, and it is their theory that he purrs with the false cords, talks with the true ones.

Sounds range from the almost inaudible purr, which is felt rather than heard, to the ear-splitting screams of mating cats. In between these extremes lie scores of sounds, each quite different, each expressing a different idea or emotion. The purr of contentment, the miaow of greeting, the demanding cry of hunger, the chirp or hum with which puss lovetalks his animal and people friends, the commanding call of the mother cat to her kittens, the wail of fear, the spitting growl of the fighting cat, the hoarse and usually piteous cry of sickness—these are just a few of a long, long list.

56

Winner of the cat talk-athons—the Siamese. He speaks in many voices and almost constantly. Some owners find this enchanting. Others long for peace and quiet.

Each cat has his own very special voice, unlike the voice of any other. Without laying eyes on my cats, and even at great distances, I can tell which one is speaking, and what message he is sending. Some cats, of course, are great talkers and some are almost silent. Different breeds vary in their talkativeness and in the tonal quality of the voice. To the Siamese must go top billing in the talkathon. His incessant chatter and rather raucous voice enchant some people and destroy others. One of my veterinarian friends says that he has constant requests from Siamese owners regarding a possible operation on the vocal cords, a type of surgery the good animal doctor does not recommend.

If you like daily dialogue with your pet, develop it. Even a rather silent cat will respond if he is talked *to*. Unfortunately, many people think that a cat must be talked *at* in a high falsetto voice, or in baby talk, or with a gush of endearments. I have a strong suspicion that any intelligent cat finds this pretty silly. The right kind of people-to-pet talk should sound exactly like people-to-people talk. Try it and see how quickly your cat begins to grasp the gist of the conversations—and to answer back.

The Signal System. Using a combination of eyes, ears, tail, and body movements, every cat talks in a silent language that is louder than sound. Often he uses all this equipment at once, and if you are perceptive, you will rapidly get cues which tell you exactly what your cat is thinking and what he plans to do. Actually cats are excellent burglar alarms. With their keen hearing and their instinctive awareness of impending danger, they usually recognize the unwanted stranger. When my cats freeze at

A cat's tail is a vital part of his signal equipment. And each tail is quite individual, and expresses personality. Chip's tail, which he wags like a dog's, always carries a question mark. Big Boy's beautiful fluffy tail waves in gracious welcome. Pete flies his tail into the wind as he runs eagerly into each new situation.

Each morning Chip cries softly and seductively to the pigeons and gulls as they swoop past his carefully screened window. Sight unseen, any owner can recognize his cat by voice and know quite exactly what his pet is saying or doing.

Watch your cat's ears carefully. They scoop up and evaluate every small or large sound, many of which you might not hear at all. As indicated by this listening-without-alarm position, the noise level is low, there are no intruders, all is well.

Often a cat operates several of his signal systems at once. Hiram, who has been interrupted in his toilet, is quietly combining eye and ear signals to warn away a friend with fun on his mind.

attention or run from door or window, I grow cautious. More than once when I lived in a city garden apartment, it was my pets who told me an intruder was coming over the wall or down a fire escape.

In signaling, as in sound, each cat is utterly individual. For example, a tail is not a tail is not a tail. Some, like Chip's, are tapering, wag like a dog's, and have a constant question mark at the tip. Some are big and fluffy and wave graciously, like Big Boy's. Some lean forward into the wind, as does Pete's. All fly erectly high when your cat is happy and welcoming. Some will droop and even drag in fear. All will bush and bristle when angry. All lie flat and lash a bit when the cat is stalking. All can curl neatly and tightly around sleeping bodies. There are as many different tails as there are cats and breeds of cats. Ears and eyes have the same wide variations, and their expressions and implications are manifold.

Particularly expressive are body movements. I envy Chip's complete relaxation as he sprawls frog-legged on his back with his legs poised daintily in midair, and as he rolls and turns and stretches in drowsing, luxurious comfort. All this lovely repose can vanish if your pet is sick. Hunched up like a rabbit or crouched uncomfortably into a corner, he becomes a picture of utter misery.

The Touch System. As he winds about your feet or snuggles into your lap, your cat is doing rather ordinary things that do not stretch his imagination. And as he "makes bread" with his paws and claws on you, your clothing or some kind of material that excites him, he is simply repeating the sexual movements he began as a kitten when he kneaded his mother's breast to stimulate milk flow. It is the cat who touches you rarely and in unusual ways who is being most intelligent. An occasional gentle touch with the paw, sometimes on your hand, sometimes on your eyelids closed in sleep, the thank-you nuzzle with the head, a soft nip of your nose or finger, a kind of restrained affection has far more significance than lavish outpourings of emotion.

The Radar System. I always hesitate to dwell on this, for to many people it sounds zany and unbelievable. From personal experience I know that lost cats trying to get back to you, their favorite person, somehow signal you when you are far separated. A number of times when my free-roving pets have been "lost," I have known instinctively that they were in trouble. How can I explain the sure sense that has told me my cat was calling to me from somewhere? And how can I explain an equally sure sense that has taken me to the right somewhere? This sense, or perhaps you would call it nonsense, has carried me miles in the country and over block-long garden complexes in the city. This whatever-you-call-it has some resemblance to the homing instinct of pigeons. Even in unfamiliar territory I have known where to search and have bailed my pets out of traps in the woods, excavation ditches, city alleyways, and basement labyrinths never before seen. At the point where my mental "scent" got hot, I have always called, and my calls have been answered, often from far away.

Communication is a two-way street. If you can establish this you are in for some extraordinary and most rewarding experiences. Remember that the cat is a provident animal. If one communication system seems to be all that is required, he will not strain himself. If, on the other hand, he has trouble getting through to you, he'll pull out all the stops. You get exactly what you give, just as you do in your daily relationships with family, friends, and business associates.

It is in his touch system that the cat is at his sensitive best. Often swift and light, Chip's head touch says many warm and endearing things.

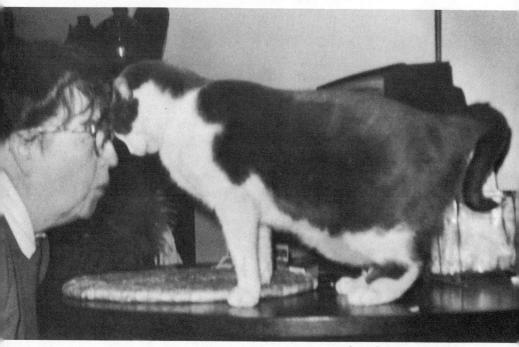

Photo by Ann Purtill

7

Food and Drink

A. A NEW LOOK AT NUTRITION

Some Myths About Cat Feeding. All through the past and current literature on cat feeding, I keep stumbling over theories that are not only out of date, but almost completely inaccurate.

First of all, there is the cat-and-mouse myth. In his natural state, so many writers insist, a nice plump mouse made a perfect meal for kitty, a well-balanced meal that he ate with relish, beginning with the most delectable portion—the innards, which happen to be rich in vitamin B, for which the cat has a high requirement.

Moving from mice to canned cat foods, most writers have given this subject small shrift—a paragraph or a page at best. "If your cat will eat canned food," say they, "give him some, but don't be surprised if your cat refuses. My cat does." Most current writers concede that commercial foods have improved, but how or why is rarely defined.

The third old saw relates to table scraps. No discriminating cat, say the writers, will enjoy that medley of meat and potatoes and vegetables left over from the family meal. And, they add, this collection probably won't supply the nutrients needed for health and growth.

Stop for a moment and examine these three dogmas. Take the mouse myth. Even before the day in which lethal poisons were used to destroy

What your cat eats and drinks plays a major role in his growth, physical and mental, his vitality, the health of every portion of his body, his ability to withstand or fight off disease, and his longevity. You are the prime factor in your cat's continued good nutrition. In effect, you determine how long and how well your cat will live. Pink was seventeen when this was taken.

mice and rats—poisons also lethal to the mouser—rodents have lived in filth. If you have run a farm as I have, cleaned barns and poultry houses, you would not consider a mouse or rat a safe, sanitary, and healthful meal. A vast number of cats would not eat one, just stalk and play to satisfy a basic hunter instinct.

As a matter of fact, most modern cats are more familiar with the sound of a can opener than with the rustle and squeak of a mouse. And let's face it, modern food industries have spent untold dollars developing many canned and frozen products that contain essential nutrients in pretty good balance. In addition to canned and frozen food designed especially for the feline, there are scores of canned products processed for dogs or human consumption that make fine cat foods when used occasionally.

If you were to check with many of the major animal care centers, you would discover that most of them use well-balanced canned products only, not just for adequate maintenance, but in cases where high nutritional levels are essential to fight illness and disease.

As for the third concept, that table foods are unappetizing and lacking in the nutrients cats need, this is true only when the family diet is lacking in quality. No cat likes a mess of scraps that anyone in the family would reject. But if there is anything wrong with roast beef, roast chicken, hamburger, stew, mashed potatoes, well-cooked vegetables, why do you offer your family such an array? All these family foods are on the preferred list for cats. And serving puss as you put your own well-balanced dinner on the table is simple and time-saving.

At Last—Recommended Daily Requirements. In all justice, there is a reason for this confusion on what to feed cats. Only recently have studies indicated what nutrients, and how much of each, cats need. With increasing accuracy, researchers are now able to set at least some of the minimum daily requirements for kitty, and they have discovered, as they might have expected, that the cat is an individual. He has special needs that even his near cousin, the mink, does not share, and requirements that are quite different from those of the dog.

Perhaps it seems odd that it has taken so long to compile and report hard-core information on feline nutrition. Growers and breeders of cattle, hogs, and poultry have been equipped for years with exact formulas designed to put on so many pounds of weight per day, keep young and adult in top health, increase fertility, and ward off old age. For the homemaker who guards her family's welfare, there has also been a wealth of accurate foods and feeding information. Data on cats have been much more sketchy and far less specific. It is only in quite recent literature that we find experts labeling food as the "criminal" in a long list of cat diseases and reproductive problems.

Why this lag? Well, for one thing, it has taken a change in status to turn a full spotlight on feline nutrition. There have always been highly prized cats who lived in the lap of luxury, but most of the army have been workers, mousers in country or city, strays that wandered the fields or the city streets, and laboratory animals used by scientists. When cats graduated to a primary position as one of the nation's major pets, their economic importance brought to them what was needed for a long time— an educated as well as an emotional analysis of their food needs.

Some Condensed Guidelines to Good Diet. Before getting into the full details of good nutrition, let me pinpoint some of the recent findings that will help you shape a sound feeding program for your cat.

. . . Kitty is a protein eater, and must have much more protein than you and I need. Plenty of muscle meats, organ meats, milk, cottage cheese, eggs, and cereals give him the high protein diet he requires, and in addition supply complete protein plus some of the most essential vitamins.

. . . Quite a lot of fat won't hurt your puss. In fact he needs it.

. . . Don't hesitate to feed some things like rice and potatoes and macaroni. Don't overdo this, but mix some of these starchy foods and also some vegetables with the meat you are feeding. Note: All these stretcher foods, which also supply energy, must be cooked.

. . . Good nutrition must begin before birth. The diet of the queen contributes greatly to the health and vigor of the kittens.

. . . Growing kittens and young cats need much more food—and a higher percentage of food nutrients per pound of body weight—than do adult cats or old cats. What's more, the four-week-old kitten needs four times as many calories as the adult cat.

. . . A number of extensive studies indicate that cats thrive better on raw meats and raw milk than on cooked meats and pasteurized milk.

. . . Many cats cannot drink milk. They may be allergic to it, or, due to its lactose content, the milk may ferment in the stomach and cause diarrhea. When whey is an ingredient in processed foods, it may cause the same reactions. Kittens on cow's milk may suffer from malnutrition. Powdered milk at twice the concentration used for babies can be used successfully in the kitten stage, and many adult cats enjoy and tolerate this brew.

. . . Water—plenty of fresh, clean water every day—is a must.

. . . When family table foods are fed to cats, it is best to avoid the highly spiced ones.

. . . "Fish only once a week," that's what many authorities on cat feeding say, loud and clear, and largely to stop owner from feeding an all-fish diet. If blended and balanced with other foods, fish can be used more frequently.

Water, lots of ever-fresh, clean water in the kind of bowl that cannot be easily overturned, is a number one need for your cat. He can go without food for days, but water he must have to survive— water, not milk, which many cats cannot tolerate.

. . . In buying canned cat food, read the label very carefully to see that all the essential nutrients are mentioned. Often the more expensive foods are a better blend and well worth the extra money, except the gourmet foods, which are not balanced and cause the cat to develop fixed eating habits. The sample labels illustrated can be used as a guide in the selection of products.

. . . Although we now know more surely the nutrient requirements of cats at various ages and weights, there is no exact rule on how much to feed. Some cats are dainty and finicky eaters. Others are pigs—constantly hungry. Like some humans who eat mountains of food and still look like string beans, some cats can eat and eat and stay thin. When pussy begins to look pudgy, better cut back on quantity, or you may end up with a fatty who loses interest in healthy, active play.

The one kind of cat you can rarely overfeed is the pregnant mother who becomes the nursing mother. In the building of body and bone, in supplying adequate food for growth of the newborn, the cat mother's nutritional reserves are rapidly depleted. She may eat and get thinner unless you see to it that she gets all she will eat of a good-quality diet.

. . . Variety in diet is important and sensible. Don't let your cat get hung up on a one-food diet. This will not give him the balance of nutrients he needs and will cause untold troubles if some circumstance forces a change in diet.

Acceptability. In the final analysis, acceptability plays a very large part in your pet's diet. However hard you work for best nutrition, however faithfully you train• your cat to a varied diet, you will at some points come upon a stone wall. Puss, being an independent soul with a mind of his own, may consistently and forever refuse certain foods. Taste, texture, smell—something is obnoxious to him. Unless this disliked food is vital to health and maintenance, don't keep on forcing it. My Pete gets one smell of clams and almost runs away. Chip loathes chicken. Each can live a long and happy life without either of these foods, so I don't make an issue of the business anymore than I would force a guest in my house to eat oysters if he thoroughly disliked them.

In one of the quite technical books on cat feeding I recently ran across a small poem * which states the situation quite exactly:

* From "Rum Tum Tugger," from *Old Possum's Book of Practical Cats,* copyright 1939 by T. S. Eliot; copyright © 1967 by Esme Valerie Eliot. Reprinted by permission of Harcourt, Brace & World, Inc.

. . . If you offer him pheasant, he would rather have grouse . . .
If you set him on a rat, then he'd rather chase a mouse.
Yes, the Rum Tum Tugger is a Curious Cat—
And there isn't any call for one to shout about it:
For he will do
As he will do,
And there's no doing anything about it.

B. THE NUTRITION STORY

Progress Report. A flood of information on the nutritional needs
and requirements of cats is now coming in from all over the world. And
just as "flood" accurately describes the volume of information, so "fluid"
describes the character and change of the information. Data published by
the National Research Council in 1962 are now in revision because of
newer knowledge. In dozens of research centers, many in major universities both here and abroad, the search goes on to discover not only the
best diet for health, growth, and maintenance, but how diet affects reproduction, ensures strong, healthy litters, and above all else, how diet can
prevent or control the disease of cats.

The Interlock of Nutrients. One of the most fascinating facets
of the nutrition story concerns the interplay—the interlock—of nutrients.
Unless you are a technical person, you will never understand this fully,
and even technical people admit that it is difficult to grasp. The fact re-
mains that in some marvelous fashion of creation, every nutrient works
with other nutrients. Like members of a family, they spare each other,
support each other, occasionally fight each other.

The nutrients your cat needs are the same nutrients you need—proteins,
carbohydrates, fats, vitamins, and minerals. As in the human diet, these
nutrients must all be present and in a certain balance. Your cat differs
from you in the amounts of each nutrient he must have. A good sound
knowledge of human nutrition will make you more successful in feeding
your pet, but to do the job really right, you must take the final step—
learn your cat's special needs and the "why" of these needs.

The Energy Requirements of Cats. Three types of nutrients
play important roles in satisfying the energy needs of cats—protein, carbohydrate, fat. Energy needs increase and decrease depending on a number
of factors—age, body weight, activity, and periods in the life cycle, such
as pregnancy and lactation, state of health, even weather.

The baby cat who doubles his body weight in seven to nine days has four times the energy needs of the normally healthy adult cat. As a matter of fact, all the newborn's nutritional needs are special, for the entire composition of his body is changing during the early weeks of his life.

For simplicity in figuring, the energy needs of the cat are expressed in calories and related to body weight, very much as your own calorie needs are figured. The following calorie-weight-age chart * may be used as a a guide by owners and breeders.

Calories per Pound of Body Weight
(Daily)

Age	Calories
4 weeks	125
10 weeks	100
14 weeks	70
24 weeks	65
30 weeks	50
Older tomcats still growing	40
Adult cats	30

It would be quite simple if we could stop here, but nothing in nutrition is that simple. The nutrient source of energy for kitty is almost more important than the amount. It has now been established that 30 percent of the energy requirements of the kitten, and 20 percent of the energy needs of the adult cat must be met by proteins. The reasons for this high protein need even in the energy area will become apparent as we examine the many functions and great importance of protein in the health-growth pattern of the cat.

Protein. Protein has been called the "stuff of life." When you take a look at your cat, practically everything you see is protein—and so too are many of his parts you don't see. Hair, eyes, claws, whiskers, teeth, muscles, vital organs, blood, bones—all are, in part, protein.

Protein is linked with the health and growth pattern of the cat throughout his entire life. But protein needs vary at different stages of the cat's life cycle as the requirements for building and repair materials vary.

Chemically, protein is made up of more than twenty amino acids, some of which the body—the cat's body, like your own—can manufacture. Some of these amino acids cannot be manufactured by either man or animal.

* Scott, P. *Feline Medicine and Surgery* (Wheaton, Ill.: American Veterinary Publications, Inc., 1964).

Calorie Count of Foods Often Used in Feline Diets

This list of foods, with portions and caloric value, will assist the cat owner in understanding "food energy." Because of the cat's specific nutritional needs, which must be satisfied with a well-rounded cat diet, no one food in this list is recommended for regular feeding as a total meal or total diet. Balanced canned cat foods, not the gourmet foods, use a careful blend of many of these foods. Some family dishes are included because many cats are fed from the family table. In general, homemade diets lack the necessary balance of nutrients.

	Portion	Approx. Calories	IMPORTANT FOOD NUTRIENTS
RAW MEATS			
Beef (trimmed for retail)		257	complete protein, fat, niacin
Veal (trimmed for retail)		156	complete protein, fat, niacin
Lamb (trimmed for retail)	3½ ozs.	247	complete protein, fat, calcium, niacin
Liver (beef)		140	complete protein, fat, vitamin A, riboflavin, niacin
Kidney (beef)		130	complete protein, fat, vitamin A, riboflavin, niacin
Heart (veal)		124	complete protein, niacin
COOKED MEATS			
Beef (pot-roasted)		327	complete protein, fat, niacin
Veal (stewed)		216	complete protein, niacin
Lamb (roasted)	3½ ozs.	300	complete protein, fat, niacin
Liver (beef, simmered)		174	complete protein, vitamin A, riboflavin, niacin
Kidney (beef, simmered)		170	complete protein, vitamin A, riboflavin, niacin
Heart (veal, simmered)		164	complete protein, niacin

	Portion	Approx. Calories	IMPORTANT FOOD NUTRIENTS
POULTRY			
Chicken (roasted)	3½ ozs.	188	complete protein, fat, niacin
Turkey (roasted)		200	complete protein, fat, niacin
Chicken liver (raw)		129	complete protein, vitamin A, riboflavin, niacin
Chicken liver (simmered)		165	complete protein, vitamin A, riboflavin, niacin
Chicken (boneless canned)		195	complete protein, fat, niacin
FISH AND SHELLFISH			
Mackerel (canned)	3 ozs.	155	complete protein, fat, calcium, niacin
Tuna (canned)		170	complete protein, fat, calcium, niacin
Shrimp (canned)		100	complete protein, calcium
Clams (canned)		45	complete protein, calcium
Swordfish (broiled)		150	complete protein, vitamin A, niacin
Salmon (canned)		120	complete protein, fat, calcium, niacin
CEREALS			
Corn, rice, wheatflakes	1 oz.	110	protein, carbohydrate, niacin
Oats, puffed	1 oz.	115	protein, carbohydrate, calcium
Oatmeal (cooked)	1 cup	130	carbohydrate
Rice (cooked)	1 cup	185	carbohydrate, niacin
Macaroni (cooked)	1 cup	190	vegetable protein, carbohydrate, iron
Bread (white, enriched)	1 slice	60	vegetable protein, carbohydrate, calcium, niacin

VEGETABLES (Cooked)	Portion	Approx. Calories	IMPORTANT FOOD NUTRIENTS
Carrots	1 cup	91	carbohydrate, calcium, vitamin A
Potatoes (white, boiled)	1 potato	90	carbohydrate, calcium, niacin
Beans (snap)	1 cup	30	calcium, vitamin A, vitamin C
Beans (lima)	1 cup	180	vegetable protein, carbohydrate, calcium, vitamins A and C, niacin
Asparagus	1 cup	35	vitamin A, niacin, vitamin C
Tomatoes (canned)	1 cup	50	vitamin A, niacin, vitamin C
Peppers	1 pod	15	vitamin C
Spinach	1 cup	40	calcium, vitamin A, niacin, vitamin C
Corn (canned)	1 cup	170	carbohydrate, vitamin A, niacin, vitamin C
Peas (cooked)	1 cup	115	carbohydrate, calcium, iron, vitamin A, niacin, vitamin C

MILK AND RELATED PRODUCTS

	Portion	Approx. Calories	IMPORTANT FOOD NUTRIENTS
Milk (whole, cow's)	1 cup	160	complete protein, calcium, vitamin A
Evaporated (undiluted)	1 cup	345	complete protein, fat, calcium, vitamin A
Dry (nonfat)	1 cup (fluid)	80	complete protein, fat, calcium, vitamin A
Cheese (grated Cheddar, American)	1 cup	445	complete protein, fat, calcium, vitamin A
Cheese (Creamed cottage) skim milk	1 cup	240	complete protein, calcium, vitamin A
Butter	1 tbs.	100	fat, calcium, vitamin A
Margarine	1 tbs.	100	fat, calcium, vitamin A

	Portion	Approx. Calories	IMPORTANT FOOD NUTRIENTS
BABY FOODS			
High Protein		357	vegetable protein, fat, carbohydrate, calcium, iron, vitamin A, thiamine, riboflavin, niacin
Beef (strained)	1 jar	99	complete protein, niacin
Beef liver (strained)		97	complete protein, fat, vitamin A, riboflavin, niacin
Veal (strained)		91	complete protein, niacin
FAMILY DISHES			
Macaroni and cheese	1 cup	470	complete protein, fat, carbohydrate, calcium, iron, vitamins A
Spaghetti and meatballs	1 cup	335	complete protein, fat, carbohydrate, calcium, iron, vitamins A and C
Hamburger (broiled)	3 ozs.	185–245	complete protein, fat, niacin
Beef stew with vegetables	1 cup	210	complete protein, carbohydrate, vitamin A, niacin, vitamin C
Fish sticks	1 stick	40	complete protein, fat, carbohydrate

Sources: *Composition of Food*, Agricultural Handbook No. 8, U. S. Dept. of Agriculture.
Nutritive Value of Food, U. S. Dept. of Agriculture.

These are called the "essential amino acids," and must be supplied by food. All told, there are ten essential amino acids. Some protein foods contain all ten, some do not. When all ten are present, and an adequate supply of nonessential amino acids is also present, we have a complete protein food. When some are missing, we have an incomplete protein food.

The Cat's Protein Requirement. Cats need a diet with a high-protein content, considerably higher than that of dogs or people. As in the case of calories, kittens need far more protein than adult cats, approximately one-third more. Not only does the baby cat double his weight in one week, he trebles it in two and quadruples it in three. All the expanding new parts of his body need protein for proper growth. Contrast this with the human baby who doubles weight in six months.

Recommendations on protein go like this: 25 percent for adults and up to 40 percent for kittens, dry weight. Wet weight (70 percent moisture) protein, 8 percent for adult cats, 12 percent for kittens. These are minimum requirements, however, and the experts consider 15 percent (wet) a more satisfactory level for adults.

Quality of protein must also be considered. If protein source is egg, meat, and milk, 8 percent is adequate; if the protein comes from grains and by-products, 12–25 percent is needed.

Milk Protein. We can't talk of protein for kittens and cats without considering milk protein. The nursing cat's milk is a rich source of protein. Half the milk solids—about 20 percent of all milk is solids—is protein. As long as the little cat can depend on mother's supply, and as long as she is well fed, little cat does very well. But on cow's milk he may not live. This is why researchers are recommending a special milk mixture for the kitten who no longer gets mother's milk. Use a dry powdered milk, they say, at double the concentration used for the human baby. Evaporated milk can also be used successfully. And there are special products available on the market for feeding orphan kittens.

Major Food Sources of Protein. As in the family diet, meats, both the muscle meats and the organ meats, head the list of favorite protein foods. Beef, veal, lamb—the average cat likes any and all. All kinds of poultry belong on the list, and fish and cheese and milk. These are complete protein foods. Incomplete protein in cat foods is usually supplied by soybean meals, cornmeal, barley and other cereals, and by certain vegetables such as green beans, peas, and carrots. Many of the meat by-products used in canned and dry cat foods are also incomplete.

Carbohydrates. Most of us know carbohydrates as sugars and starches, and loosely speaking, this is correct. Cats apparently don't need carbohydrates, but tolerate some of them very well, and frequently enjoy them thoroughly. Starches and dextrins as found in such foods as rice, potatoes, and macaroni, if the foods are cooked, can make up as much as half of the dry weight of the diet.

Sugars—sucrose and lactose—are less well tolerated, and it is the lactose of milk that causes ferment in the stomach of many cats—ferment and vomiting and diarrhea. On the milk question, cats, like some people, are sometimes allergic to milk and milk by-products such as whey. Sucrose (table sugar) in large quantity can also produce diarrhea.

Carbohydrates are not without their values. They add bulk to the diet and they aid in utilization of other nutrients, as well as supplying needed calories.

Since puss does not spend hours before a mirror or weigh himself daily on the bathroom scales, just make sure that he does not overeat on a favorite carbohydrate. That too-well-rounded look which you recognize all too well in yourself may repeat in kitty, and carbohydrates can be one of the causes.

Fat Requirements in the Cat's Diet. The American public has been so well alerted to the problems of fat in the diet, that some of this may rub off in your thinking about fat in the feline diet. Your cat needs and tolerates fat very well. Even on diets up to 64 percent fat, there have been no signs of the heart and vascular problems we humans fear. Diets ranging between 15 and 40 percent fat are quite acceptable and recommended to supply the concentrated calories needed by kitty. Since fats are more expensive than carbohydrates, many cat foods are low in fat. To ensure adequate fat, give him regularly such things as butter, vegetable oil, fat trimmed from meats and poultry.

Fats are not only growth promoters but also fight fatigue. Fat acts as an insulating material to help keep the body warm and contributes to the resilience of inner body tissues. Like carbohydrates, fat aids in the utilization of other nutrients, and some fats are carriers of essential vitamins.

Perhaps you did not realize it, but the newborn kitten has practically no body fat. At first his body warmth must come from his hovering mother and his littermates. As he grows, he not only adds fatty tissues that help to keep him warm, but his body temperature slowly rises to the normal 101.5° F. of the adult cat.

Where the cat is concerned, the kind of fat he is given is perhaps most important. The unstable polyunsaturated fats found in fish oils, margarine, and soybean oil are antagonistic to one very important vitamin, vitamin E. With too many unsaturated fatty acids in fat-rich foods, the quality of fat deposits in the body can be seriously affected. The so-called yellow-fat disease can cause pain, partial paralysis, even death. So important is this finding that it has been highlighted again in the section on canned cat food, especially fish, where supplementation with vitamin E may not be sufficient to combat the problem.

Vitamin Requirements of the Cat. You and I are continuously bombarded by information on vitamins. Radio, TV, advertisements in the press, and labels all pound away at us, mainly because someone has vitamins to sell. However, I would bet that on a quiz program most of us would go down to defeat if asked to state a correct vitamin intake or to explain what each vitamin does. In feline nutrition, the confusion is much worse, for until recently even the experts have not known enough to set recommended allowances or to define the exact functioning of the vitamins.

For the moment, here is the latest information available in what I hope are simple understandable terms.

Vitamin A. Cats are dependent on their diet for fully formed vitamin A, which means they cannot, as we humans do, synthesize or manufacture vitamin A in the body from carotene, which is found in foods like carrots and other yellow and green vegetables.

Vitamin A is a very essential nutrient in the diet of the cat. It is believed to be a growth promoter. It helps in the maintenance of good skin. It contributes to proper eye functioning, and seems to guard against certain of the eye infections. Vitamin A is closely linked with reproductive activity and will make a difference in the health and strength of the newborn kitten.

As the table of nutrients indicates, a high intake of vitamin A must be maintained—at least 1,600–2,000 I.U. per day for adult cats. Nursing queens need an extra supply, since vitamin A reserves are cut in half during pregnancy, and in half again while mothers are feeding the litter. While vitamin A is important, as stated above, amounts above the requirements are of no value and may even be harmful. Be sure your cat has enough—but not too much.

Major Sources of Vitamin A. Liver and other organ meats are probably the best sources for cats. Other high-source foods are fish and other seafoods, butter, margarine, milk, and cheese.

The B Complex. The B complex family has been a growing family, and quite possibly we do not yet know all of the members. By now, however, most followers of modern nutrition recognize thiamine, riboflavin, niacin, pantothenic acid, pyridoxine, biotin, and vitamin B_{12}.

Just as the family is multiple, so its functions are multiple. All B vitamins are essential to top health. Some contribute to nervous stability. Some help to maintain good condition of the outer skin and the inner tissues. Pyridoxine (B_6) is a factor in preventing the development of urinary "gravel" and so-called calculi which cause serious trouble for probably 10 percent or more of altered male cats.

As with other nutrients, needs vary according to age and stage of life. Once again, the pregnant or nursing queen needs extra. Her vitamin requirements are double or triple those of other adult cats. In general, the cat requires twice the amount required by the dog. The prolonged use of dog foods for cats may result in B complex deficiency.

Some of the B vitamins can be destroyed by overheating, something that can happen in the canning process. One, niacin, cannot be manufactured by the cat's body and so must come in the food. And a third, thiamine, can be destroyed by an antagonist in raw fish.

Major Sources of B Vitamins. Raw meats and whole-grain cereals are good sources.

Vitamin D. We have long ago been introduced to vitamin D as the "sunshine vitamin," and so it is, for by exposure to sunshine, our bodies can manufacture vitamin D. It would seem that cats have this same ability, but apparently not in the same degree.

Actually, the cat's need for vitamin D is rather small. Some kittens born in the winter or raised in dark cellars show signs of a kind of "rickets," a bone condition similar to human rickets and related to a deficiency of vitamin D. However, adult cats live in fine and healthy condition in dark city apartments that never see even a shaft of sunshine.

Manufacturers of canned cat foods usually add irradiated yeast, a source of vitamin D. Since the needs are low, vitamin supplements containing vitamin D should not be used for cats. Here is one area where vitamin supplements can be dangerous.

Vitamin E. Some of the most impressive information on vitamins relates to vitamin E, the true vitamin E that can now be manufactured in a stable form. Not only does vitamin E play a part in general good health, but it aids proper reproductive activity, is involved in the maintenance of muscle tone, including such a vital muscle as the heart, and helps to keep the fatty tissues of the body in proper condition. Birds, animals of almost every species, and man all apparently need vitamin E.

Sheep and dogs deprived of vitamin E have suffered heart failure. Turkeys minus proper amounts of vitamin E can lay infertile eggs. Racehorses without sufficient vitamin E often have poor performance records and are retired from the track more quickly than owners would wish. And cats short of vitamin E may show signs of lameness, very painful lameness, and have a change in fatty tissues that can be sometimes felt in casual examination of advanced cases—a doughy, lumpy or granular feeling. Without vitamin E therapy, such cats may not only suffer great pain, but often die. Even with therapy, some cats never recover.

In cats, the major reason for a vitamin E deficiency is the all-fish diet. Fish oils are high in polyunsaturated fatty acids—antagonists of vitamin E. These antagonists are very efficient—they destroy vitamin E. It is doubtful whether the addition of antioxidants to fish or the addition of vitamin E to fish solves the problem.

Vitamin E deficiency can be prevented by feeding a well-balanced diet, not composed mainly of fish or other foods high in unsaturated fatty acids. Cheap canned fish foods for cats and human fish foods—tuna, salmon, sardines—should be avoided.

Mineral Requirements of Cats. As with the vitamins, so with the minerals. Cats need the same ones you do, but in somewhat different quantities and apparently in a different mineral-to-mineral balance. Actually, mineral requirements are quite low, so supplements are unnecessary unless you are feeding an all-meat diet.

Sodium, Potassium, Magnesium. It is actually not essential that the average cat owner know too much about these three minerals. The amounts of these minerals that are lost through body wastes are usually replaced by food, and an average good diet provides sufficient amounts.

Apparently there is a very delicate balance that must be sustained between sodium and potassium. Cats, being meat eaters, have a rather high intake of potassium. The dangerous urinary ailments of cats seem to arise, in some cases at least, when the sodium-potassium balance is too high on the potassium side.

Calcium. Calcium is vitally important to the full development of bones and teeth. But to do this job of building, calcium must have such teammates as protein, phosphorus, and vitamins A and D.

Kittens need much more calcium than adult cats, and I find it interesting that kittens utilize some 80 percent of the calcium provided by food, while adult cats utilize only 30 percent. An intelligent body mechanism turns off use when need declines. As you might guess, the pregnant or nursing queen has a high calcium need, and at this point in her life, she recovers her ability to use food calcium.

One of the best sources of calcium for kitty has been snatched away from him—the bones of fish and birds. Some experts say that, contrary to a lot of talk, these bones very rarely cause any harm. To be fully safe, don't take a chance, rule out bones of any kind unless they are finely ground.

For the cat who can take it, milk is an excellent calcium source. And in the canned cat food section, look on the label for the ingredient "bone meal," which is another good source.

Veterinarians meet a fair amount of calcium deficiency in their patients. Be sure to put this mineral on your list of nutrients that are truly needed and may be short in supply if you are feeding all-meat foods or the gourmet-type cat foods such as liver or kidney.

Iron and Copper. Unlike humans, cats utilize most of the iron and copper provided by food, so that iron-deficiency anemia, which one TV sponsor has talked about for years, does not haunt kitty—if she or he is on a balanced diet.

Iodine. Yes, cats need iodine, and some cats and kittens suffer from thyroid conditions if iodine is lacking. Stunted growth may be one sign of insufficient iodine. The best source is iodized salt, present in most cat foods.

Water. Your pet can live for quite a time without food, but he cannot get along without water. Many new pet owners do not know this. When I give kittens for adoption, and I have given hundreds, I always find surprise when water is mentioned. Water must be available at all times and should be kept fresh and cool, not old. One of my city-cat friends, Gregory by name, fell from the window of his apartment to the roof beneath. His frantic mistress could not find him. Fortunately a smokestack gave him refuge, and a snowstorm gave him water. Two weeks later he was discovered, unhurt, skin and bones, but alive and able to recover rather rapidly.

The water problem for cats is complicated by what is happening to all water sources. In the city some cats react to the chemicals used to keep water potable. In the country where no municipal sewage systems exist, detergents in drainage systems can make a cat very sick. And so too can insect sprays, which settle and float on water bowls or water puddles. If you use sprays inside or out, be sure to empty any water-filled containers immediately.

You don't have to teach a cat to drink. Even as a rather small kitten he moves naturally to the water bowl. The amount a cat drinks depends on a number of things—age, body weight, physical condition. Little kittens actually drink more for their size than do adult cats. The pregnant and nursing mother cat needs more water than usual. And the kind of food you are feeding your cat has a great influence on his water intake. On canned foods with a moisture content of about 70 percent, much of the essential water comes from the food. Kitty may drink no more than one fluid ounce. On dry food, he may well drink as much as seven fluid ounces. As in water drinking, no two cats are alike, so don't be surprised if your pet does not conform to any hard-and-fast rule.

There is one time when water consumption should worry you. If puss suddenly drinks and drinks and drinks, he may have a kidney or urinary problem, or be coming down with some serious ailment. Don't fail to notice this, no matter how busy you are. If your cat can't get enough water, get him to a doctor as fast as possible.

Making Nutrition Work. This is pretty much up to you. If you think nutrition is a dull dish, and some of my friends do, you may not take the time to delve into it. Actually, the basic facts are pretty simple, and once captured, stick to the mind rather well. Only in its application does a knowledge of nutrition really mean anything. The following chapters will attempt to make that application as easy as possible.

Vitamin Requirements

Adult cats—weight 5 to 7 pounds—daily food intake 5¼ ounces

Vitamins	*Amount Per Day*	
Vitamin A	1,600–2,000 i.u.*	All these daily needs, except vitamin D, met with a well-balanced diet including cooked and raw muscle meat and organ meats, cooked or canned chicken and fish, vitamin-rich cereals and vegetables.
Vitamin D	50–100 i.u.	
Vitamin B₁—Thiamine	0.4 mg.	
Vitamin B₂—Riboflavin	0.2 mg.	
Niacin—Nicotinic Acid	2.6–4.0 mg.	
Vitamin C—Ascorbic Acid	—	
Vitamin E	0.36–6.3 mg.	

* Per 1¾ oz. dry food or 5¼ oz. wet food.

For pregnant or lactating queens who often eat 10 to 15 ounces of food daily, vitamin requirements should be doubled or tripled. Big cats weighing more than 5 to 7 pounds and eating large amounts of food also need additional vitamin intake.

Source: Scott, P. *Feline Medicine and Surgery* (Wheaton, Ill.: American Veterinary Publications, Inc., 1964).

C. HOW TO FEED

Keep It Clean. How to feed is almost more important than what to feed or how much. Despite the tales of the garbage-pail cat, no well-loved and well-fed pet would do anything but sneer at a garbage pail.

Cats are essentially very clean. Watch them work away at themselves, scrubbing everything from whisker to footpad. Just as they hate dirt on themselves, so they hate dirty dishes. Figure how you would feel if you sat down to a table on which today's dinner was piled on yesterday's unwashed plate. Wash your cat's plate as meticulously as you would wash your own, and dry it so that you are not mixing food with dishwater, or dried soap or detergent, which can produce diarrhea.

For some reason which I do not understand, cats react to the surface from which they eat. Plates, for example, are preferred to bowls, even for sloppy foods. My Big Boy won't eat from dark-colored bowls or plates. Chip hates plastic plates. Pete prefers a nice clean newspaper for raw foods. The all-round favorite—a note for manufacturers of pet dishes—is a coupe-shaped light-colored salad plate. This shape lets kitty eat without spilling stuff over the side, obviously lets him see his food best, and permits a spread-out of food rather than mounds of stuff, which seems to discourage him.

Tempo. Whether you feed him once or twice a day, give your cat a chance to eat at his particular speed, and after a reasonable time, dump out what is left. This rule often has to be broken by working folks who rush off on the seven-fifty train or bus or whatever. Except for dry foods, most cats are not faintly interested in food that has been sitting around, for it quickly dries out, cakes over, and will draw flies or ants or whatever insect lives in your area. If a lot of good food is left on the plate, you can put it back in the can and refrigerate for a later feeding. This is not a perfect solution, but at the price of canned cat foods, it may be necessary.

Temperature. If you refrigerate opened cans, be sure to cover them tightly. Bring them back to room temperature before you serve the rest of the can. For a quick recovery of temperature, drop the can into a small saucepan of very hot water, and stir the contents. Extra trouble? Yes, a little, but much better than serving cold food, which is bad for kitty, or throwing away half-emptied cans.

Timing of Feedings. Cats are creatures of habit. They like to be fed at the same time every day. I have trained my tribe to eat at about six thirty in the morning. This is great on summer weekdays, when my schedule calls for getting up early. But on Saturdays and Sundays, and even weekdays in the dark, cold winter, I could kick myself. Pete, fifteen pounds of Pete, jumps up and down on my exhausted framework. If this doesn't do the trick, he goes out, sits on the wall, and howls. Knowing the reasonable protest of my neighbors, I answer this call of the wild, and promptly. Big Boy uses another technique. He comes up on my bed and purrs so loudly that I can't sleep through it.

The evening meal is less sensitive. If I get tied up on a late conference, I let the family wait a bit. If I'm held until after nine, I ask my most obliging landlady to do the honors.

Some families feel that they can go away for the weekend and leave enough food out on dishes to take care of their pets. This is far from a good idea. Food rapidly becomes unappetizing, and in hot weather actually spoils. Cats will live through periodic desertion, but it certainly does not contribute to comfort or the maintenance of good health. If at all possible, take puss with you. This may be a first step in teaching him to travel.

Where to Feed. Establish a regular feeding station. Probably in the kitchen, unless you have one of those closets-called-kitchens beloved by city landlords. Pick a spot that is out of traffic lanes, or you will be stumbling over dishes and cats, upsetting your pets and getting yourself thoroughly annoyed—not conducive to relaxed living. Keep clean newspapers under the feeding dishes and remove them after each meal. This will save a lot of cleaning up.

Keep water bowls in several places, but don't keep changing the locations. The same goes for bowls of dry cat foods. Puss likes to know exaclty where to find food and drink. Don't encourage your pet to drink from a water faucet because it's cute, and don't get so lazy you let him drink from a toilet bowl.

Don't place this feeding station outside in the cold, not even on a screened porch that is very cold, for food temperatures drop quickly. Don't feed out of doors where food draws an army of flies. If the statistics are right, more cats now live in the city than in the country, so some of the precautions may be for rural families only.

Quiet, Please. Many cats—most that I have known—hate to be fed in the middle of confusion. Sensitive ears hear what you don't hear, and kitty says, "Forget it, I'll wait." I always feed my cats before I serve myself or my guests. I try to see that they are not disturbed or interrupted until they have had their fill. I often won't answer a bell until

Establish a feeding station and, if possible, feed at the same time every day. Disposable newspapers under plates, a shallow plate from which food can be easily scooped up —and always that water bowl nearby.

There are times when you bring the food to the cat just as you would serve bedside food to a member of the family.

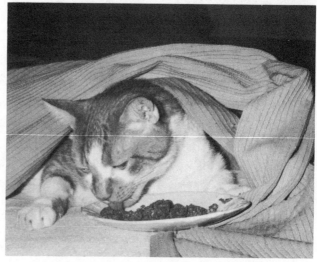

they have eaten in peace. Even if you have a noisy house, with kids making life merry, feed the cat before the sound level gets too high. The cat that is fed just ahead of the family dinner not only gets the right share of family food; but he will not hang around and beg you at the table for a handout. Many cats prefer to feed in the quiet of the night, and will clean up food rejected during the day.

Coaxing a Cat to Eat. Every book I have ever read says that this is a waste of time. I disagree, violently. A cat can be coaxed to eat and often must be coaxed. The old cat, the sick cat, the cat whose diet is being changed can be won to food.

It was with real delight that I read one sentence in a very technical book designed for veterinarians. It stated: "It has been discovered that the handling of food by attendants will frequently make it more accept-

Raw food must be cut into small pieces so that they will not choke a cat. Pete, who uses his paws like hands, is reaching for that half-inch liver—raw—which is a cat-size bite.

Teach your cat to eat from your fingers. This may be very important some day when he will accept food no other way. The experts say that a cat senses when he is being fed by a loving hand that has handled the food offered him.

Most cats instinctively eat grass to clean out an upset stomach. For the city cat provide a grass box which will grow for months if watered and clipped as your lawn would be.

able. Cats also seem to respond better to women attendants than to men."
How true. To this, another expert has added an interesting note which
says, "By the smell of the hand that feeds him, the cat can tell whether
he is being fed by someone who loves him."

When my old Pink went through a very dangerous spaying at age
fifteen, she would eat nothing. Or if she tried, she whoopsed it up. For
six months I hand-fed her. Little tiny bits at a time. Her most favorite
foods. Warm milk from my finger. Even raw fish, which is completely
taboo, but at one point, that was the only thing she would touch. It was
a long hard struggle, and at times I said to myself that life wasn't very
good for her or for me. Two years later she was just fine.

My Pete, my young'un, the big-little guy with a urinary problem, had
to have a diet change. No fish, so the doctor said. Pete agreed to this
quickly, but then he would not eat anything. Finally I discovered the
answers. If I held the plate, he would eat almost everything. If I fed him
on his favorite chair, a place where he felt secure, he would eat the same
food he would refuse in the kitchen. Like the noble Romans, he has
acquired the neat habit of eating while he lies down. Nonsense, you say.
Just the silly idea of one of those cat people. Remember it when you
have a difficult feeding problem.

Changing Diet Habits. I have one of the best veterinarians in
the world—I have found him practically infallible, but on one point, the
business of changing diet habits, I disagree with him. Says he, and wisely,
"Put the new food down, and if your cat won't eat it, take it away. When
he gets hungry enough, he will eat what you serve." Sorry, Doctor, this
may work in a caged environment, but with at-home pets, it is not the
only answer.

In the eat-it-or-go-without method, a cat may lose a lot of weight, come
up with a bad case of diarrhea, and if he is a stubborn one, still refuse
the new food. In the substitution method I prefer, the number of feedings
may be increased for a time, and the total food intake may fall, but there
is less upset to the cat's metabolism.

The Multiple-Cat Feeding Problem. It must be completely
obvious by now that my current cat family numbers three. Once, I must
admit, I had twenty-four, all at one time. Let me hasten to add that then
I lived on a big farm. Just the same, if there is anything about multiple-
cat feeding that I have not encountered, I don't know what it is.

To those of you who have more than one—and most cat lovers do—here
are a few suggestions born of long experience.

If your family of cats love one another, they will often eat better to-

Companion cats often eat best together.

gether, from the same dish. When Big Boy sees Chip digging in, he digs in. Not unlike the family situation where that thing called "togetherness" quite definitely contributes to the group enjoyment of a good meal.

Contrariwise, some cats will eat only all by themselves. A dish for each guest. This is particularly necessary when you have timid eaters, bold eaters, and ladies and gentlemen all mixed up with hoboes. You must not let one cat get all the food, and this can happen.

Sometimes there is a special kitten in a litter, a little one that does not grow, maybe won't follow the normal pattern of food acceptance. I had such a one, a small black one who seemed to get smaller, not larger. For weeks he refused all solid food. When at last he tasted a bit of baby food, I began tapping the glass jar each time I was ready to feed him. Soon, on signal, my kitten was jumping to the top of an end table where, completely alone, with no need to fight his husky littermates, he ate with increasing heartiness.

There is one angle of the multiple-cat feeding problem that can throw you. Very rarely do two cats like the same thing. And most cats can't be forced into eating foods they actively dislike. Even with my current threesome, my feeding station often has the look of a smorgasbord—cooked beef for Chip, raw liver for Pete, and cooked liver for Big Boy. Fortunately, they all agree on many other things, and demand their favorites at only one time of the day. Chip won't touch raw beef in the early morning, but looks for it as an appetizer course at dinner.

If possible, find common-denominator foods, as you do for your family —something everybody likes. Then pander to special appetites as far as you can without being ridiculous about it. I heard just yesterday of a cat owner with eight cats who spends practically his entire day preparing different menus for each cat. I forgive him only because he is a breeder.

D. CANNED AND PROCESSED FOODS

Cat Foods, Canned. A relatively short time ago the supermarket shelves blossomed with a great array of food canned especially for cats. Want a clam dinner tonight? Liver or kidney in cream sauce? A tasty beef meal? Horsemeat that smells good enough to serve the family? Chicken alone or blended with other high-protein food? Fish? Take your pick of these and a lot more.

Most of these canned foods move off the shelf almost as fast as they move on. Not only are there waiting pets at home, but cat lovers everywhere are feeding strays. I recently watched a purposeful lady scoop up twelve cans of fish. When I ventured a polite question, she announced sternly that she was off to feed "sixteen cats from down on the wharf."

How to Read the Label. By law, all of these canned foods carry labels that list nutrients and chemical analyses. This chapter contains sample labels and a chart that will help you to judge whether the ingredients listed are recommended for cats and are included in the adequate proportions.

Vitamins are mentioned on practically all labels, but amounts are not given. If you read the section on nutrition, you know why—a lack of accurate recommendations until just recently—and then not total agreement by all "experts." Actually, telling you what vitamins have been added to canned food would do you little good. Some new reports from England tell us that overheating, sterilization, and the preservatives used can all destroy up to 50 or more percent of vitamin A and a fair percentage of the B vitamins. Manufacturers are aware of this problem and are doing their best to solve it. For the moment, there may be good sense in the recommendation for regular use of a vitamin-mineral supplement that can be mixed with canned cat foods. This is not essential if a good, varied diet is sustained.

If you depend on canned food only, try to blend some of the gourmet or all-meat or fish foods with some of the cereal-based foods. Both meats and cereals are needed to provide nutrients important for your pet.

A number of canned foods now on the market are labeled for feeding both cats and dogs. Since the nutritional needs of cats are quite different from those of dogs, do not use these foods as the mainstay of the diet.

Make sure to read the label on cat foods. In addition to an analysis of content, many labels carry additional feeding directions. Increasingly, foods containing fish mention vitamin E supplementation. This is the vitamin lacking or in short supply in fish foods.

Remember, too, as you read the label, that quality of protein is more important than just quantity. Unless you know the source of the protein, "10 to 15 percent" doesn't mean a thing. The label that says clearly BEEF, BEEF BY-PRODUCTS, or TUNA or CHICKEN tells you much more than the label that says rather vaguely MEAT or FISH. Frequently these labels add SOY-BEAN MEAL, CORNMEAL, BARLEY, or some similar combination of cereal foods. If the proportion of cereals is high, much of the protein in these cans is the incomplete kind, lacking in those essential amino acids. Experts say very clearly that incomplete proteins, in cereals, for example, are good and inexpensive sources of energy, but do not have the body-building qualities of the complete proteins in meat, poultry, fish, and dairy products.

How Good Is Good? Just how good are these canned cat foods? Very good indeed, the best of them. They have been formulated carefully by teams of scientists working for good food manufacturers constantly striving for improvement. It is fair to say that most cats live and thrive on a largely canned-food diet—*if the best of the canned products are selected—and if they are fed in variety and in quantities to satisfy caloric needs.*

New Gourmet Foods. Recently, types of so-called gourmet cat food have appeared on most supermarket shelves or are featured by specialty food shops. These gourmet foods lay their claim to fame as "high protein" and "all-meat," and say very clearly how they are blended and seasoned to tempt the most finicky cat. Their advertising makes quite a point of the omission of cereals and other "filler" foods. Gourmet food prices are high, but despite this their popularity has grown. In buying these new products, just remember that they do not attempt to put a balanced diet into the can. Their taste appeal can easily make them habit-forming—and often a bad habit. When being used, they should be extended or mixed with other formulated cat foods that are cereal-based. Now you have quality protein in a reasonably well-balanced ration.

As other extenders for gourmet foods, use rice, potatoes, macaroni, or some of the green and yellow vegetables. Meaty Italian green beans head the list in my house. But on occasion there are other favorites—string beans, baby limas, peas, carrots, even winter squash. I have watched my Pete carefully pick the broad beans out of the dish and leave the meat. Since most cat foods are low in fat, it is a good idea to add to each pound of cat food one tablespoon of corn oil or other salad oil. Bacon drippings or other kitchen fat is also good.

Dog-Cat Foods, Canned. Some of the canned foods sold for dogs are reasonably acceptable to cats. Some cans are even marked "for dogs and cats." Here you are pretty much on your own. Experiment and see which foods your cat goes for. I have found a canned beef liver that my Chip—who hates liver—will gobble up and ask for more. There are also some of the meat-and-vegetable combinations that my cat family will take occasionally. Because of the large can size in which the dog foods are packed, I find myself throwing away part of every can. Cats have very specific requirements, much more exacting than dogs, so use the dog-cat foods only occasionally.

People Food for Cats. Last night my gang had roast beef and green beans and boiled potatoes for dinner, all of it people food. The roast beef came out of a can, since I don't have time, except on a weekend, to roast beef. Every last bite was licked up, including the jelly-like juice. Expensive? Not really, when you figure this meal served one person and three cats.

Try canned meats and chicken. Try hearty meat soups and roast beef hash. Chip is eager for New England clam chowder, and all the tribe go occasionally for beef stew and beef goulash—not every day, but a couple of times a week.

For kittens, baby food and junior foods—the meat ones especially—are great, and recommended, but very expensive. Some cats are kept on baby food forever. Many food experts do not approve of this because baby foods require no chewing, and chewing is what the cat has been built to do. Adult cats on baby food often have serious tooth and gum problems, and at an earlier age than would have been likely on a different diet.

All About Fish. Most cats like fish, and some are passionately addicted—"hooked," as the current word goes. There are probably more canned-fish foods for cats than any other kind. Either all-fish, or fish and another protein food, or so-called meat-flavored items that are basically fish. Much of the fish used is red tuna, and the can says so. This is the poorer tuna not packed for human consumption. Some packers mix white and red tuna to make a better product. Some add carrots, peppers, onion, and tomatoes. Many add cereal foods. But be not misled—you are still buying fish.

Increasingly, canned-fish foods for cats bear a larger-than-usual special label saying "vitamin E added." And here we hit the crux of the fish story. If you remember the vitamin E discussion in the nutrition section, you will remember that polyunsaturated fatty acids in fish are antagonists of vitamin E, and either destroy or render this vitamin ineffective. Don't feel completely assured when the can stresses a vitamin E additive. It is highly doubtful whether this addition does enough for the fish product to make it an acceptable food for puss on an everyday basis.

Many doctors believe that a lot of animals who don't like too much handling may have a minor vitamin E deficiency. Discomfort, but not disaster, if the feeding schedule is changed.

Hopefully all of this will alarm you, but don't become so alarmed that you banish fish forever. Remember the iodine in fish and the good calcium in the *small* bones you see in many of the better packs. Don't pick out these bones. Kitty can handle them. Fish can play a minor but regular role in any well-balanced diet. Or you can make it a rule to feed fish only once a week.

Red tuna is usually considered the culprit, and many cat lovers confidently buy mackerel, sardines, herring, and salmon. Fish is fish, as far as vitamin E is concerned. All of which means that as you load up on canned cat foods, limit the number of cans of fish foods, and check the labels to make sure that you have not been confused as to the real contents.

Prescription Diets. There are a number of very carefully formulated complete diet foods now available for cats. These have been scientifically developed to provide all of the essential nutrients in the right proportions, and are further planned to protect puss from certain ail-

Through your veterinarian you can secure a properly balanced prescription diet. This is expertly blended to satisfy the cat's very special nutritional needs. Some cats will refuse it. Some will accept it as their standard diet.

ments that are recognized to be diet-connected. The best known of these foods is Prescription Diet®—a canned product—created by Mark L. Morris, D.V.M., and available through veterinarians only. It combines horsemeat, meat, and meat by-products blended with whole fish, egg yolks, cottage cheese, and certain cereal foods. The mineral and vitamin content is excellent. Designed originally for cats with a urinary problem, the food soon demonstrated its value in prevention or control of other diseases. Finally, demand, both professional and popular, brought about the manufacture and wide distribution of Prescription Diet c/d®, as the diet is called.

Many of the animal centers depend upon Prescription Diet c/d® and use it extensively, sometimes in combination with a variety of commercially canned foods. Many pet owners swear by the diet and report excellent results—happy, healthy cats with a minimum of ailments. Some owners find the diet too expensive and think they cannot afford it. The higher caloric density, however, reduces the quantity eaten, thus there is little difference in cost, especially if veterinarian bills are considered. Cats, being cats, either like it or don't. Usually, if trained to the diet from kittenhood, puss rarely yearns for the foods he has never tasted. The track record of the diet is a fine one. It is also interesting to note that cats on Prescription Diet c/d® seem to develop far fewer urinary problems, which cause the cat family so much trouble. There are other less widely distributed feline foods, usually devised by breeders whose interest in the cat they sell does not end with the sale. One of the better known of these is a frozen product—a combination of raw chopped kidney, a small amount of fish, meat products, and egg yolk, with mineral and vitamin supplementation. It is marketed in neat plastic containers, each container a single meal. The cost is greater than the cost of commercially canned cat foods, but like the canned Prescription Diet®, it provides a balanced meal with everything your pet needs and in the right proportions. City dwellers who have little time to spend as they rush to business are high on this and other complete foods.

These special diets now on the market are not the total answer and may not be your answer. You can do it yourself, less expensively, if you make it your business to understand your cat's nutritional needs. But these carefully formulated foods are a big step in the right direction. Hopefully, we will soon be able to walk into a supermarket and purchase at reasonable prices a lot of products that do a fully competent job of good feeding. This is the direction in which the big commercial manufacturers of pet-food products for cats are moving, and strongly.

Don't Overstock on Canned Foods. If you find a canned product your cat thoroughly enjoys, make sure you have a small supply on hand, but don't make the mistake of buying by the dozen. Although cats do establish strong food-habit patterns, they can also show a fickle fancy; they may suddenly refuse what has been a favorite food. The good beef dinner your cat cried for last night, he may well walk away from tomorrow.

Never stop trying for a varied diet, something different each day of feeding. Make every effort to use up a can fast. Many cats will not eat food from an opened can, even if it has been refrigerated and brought back to room temperature. And throwing away half-used cans can run up your food bill alarmingly. I suspect that some of the volume of the canned cat food business rests on the discard of partially used cans.

Dry Cat Foods. There are a number of good pelleted dry foods. Again, the nutrient analysis is on the box. I have heard, many times, that with water and dry cat food, puss can survive comfortably. This may well be, in an emergency, but the consensus of expert opinion places the dry foods in the free-choice class—available at all times, but not to be counted on for full feeding. There has been a notable increase in urinary calculi in cats fed exclusively on dry foods.

Chewing these hard pellets is apparently good for the teeth and helps to counteract tartar, which will form if only soft foods are fed. One note of suggestion—make sure the dry foods are fresh. If they sit around, they pick up moisture and get stale. Empty out a dish and fill it with fresh food—then watch your cat move in. Remember, too, that cats eating dry foods need lots of fresh water.

What to Look For on a Label

WET-WEIGHT ANALYSIS OF FOOD

	Meat, poultry, or fish-based food	*Cereal-based food*
Protein	min. 80%	min. 15%
Fat	min. 4–5%	min. 4–5%
Fiber	max. 1%	max. 1%
Ash	max. 3–4%	max. 3–4%
Moisture	max. 74%	max. 74%

Typical Ingredients

Meat, poultry, or fish. Sauce of wheat flour and water. Ground bones. Brewer's yeast. Onion or garlic powder. Carrots, bell peppers, tomatoes, spinach. Iodized salt. Vitamin supplements.

Meat by-products. Soy grits. Pearl barley. Cornmeal. Wheat-germ meal. Bone meal. Vitamin supplements. Iodized salt.

DRY-WEIGHT ANALYSIS OF FOOD

Protein	Min. 21–24%
Fat	Min. 5%
Fiber	Max. 4.5%
Ash	Max. 11–12%
Moisture	Max. 10%

Typical Ingredients of Wet and Dry Foods

Ground yellow cornmeal, wheat middlings, meat and bone meal, wheat germ meal, fish meal, dried skimmed milk, animal liver and glandular meal, iodized salt, mineral and vitamin supplements.

Note: Both dry and canned cat foods now include vitamin E in addition to B complex vitamins, and irradiated dried yeast, source of vitamin D.

E. RAW AND COOKED FOODS

Raw Meats. Ideally, your cat should have plenty of meat—both the muscle kind and the organ meats—lungs, heart, brains, liver, and kidney. Meats, both raw and cooked, not only supply the right kind of protein—the complete kind—but are good sources of essential vitamins, vitamin A in the fatty meats, and many of the B complex family. Cooking meats, as in canning, destroys vitamins to a small degree. Do check your veterinarian on raw versus cooked meats. Current research indicates that raw meats can be a source of infectious parasites which may be transferable to humans. If you do feed raw meats, here are some how-to suggestions:

. . . Quite a lot of cats will eat small chewy pieces of beef when they refuse hamburger. There is probably some long-established instinct that invites them to tear meat into chunks. After all, the meat grinder is of rather recent origin, somewhat younger than the cat family. In one of my very low-budget days, I used to get beef fat from the local butcher, presumably for the birds. The birds got most of the fat, but the cats got all the lovely little pieces of meat that a careless knife had not cut off. Saturday morning was the big-treat day, and my cat family sat around in a circle while I salvaged every last little bit of fresh red beef, divided equally, of course. Try tossing the chunks to the cats. The feeding can have the added lure of turning into a game of catch-as-catch-can.

. . . Dice raw kidney and mix it with hamburger. This may get the hamburger down, even if kidney is the favorite.

. . . Feed raw meats as an extra to a basic balanced diet, a snack in the middle of the day. I am sure the snack makes pets feel loved. It is a special-attention gesture.

More About Organ Meats. Especially in feeding the organ meats, there are a few things to remember. In general, cats prefer kidney to liver, or perhaps I should say that more cats will eat the kidney than the liver. My family likes beef kidney better than any other kind, but lamb kidneys and the more expensive veal kidneys are highly desirable. Good steer liver is sweet and tender, but again some cats will refuse this and accept chicken livers only. Raw, both kidney and liver can cause diarrhea, if too much is fed.

All the raw meats, but especially the organ meats, should be cut up in about half-inch pieces. You may find that it is quite a chore, early in the morning especially, to slice up a glistening red kidney, or a firm resistant heart, or a hard-to-conquer chicken gizzard. Don't fail to do the job correctly. Too big a piece can choke a cat to death, as it once did the prize breeder female belonging to one of my friends.

While kitty is chewing up these delicacies, don't suddenly frighten him. In fear or disturbance, he may fail to chew and try to swallow something he cannot handle.

Since these meats must be refrigerated, I make a point of running them under very hot tap water before cutting and feeding. Cold foods, as you know, are not for cats. My Big Boy will simply vomit the stuff back, if the temperature is not right.

Cooked Meats. Any of the muscle meats—beef, lamb, veal, pork —plus chicken and fish—can be fed cooked, depending on which your cats prefer. Liver must be cooked quickly and lightly so that it is still very tender and juicy. Pork must be cooked to avoid the dangers of trichinosis. And so too with fish. Fish must be cooked to protect against the danger of certain parasites whose larvae live in raw fish and also to destroy the harmful enzymes that cause thiamine deficiency. This also goes for shellfish. For the most part, leftovers from your family table should supply these cooked foods.

Starchy Foods and Vegetables. This is a repeat, but worth it. Rice, potato, macaroni, fall into the "served cooked" class. So do all of the starchy vegetables, and almost any vegetable. Corn is an exception. Very fresh corn, just pulled from the stalk, is a real treat, but it must be right off the stalk. When I lived on a farm, I could hardly get the corn from the field to the house. At the first sound of a husk being ripped off the ear, I had a gang of customers. Many cats adore cream-style corn, but it does not agree with all pets. Corn may scratch tender linings of stomach and intestines, just as it may in your own digestive system. In canned cat foods, corn is a good starch ingredient.

Cereals. One of the processed high-protein cereals often used in baby feeding is equally good for cat babies. Mix the cereal with either water or milk, whichever the little ones tolerate best. I have no authoritative information on things like oatmeal and Cream of Wheat, but have used both, cooked, for both big and little cats, as extenders of high-protein foods.

Dry cereals are great favorites with many cats. Since most cereals are vitamin-and-mineral rich, don't hesitate to include them, if your cat goes for this kind of thing. Cereals belong in the balanced diet.

Bread—bread and milk—was once a favorite food for farm cats, partially because it was cheap and always available. There is no evidence that bread is a good cat food, and most of the cats I have known refuse it, unless it appears as stuffing from poultry—in other words, cooked.

Special Home-Cooked Rations. I read about things like this, and then walk away. First of all, home-prepared formulas call for stewing and brewing. I suspect these home-created items satisfy the owner more than they do the cat. Most of us are too busy in this busy world to concoct such brews. Unless you are a breeder, there is usually no reason, except for a kind of self-satisfaction, or that other thing called a "conversation piece." If you want to spend your time working up a formula, and if your cat will eat what you have cooked up, and if it supplies his needs, have fun. But don't expect to set a style.

Cheese. Let us not overlook cheese. Little kittens, and big ones, too, often love cheese. My Old Pink liked Cheddar, the old-fashioned "store" cheese kind. Pete prefers macaroni and cheese—cooked cheese. Lots of cats will accept and enjoy cream or cottage cheeses. Fine and dandy if they do. Cheese supplies calcium, complete protein and fat —all right for him. If you don't have a cheese cat, don't make an issue of it.

Eggs. When I lived on a farm and kept a laying flock, my cats got a fair share of the "cracks." They relished both whites and yolks—if the eggs were completely whipped. Some experts give directions for feeding yolks raw and whites cooked, a method with which many cats agree. Unless you are a poultryman, you won't have a wealth of eggs to feed. What's more, your cat may have little or no interest in eggs. If you can, feed once or twice a week. Mix raw egg yolk or diced hard-boiled egg with some food you are serving. If you skip eggs, don't get excited. If the rest of your cat's menu plan is good, he will live long years without ever meeting an egg.

Family Diets Not Suited to Cats. If your family is on a special diet for health or religious or any other good reasons, or if you are playing with some kind of a get-thin-quick or add-pounds diet, don't ask kitty to join you. Your pet's food requirements make it impossible for him to be a vegetarian. Highly spiced foods, which do him no good, make it undesirable for him to eat in many languages. And he doesn't understand fast days.

How to Check Nutrients in Raw and Cooked Foods. When you feed raw or home-cooked foods, it is very simple to figure out the percentages or units of essential nutrients and the calorie count of the amount fed. With reference to the two charts shown on pages 69 to 73, the one a "portion" chart, the second a "composition of foods" chart, you are in business. Once again, as with canned food, make a list of the foods you feed most frequently so that you don't have to run for the book and exasperate yourself every time it's mealtime.

The Economics of the Business. When I mentioned to a friend of mine that something should be said in this book about money, and what it costs to feed a cat, I got a loud cry. "Don't mention cost," he said. "This might be negative." Well, come now, how unrealistic can you be. Of course it costs something to feed a cat, and this is multiplied by the number of cats you have. I can't afford sirloin steak every day, nor do I need to pat myself on the back by assuring friends that my cats refuse

How many cats are too many? To cat people that is a difficult question to answer. Sometimes it comes down to sheer economics, for a family like this, even on an economy diet, will eat fifty cents' worth of food daily.

everything except sirloin. Don't fall into the status-seeking area, via your pet.

In today's marketplace it may well cost you as much as thirty to fifty cents a day to feed your cat with fresh and canned foods, unless you rely on sharing family food with kitty. With intelligent thinking and buying you can cut this cost in half and still do very well by your pet.

F. HOW MUCH FOOD AND HOW OFTEN

Adjusting Food Needs to Suit Your Cat. How much to feed and how often have a direct relationship to the age of a cat, to his weight, to his activity, and to his state of health. A secondary consideration is temperature, since weather, provided by the sun or the living-room radiator, may well take the edge off normally eager appetites. My three couldn't care less when the thermometer soars. But you should see them dash in, after having a ball in a snowdrift. They eat the spots off the plate.

The Nursling. In one swift year, the kitten grows from his birth weight of about three and a half ounces to an eight-pound—or better— adult. And more than two-thirds of this giant step is taken in the first six months. To build bone and muscle and tooth and furry coat, plus an assortment of vital organs, little puss will consume what at times looks like a mountain of food. For the first four weeks, of course, he sucks madly on mother, kneading her breasts to stimulate milk flow, and purring loudly in contentment. Incidentally, it is a question who likes the nursing best—mother or baby. Just watch the beatific expression on the mother cat's face as the kids tear in for dinner.

At this stage, you have no problem on how much or how often as far as the kittens are concerned. Whenever they feel the need, they suck, with mother inviting her family as the teats swell full of milk. If the queen has been well fed, mother's milk is rich in protein, a high-quality protein plus other nutrients and protective factors that nature has balanced almost perfectly.

At four weeks, the weaning process should be in full swing, although some mother cats who love to let the little ones nurse will prolong this happy babyhood. However, at about this point, your job begins, first of all to get the youngster off to his adult diet, and secondly to spare mother, who can deplete all of her reserves unless properly fed. The very special problems of the pregnant queen and the lactating mother will be detailed later.

Milk is usually the first food to which you introduce baby—milk in a dish. By dipping in little cat's mouth, while he splutters and objects, you start the drinking habit. Some small ones will never take milk—and remembering the problems milk can cause, don't force milk if the kitten fights it too much.

To repeat a recommendation already given—don't give the kitten just cow's milk. It lacks the high-protein content of mother's milk, and is inadequate for full nourishment of the growing youngster. Use powdered milk instead, in twice the concentration given human babies, then graduate to evaporated milk diluted with water—50-50. The kind of milk you and I drink is apparently suitable only for adult cats.

Quickly add human baby foods, the meat (meat-vegetable or meat-cereal) ones, or feed finely ground chopped meat. This is the great moment to establish your cat's raw meat diet and to develop his taste for many things. Continue milk and gradually try the youngsters on some of the good canned cat-food products, since ultimately you will depend largely on these.

As to how much, remember that the baby cat—four weeks old—needs four times as many calories as the adult animal. Since he also needs more of all the nutrients for his big growth push, don't be surprised if he seems

When you see your pet trying to cover up the food you have offered as he would try to cover up something in his litter box, you will know that you have served the totally unacceptable meal. Accept this supreme rejection without argument.

Every well-mannered cat always washes his face after he has dined—and for good reason, so folklore tells us. Long ago, as puss prepared to sup on a succulent sparrow, he washed before eating, at the suggestion of the wily bird, and so missed his dinner. Never since has he made such a stupid mistake.

to have a hollow leg. Expect some kittens to eat much more, some much less. As for how often to feed, the small kitten needs as much as four feedings a day. Indeed, you can feed him ad lib as much as he will eat.

The Adolescent Cat. As time goes on, the number of feedings can be reduced. By now you are probably down to two meals a day. Again be sure to watch the caloric intake. Adolescents are still eating heartily. Keep on working very hard for variety. Don't get hung up on a single-food diet because it is easier. Cat food, dog food, family foods, try them all and vary them. Add fat for increased energy need.

The Adult Cat. For adults, once-a-day feeding is often enough, although many cats prefer two meals. I personally prefer two feedings and a snack for my cats.

The average adult cat has a stomach that will accommodate four or five ounces of food at one time. Replete, with a full stomach, kitty can last twenty-four hours. Bigger cats—my Big Boy weighs twenty pounds—have bigger stomachs and need for food.

Scientifically the amount needed can be calculated according to the body surface. Since you are not about to take such measurements, work on the weight basis. For every one pound of weight the adult cat needs about 30 calories. Weigh your cat, multiply 30 by his weight, and you have the answer. If your cat is overweight, figure his needs on his correct weight and start him on a reducing diet. A list of foods and their calorie values will help you in your diet planning.

The Pregnant and Lactating Queen. The nutritional needs of the pregnant and lactating queen are very special. Unless she is full-fed, far more than usual, and has a high-quality, balanced diet, the pregnant cat will give birth to small, weak litters. A shortage in even one nutrient —vitamin A, for example—has not only cost breeders profitable kittens but impaired the health of the mother cat.

In the lactation period, the cat mother, like the human mother, drains on her body reserves to produce milk. She subtracts from body fat and muscle protein and calcium reserves to manufacture an unusual milk supply that meets the needs of her babies. As you have already read in this section, nature makes it possible for her to utilize more of the available calcium in her food than she would absorb at any other time in her life cycle. But she can get all and enough of the nutrients she needs only if she has your intelligent cooperation.

One very famous cat authority says that a lactating cat cannot be over-fed. If she is feeding four or more kittens, states Dr. Patricia Scott of the University of London and the Royal Free Hospital School of Medicine, she may consume a pound of moist food each day.

Without a plentiful food and liquid supply, such a nursing mother can lose weight rapidly, and if food is poor or inadequate, her milk flow can be cut to a point where there is not enough to sustain kittens. Just as the growing weanling kitten should be fed ad lib, so should be nursing queen be allowed to have all she wants of a balanced ration. If she seems to be stealing food intended for the youngsters or for other cats in your house, just put some more on the plate and let her have her fill. In the first few weeks, an ardent mother—and most of the queens I have known are dedicated—will hardly leave her kittens, even for food. I make it my business to get food to the cat, not the cat to the food when there is a nestful of hungry, suckling babies.

Nature being the magnificent thing it is, the mother cat can regain her body weight and nutritional balance rather quickly once her youngsters discover the delights of eating from plate and bowl. In no time at all she will be her sleek, slim, fashionable self.

The Old Cat. More and more cats grow old today, and gracefully, because their owners have learned how many years can be added to a life by good care and good nutrition.

In many ways, feeding the old cat is somewhat like feeding a kitten. Don't insist on regular meals at regular times. Let your old lady sleep late if she wishes, and as with baby cats, let her have any number of small meals through the day, whenever she shows interest in food. Since the caloric needs of the old cat are far less than those of the active kitten or young adult, the total amount of food needed by the old cat is likely to be small, even with multiple feeding.

Pamper your old friend with favorite foods, but keep a very wary eye on nutritional balance. Talk over diet with your veterinarian and get his recommendation for any special feeding techniques. Old age is often the time when vitamin supplementation is needed more than at any time in the cat's entire life-span. And it is also the time when loss of appetite is a dangerous and disturbing symptom.

The Working Cat. The working cat is often the most underfed cat in the world, except for the stray. In the country, he is relegated to the barn. Given cow's milk—warm, thank heaven. Bread. Table scraps, maybe. The old theory, still prevalent, says that the working cat must be kept hungry so that he will catch mice and rats. A vast number of barn cats never live to catch a mouse. And those that do may be so malnourished that they have no strength to hunt. The barn cat's city cousin usually lives in a basement, a smelly basement in a store or restaurant. Although he may never see the light of day, he eats a bit better, unless he must dine on heavily spiced foods.

The best-fed working cat lives in a butcher store or a delicatessen. He may be lonely on weekends, when his folks leave him in charge, but he usually gets the goodies—fresh meats, liver, cheese, milk if he likes it, canned cat food or canned people foods. And so, well supplied, he does what a working man should do. He performs as a vigilante. No marauder, be it sewer bug or mouse, escapes him.

Remember that the working cat is one of your employees. Keep him happy, see that his comfort is ensured. Feed him twice what you give the pillow-sitter, and he will be one of your better workers—bright-eyed and bushy-tailed.

I must add one kind of storekeeper to the list of perfect employers. A carpet shop near me, specializing in Orientals, has a sleek yellow-and-white who sleeps in the window, lending color contrast to the Orientals. With every movement, he invites the customer. I might add that the rug shop is flanked by a butcher store and a delicatessen.

The Sick Cat. The sick cat represents the most difficult of feeding problems. Some of the special techniques have already been discussed in the section on "Coaxing a Cat to Eat," and these hand-feeding and pampering methods will work if the cat is mildly sick or convalescent. The very sick cat cannot be coaxed. Sickness not only changes his eating habits but his whole personality. The loving animal that usually winds around your feet will crawl off to a corner or crouch by a door, barely moving a muscle, a furry lump of misery. Or he will do the more frightening thing, run away, disappear, refuse to answer calls. If possible, you must search him out and pen him up. His need for liquids and a highly nourishing diet reaches the peak in time of severe illness. Your ability to get him to eat may determine whether he lives or dies.

If you have a very sick cat, get your pet to the doctor immediately. Don't try to force-feed him on your own, in the frantic hope that some good solid food will make him well. When you don't know the ailment, you may be making matters much worse by your ministrations. It may well be that the doctor will decide on hospitalization for a period, and he is fully equipped to employ force-feeding or infusion or whatever the diagnosis dictates.

If the illness is not too serious, you may find yourself carrying kitty home with feeding instructions that include force-feeding. Chances are your doctor may suggest a baby food, one of the all-liver kind, or a new food called Initol, specially designed for sick cats.

I find a large eyedropper the best implement. Try to insert this at the side of the mouth, back of the saber tooth. Remember that easy does it, little amounts at very frequent intervals. And don't let your patience wear thin. Call up the boss and say very clearly that a member of your family is sick and needs constant attention. Nothing could be truer. How much liquid and nourishment you can get into your pet may well determine whether or not he will live.

Taking care of kitty for one dedicated day is not the answer. Most veterinarians will tell you that a lot of cats die because of nonperformance on the part of their owners. If your child has pneumonia, you don't maintain a tight ship for a day, and then walk away from the routine. If you can't keep up the very special attention your cat must have, he is better off in a cage at the doctor's, despite the fact that this is not the perfect place for him. This maintenance of routine is something you have to work out to fit your pocketbook and your living pattern, but if you want a live cat, work it out.

With the first flicker of interest in eating anything from a dish, press your advantage. Tempt, pamper, invite, pet, encourage, until puss is competent again.

8

Choosing
Your Veterinarian

As a pet owner, one of the most important decisions you will ever make is your choice of a veterinarian. The health and well-being of your pet family are directly related to the veterinarian you pick, the relationship you develop with him, and the relationships he develops with your pets. All too often, you—or any other pet owner—are apt to meet a veterinarian for the first time in the middle of a frantic emergency, and all too often, you are ready to blame this total stranger for not performing some miracle.

Instead of making a random choice from the Yellow Pages and in a moment of distress, you should go about choosing your veterinarian as you would your own physician. This will take time, because the right veterinarian for you should be someone you feel you can like and respect, someone who will understand you and like you. He should be a man (or woman) with a degree (D.V.M.—Doctor of Veterinary Medicine) from a good school of veterinary medicine. Your chosen veterinarian will have his diploma—and license where required—hanging on his office wall, as does your own physician. Preferably, the man you pick will be both general practitioner and surgeon—most veterinarians function in this dual capacity. If the services of a veterinary specialist are required, your veterinarian can direct you to such a person.

Your vet's office will tell you quite a lot about your man. It need not be pretentious, but it should be orderly and scrupulously clean, both the waiting room and the treatment rooms. If possible, ask the doctor to show

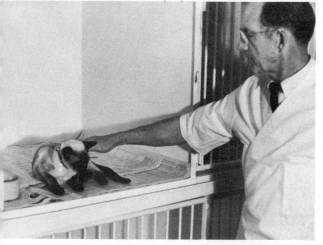

Your choice of a veterinarian may well be one of the most important decisions you make. Pick a man you like and trust, a man who likes animals, a man with reputation and training. Incidentally, the man may be a lady doctor, and you can tell whether your chosen vet has a rapport with animals as soon as you watch how he or she handles and talks to your pet.

If possible, have a look at your veterinarian's boarding or holding facilities. Cages should be fresh and clean and large enough for comfort. One cat to a cage, unless it's kittens.

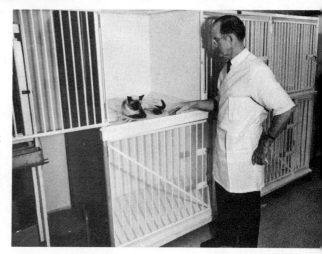

you his facilities for holding or boarding animals. Good holding cages are kept fresh and clean and equipped with water bowls and a kept-clean litter box. Don't be upset if cats and dogs are alternated in adjoining cages. Even if your cat has never met a dog, he will soon adjust. And alternation is often for a purpose. Some doctors feel that this spacing arrangement helps to prevent or check the spread of contagious disease from one cat patient to another. Good lighting and good ventilation of a cage room are also important. In facilities like these, you need not hesitate to leave your cat.

For convenience it is best to find a doctor who is not too far from your home. Traveling almost always disturbs animals and, in an emergency, closeness to an office is a great boon. Don't make this an absolute rule. If the best man in town is miles away, choose him in preference to the doctor down the street.

Young veterinarians will have some advantages over the older ones, simply because so much new research and knowledge about cats have developed in the last few years. But the older man has years of experience for which there is no substitute. Incidentally, some of our best cat doctors are lady veterinarians, just as many of the great cat research people are women. Women seem to bring to small-animal care a special warmth and sympathetic understanding of both pets and their people.

Make sure to find out your doctor's treatment hours and his timing for surgery. Discover whether he is available at night and on weekends— times when animals, like people, seem to need medical care most. If he is not available on off-hours, get his recommendation for treatment facilities you can depend on if you have need of a hurry call. Most good veterinarians will accept essential telephone calls, even at home, and no matter the hour or day. Their interest in a patient does not end when they finally take off a white coat and get out of the office. A good phone contact with your chosen veterinarian is really a vital link. Many is the time I have made a telephone call that has saved me and the doctor valuable time and ensured my cat intelligent care.

By all means check the fees your veterinarian will charge. These vary from city to country, from daytime working hours to night, weekend, or holiday calls—as they should. Usually the doctor's fee includes examination, treatment, and enough medicine to continue care at home. There are, of course, special charges for operations such as castration and spaying. If the doctor's fee is more than you can afford, say so. In many cities and towns there are animal care centers that provide excellent services at modest prices. Often these centers have some free clinics for pet owners who can qualify for care without charges. Unless you need free services for your pet, don't ask for them, and if you do apply for free care, don't resent the questions that will be asked about your financial situation, your job, and salary, if any.

One of my veterinarian friends tells a hilarious story of a family with five children and ten cats, a pet-and-people group who used to arrive regularly four or five times a year, and in a body. Each·time they put on an act. The children wept and begged the doctor's help for their pets. The older folks were full of gratitude and promises of payment—promises never fulfilled. Finally a very kind but put-upon doctor had to shut the door in their faces and warn his county colleagues to do the same.

Above all else, your veterinarian should be a person who likes animals.

And may I say that most do, or they would never have chosen their profession. I have watched veterinarians in action for many years, and I know just how tough and grueling and demanding and emotionally exhausting this job can be. My country doctor, who has served me magnificently for some thirty-odd years, often made a ten-mile trip, day or night, and several times a day when I had a critical case. And when he lost a patient, he was quite as upset as I was.

Just how can you tell whether a veterinarian likes animals? Even on a first visit, a quality of interest plus affection will come through. It will stand out loud and clear as you watch your chosen man or woman handle your pet, gently but firmly. Don't look for some phony bedside manner, just sit quietly, listen to the tone of voice as he calms your cat's fears, and watch for swift skill in his hands as he examines, treats, and deals with even painful injuries.

The people who work for your doctor will also give you many a cue about the man you have chosen. Recently I watched a great testimonial to the quality of my veterinarian's staff and facilities. I was waiting my turn when one of the kennelmen came down the stairs. Immediately a very quiet little dog next to me began to whimper and jump with delight. She strained at her leash and finally jumped into the arms of the attendant. It seems that she had been a patient for a period of some months— but almost a year ago. Her obvious affection for the man who had cared for her, and his equally frank affection for her told me a great deal about the doctor who ran the office.

Generally speaking, there are two classes of veterinarians—the large-animal doctor and the small-animal doctor. Often, in rural and small-town areas, the lines between these two types of practitioners merge, for the man who treats your cow or pig knows how important a dog or cat may be to his client and is well informed on small-animal care. The small- or big-city veterinarian rarely meets anything except small pets, and often has great expertise with the small ones.

Where to Find Your Veterinarian. If you don't know where to find a veterinarian, begin by asking around. Let's take a really tough situation. You arrive in a strange town with a sick cat. If you come by plane, go straight to the management office of the airline. Airline people are quite wonderful. They live competently with emergencies. They travel animals daily. They know an immense number of things about the facilities in the communities that surround the airport. Usually they can either tell you where to start your search or will direct you to a veterinarian. Failing airport information, check the telephone book for a local branch of the ASPCA or a Humane Society. Centers like these can give your cat emergency attention or provide you with the names of good local veterinarians. If the town is small, try the police. You may well find that the lieutenant in charge has pets of his own, and certainly he knows the local veterinarian very well. In a college town, the head of the veterinary school is a sure-fire source of information. And one other suggestion. Before you leave home with a pet for a long trip, ask your regular veterinarian for recommendations in the city or town to which you will be traveling.

When the situation is not emergency, a search for a doctor can be more relaxed. Once again the major animal health-care centers should be checked to find out what services they can render and how promptly. Cat-owning friends are an excellent source of guidance. Even cat-owning strangers. Local veterinarians who have a solid reputation in the treatment and care of little animals are widely known. Take the great city complex of New York as an example. In supermarkets I have deliberately spied on people who are buying cat foods and cat litter. And I have deliberately struck up a conversation. "Who is the vet you like?" I have asked. And again and again I have heard the names and addresses and even telephone numbers of veterinary men long familiar to me as practitioners who "have a way with cats." If this kind of information can be quickly available in the jungle of New York, it is simple to obtain in smaller communities where everybody knows everybody.

It has been my experience that unusual animal doctors are often better and more widely known than are human doctors. About a year ago, speeding along an Illinois highway to the airport, I discovered that my seatmate was a research veterinarian. New Jersey was his home state, as it was mine. He had chosen his profession, he told me, because of a small-town veterinarian who had given him in his high-school days a job as kennelman in an animal hospital. A remarkable small-animal man, my traveling companion told me, as he mentioned the doctor's name. To my amazement, it was the name of my own chosen New Jersey veterinarian who had pulled one of my best-beloved dogs through an impossible injury.

Communicating with Your Veterinarian. Communication between you and your veterinarian—real communication—is a two-way street. You must be able to provide him with sensible information about your cat and his health problems. He in turn must be able to make you understand the nature of any problem, its seriousness, and the kind and importance of the follow-through care you will have to give.

Whether you are a new or an experienced pet owner, it is only intelligent to buy a book which gives you simple and up-to-date information on warning signs of disease, the common ailments of cats, and rules of good management and good nutrition that will help to prevent illness. Don't let a rush of knowledge go to your head. Don't try to become one of those self-made experts who tells the doctor what to think. With a small amount of homework, you can learn just enough about your pet's physical makeup so that you can help and not hinder or confuse the doctor.

One excellent idea is to make a checklist like the one at the end of Chapter 8. Before you take your cat in for an examination, check any and all of the symptoms you have observed. When you get back from the doctor's office, write down his diagnosis and the date, then put the same date on any envelopes or tubes of medicine he has given you. On the same list, note the dates of distemper vaccination and subsequent booster shots. If other vaccinations have been given, enter those also. Now you are building a permanent health record for your cat, and will your veterinarian love you! This kind of orderly report, which gives him a true picture of his patient, may make a great difference in the depth and accuracy of his diagnosis.

Most veterinarians try to make the simplest possible explanations. They anticipate that many pet people who will come to them are not familiar with technical terms. Occasionally, they slip into the language of medicine. I am told that one of the most common misunderstandings occurs when the doctor asks for a "stool" sample, meaning of course a sample of a bowel movement which is taken from the litter pan. When your veterinarian uses a word you do not understand, don't feel silly if you ask for an explanation. If the cases were reversed—if your doctor were ignorant of the terms and words of your trade or profession—you would certainly not consider him a fool if he asked for interpretation.

Don't ever fail to tell the veterinarian if your cat has bitten you. If such a bite happens in the doctor's office, he must, by law, report this to the city or town health board in most areas. Rabies, tetanus, and certain other diseases can be transmitted or caused by bites. While rabies is not too prevalent in United States cats, safety rules call for an examination of the cat about ten days after the biting incident, as a protection for you, the owner. I listened in on a telephone call that came to my veterinarian recently, a call from a cat owner whose pet had bitten her not once but several times. She wished to have the cat put to sleep, and immediately. The veterinarian wisely urged against this step. He doubted that the cat had rabies. However, he urged a ten-day wait until a competent check could be made. This would ensure the health safety of the owner and not leave her in doubt. If the animal continued to be vicious, then he could with sound judgment make the only proper decision.

Don't Blame Your Doctor When You Are to Blame. Blaming the doctor is a great American sport, be he your M.D. or D.V.M. I have listened to loud complaints from friends and neighbors about the dire mistakes of Doctor So-and-So. Some of these complaints are probably justified, but usually they are not. All too often, those who scream the loudest are really the guilty parties. Many a farmer or pet owner has failed to call a veterinarian in time, waited until the animal was dying, and then put the onus of death on the veterinarian who arrived after the damage was done. Many a time, cheap, homemade remedies are tried, remedies that are not remedies at all. Or pet owners will do that other stupid thing, keep searching for a new and unfamiliar veterinarian who will agree with them.

Some errors in judgment by the pet owner are honest though misguided. They have read a book on cat poisoning, let us say. The book says give an emetic immediately. Make the animal vomit. True, getting poison out of the stomach as quickly as possible seems logical and desirable. But in vomiting, a cat can get some of the vomit into the lungs. The almost sure result is pneumonia—swift, deadly pneumonia.

This pneumonia hazard is a very big one. Let me give you another case history, which I hope will scare you. Recently a woman brought her cat to my vet's office for a diagnosis. Fleas, an army of fleas, proved to be the problem, nothing else. The veterinarian gave the lady a flea powder which was completely harmless to cats but death to fleas. He gave her explicit instructions on applications. But the lady knew better. She went home and forced two teaspoonsful of mineral oil down her pet's throat. Soon she was on the telephone, screaming that the cat could not breathe, the flea powder was at fault. She demanded a home call, which the doctor could not make. Then there was silence for twenty-four hours. When she finally turned up at the animal hospital, she brought in a dying cat. She had had to get some sleep, she said, and after all, what could flea powder do? Her cat died of what is called "inhalation pneumonia." Liquid, the mineral oil which she had forced, had reached the cat's lungs, not his stomach. She went away berating the doctor for giving her a poisonous flea powder, and she will doubtless tell all of her friends to avoid that inhumane doctor who killed her cat.

Good Manners in Your Veterinarian's Office. Start off on the right foot by making an appointment with your veterinarian. This will save you time, get your pet more prompt attention. Don't expect your appointment to be kept if there is a greater emergency in the house. I listened to a woman who brought in a cat for a simple claw clipping and was delayed by an emergency operation. She tromped up and down the waiting room, telling everybody what she thought of the doctor, the center, people in general. Finally the doctor dealt with her, and although he is a quiet and controlled man, he told her off. She marched out breathing fire, and with her cat's claws unclipped, urging all other clients to follow her. This kind of ridiculous scene gains nothing for pet owner or pet.

Bring your cat to the animal hospital in a carrying case of some kind. And keep him in it while you wait. The carrying case can be a box from a supermarket; it doesn't have to be an expensive container.

Don't take your pet out of the case and expose him to other patients in the doctor's waiting room. And don't let children and overcurious adults try to pet your pet. Remember that most of the animals in a doctor's waiting room are there because they are sick. If you want to expose your cat to all kinds of infection, the best way to do it is to encourage handling or contact with other people and other pets.

When you get into the treatment room, work with your doctor in examination of your cat. Your hands on your pet will make this examination easier, provided you perform correctly. If you are unsure of your ability to help handle your cat, tell the doctor and ask him to get help from one of his trained assistants. An unsure hand is worse than none.

However upset you may be about a sick cat, don't take hysterics into the treatment room. Any sick animal, like any sick person, is already under stress. You will only increase that stress and make the doctor's problem more difficult if you walk in with your emotion showing. Also, your pet will likely sense your distress, and this will make him more difficult to manage.

If your pet has to stay for a time in an animal hospital, don't insist on going to see him. A very wise doctor taught me this a long time ago, a longer time than I want to remember. It was a dog, not a cat, I had had to hospitalize, but the same goes for all animals. Von, a great German shepherd, had run over a newly cut woodland and torn out her side on sapling spears. It took months of care and skin grafting to save her. My doctor explained that a visit to Von would simply upset her and make her long for home. Twice a week my husband and I drove sixty miles to watch through a window as the doctor changed dressings. We never called Von or touched her. She had learned to love and trust her doctor. Had we insisted on a personal visit, we would only have delayed her recovery. All a visit to a hospitalized pet can do is to make you a bit happier. Why pamper yourself at the expense of your pet?

Take your cat to your veterinarian in a secure carrying case, and keep him in that case until you and your pet are in the examination room. Involve your children in this visit to the doctor. It will help them to learn how to handle a cat.

Watch your veterinarian as he makes body examinations, and ask him to explain what he is doing and why. If he uses words you do not understand, don't feel foolish if you request an explanation.

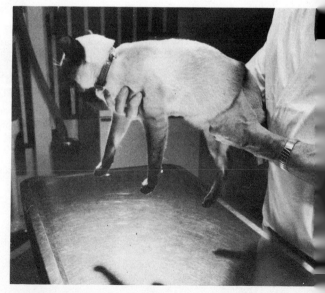

Claw clipping is most efficiently and correctly done by your veterinarian. He can show you how to extend the claws . . .

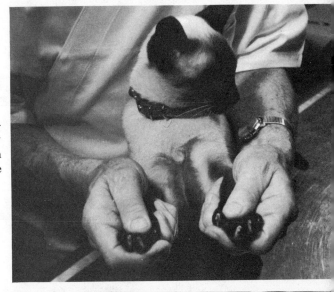

. . . introduce you to the right kind of clipping equipment . . .

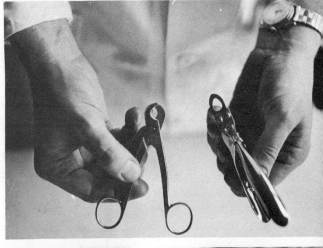

. . . and demonstrate how to do the job. Unless you feel completely competent, don't tackle the job. Bad clipping can do damage.

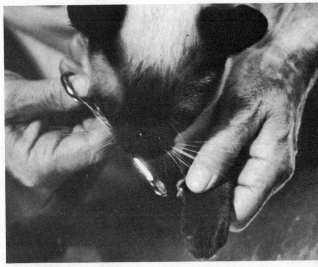

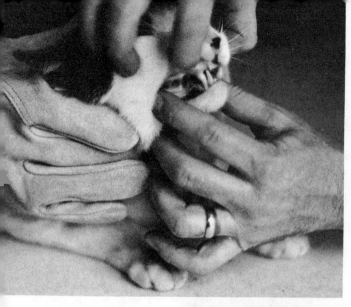

Learn how to help your veterinarian make an examination and give treatment. He will show you how to hold your pet. And, if need be, he will suggest that you wear gloves.

Frequently your veterinarian may have to give medication by hypodermic injection. Done swiftly and expertly as your doctor can do it, such treatment will hurt your pet very little. Your calm hands and calm voice will help to make a small discomfort smaller.

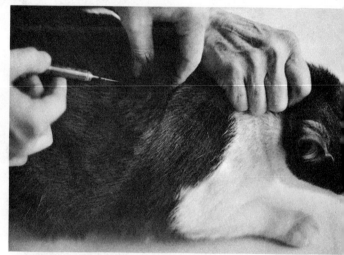

Your veterinarian may handle your cat somewhat differently than you do, and partly because he is handling strange cats every day. Lifted this way, with chest well supported and the body of the cat held firm against the doctor's body, even a struggler can be controlled.

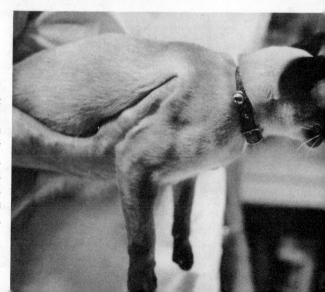

9

What to Do Until the Doctor Comes

A. WARNING SIGNS OF HEALTH PROBLEMS

Millions of cats lead happy, healthy lives with a minimum of medical care. Except for routine examinations and "shots" to protect against distemper and some of the respiratory ailments, puss may never meet a veterinarian. If and when he does, that meeting is almost sure to take place in an animal health center or the office of the private practitioner, for in these modern days, the doctor seldom comes. House calls for cats are just about as obsolete as are house calls for humans.

This puts the burden of your cat's health rather squarely on you. It leaves you with the responsibility of learning how to recognize warning signs, how to evaluate them, how to report them quickly by telephone to your veterinarian, and how to follow his orders intelligently and consistently.

Ability to know a real symptom from a false one may save your cat's life. You don't need a lot of technical knowledge for this job, just keen powers of observation, intelligence, and an ability to make decisions.

When Is a Symptom a Symptom? (In animal medicine a symptom is a "sign.") No two cats are exactly alike, not even littermates. They

115

behave differently, like different foods, express emotions in different ways, and use their own special methods of saying they are sick. So first of all you must know your cat or cats, as the case may be. To confuse the issue, what looks or sounds like a symptom may not be a symptom. You, for example, will sneeze if you get a noseful of dust. So will puss. An occasional sneeze does not necessarily mean a cold or one of the difficult respiratory ailments. Often, as with you, it takes a combination of symptoms to spell out real trouble. Difficult? Quite a bit, at first, but you'll get the hang of it very quickly. Perhaps this list of signs or symptoms will help.

Loss of Appetite. Some cats are finicky eaters. They literally turn up their noses at all but very favorite foods fed by permissive owners. Others dive into a full plateful as if it were the last on earth. If by six in the morning Petey has not jumped up on the bed and let loose a hunger howl, I know he is sick. If Big Boy sits majestically by while everybody else gobbles, I have no concern. He is waiting for a dish of his own and a moment when he can eat at his pace without competition. If Chip is slow to the dinner bell, he's busy doing something else. His morning toilet. Bird-watching by the window. A fascinated investigation of a dripping faucet.

Then there are days when no intelligent cat will insult his stomach, even with a delicacy. A day, for instance, when the thermometer climbs over ninety, or a logy, high-humidity day when it is an effort to move. Don't even open a series of cans on days like this, unless you want to throw the stuff away. Kitty will live happily on dry pelleted food and liquids. Likewise on the day when you have pushed puss into a box or case and carried him yowling to the health-care center for a shot, don't expect a hearty appetite. Any day when something unusual or disturbing happens to him, your cat's eager yen for food may vanish.

But if he looks at you with listless eyes on just an everyday day and refuses food from morning to night, you have a problem. One day without food won't hurt, especially if your pet continues to drink. A second day of the same thing, and with no interest in liquids—well, you had better call the doctor and get advice. It could be something as simple as a sore mouth or a hairball. Chip went for four days without food because of a build-up of tartar on his teeth—two days before we got the tartar off and two days after we relieved him. More likely, loss of appetite suggests brewing illness. Incidentally, the doctor may talk to you of "anorexia"— loss of appetite, that is.

Vomiting. Cats have the neat ability of dumping out the stomach voluntarily. If Big Boy gets cold food, summer or winter, he upchucks very thoroughly and immediately, usually on the rug. Five minutes after he has watched me do a clean-up, he is ready for some nice warm food that is kind to his stomach.

This sort of immediately-after-eating vomiting means little, usually, except good cat sense. Why live with a bellyful of discomfort when it is so easy to solve the problem? Unfortunately, we humans don't have the same wisdom.

Involuntary vomiting is something else again. When a cat gags and retches painfully, and when he repeats this disturbing operation a number of times, there is something wrong. If you have a strong stomach, and pet people must learn to have one, examine the vomit.

Perhaps your cat has brought up worms. Save them in a clean little bottle, preserved in rubbing alcohol, and take them to the veterinarian for diagnosis. Worms are not only bad for kitty, they might be bad for you. Perhaps he has brought up a hairball. If so, it's your fault for lack of proper brushing and a simple dose of intestinal lubricant, such as Vaseline, once or twice a week. Many cats will lick the Vaseline from your finger, as does my Chip.

Perhaps nothing but frothy stuff comes up. No clue, except that vomiting of this kind is not normal and goes along with a wide number of dangerous ailments that you are not competent to diagnose. P.S.: Country cats will often eat grass as an aid to voluntary vomiting designed to clean an outraged stomach. A grass box in a city apartment is an excellent idea, easy to provide, and kitty will love it.

Sneezing and Coughing. Some cats sneeze frequently, and all cats sneeze or cough at some times without a flicker of sickness. Sneezing and coughing associated with one of the nose, throat, or lung ailments, some of which can endanger life, are easy to recognize. I have waked up in the night to hear a single sneeze—without worry. If the next day the frequency of the sneeze increases, I know we have a "bug." If it is a day when medical help can be reached, I don't waste a minute. I get my cat to the veterinarian as fast as possible, for I have had sorry experience with a whole list of contagious nose, throat, and lung illnesses. If it is a weekend, I go back into a well-stocked emergency chest and use the pills that were ordered for a similar situation. Incidentally, if you keep leftover medicines, be sure to mark the envelope with the date received and for how long the medicine is good, the name of the drug, the name of the patient, the illness for which it was given, and the dosage. If held too long, drugs lose potency or may actually become harmful.

Sneezing, continuous sneezing, frequently forecasts one of the epidemic ailments that will travel through your whole cat family. Even with correct medication and doctor's direction, you must be prepared for several weeks of popping pills into unwilling mouths, and extraspecial efforts to keep appetite good and liquid intake adequate. In any contagious situation, some cats will be resistant: some mildly sick, some very sick. Remember when all the family had a cold, and you alone escaped? In coughing, the tone of the cough may tell you where the trouble lies.

Interestingly enough, new research, which will be detailed in another chapter, indicates that good nutrition and an especially high intake of vitamin C may help to speed recovery from these respiratory ailments. Once this vitamin was considered unnecessary for cats, but as with humans, vitamin C for cats seems to have both preventive and curative values, at least in some instances.

Difficult Urination. All too many cats suffer from urinary problems, but especially male cats. And castrated males head the list. Somehow, and no one is quite sure how, cats manufacture "gravel" or small mineral and mucous particles that can clog the tiny ducts that carry urinary wastes. *One misplaced bit of gravel that stops a passage can kill a cat in twenty-four hours or less. Kill.*

Here you must invade your cat's privacy. Many cats do not like to be watched as they use the litter box; they prefer to be alone in these basic activities. But do watch your pet as he eliminates. If he strains and strains and gets rid of nothing, he is in trouble. Even if he goes to his box too frequently, you should be alerted. And if he starts drinking an abnormal amount of water, watch out. The instinct to wash away the trouble is strong, but excess liquid sometimes intensifies the ailment, especially if the cat is "plugged."

Here I have two remarkable stories to tell. My Pete did none of the standard things to say "urinary difficulty." But as I picked him up one morning, a morning in which he had not eaten with relish, I noticed his tail was wet. I thought he had accidentally dipped it in the water bowl. An hour later I found him on my bed, and the cover was damp. In twenty minutes we were at the veterinarian's office. The diagnosis: urinary calculi—gravel. The treatment: one pill, or more, a day for all the rest of his life. After a year and a half he is doing fine, has never had a full recurrence; for I watch with an eagle eye and increase his dosage even on suspicion.

Invade your cat's privacy and watch him at his litter box. Is he straining? Does he seem to have problems in urination? What is the consistency of the stool and what is its color? Such simple checks can save your pet a lot of discomfort and help your veterinarian in treatment if it is needed.

Padraic, a cat out of my family line who went to a friend of mine, was castrated late (at nine months), after he had sired four litters of healthy kittens. Late castration is often advised as a possible deterrent to urinary problems. Padraic was a clean and fastidious cat. But one morning he startled his mistress by raising his tail against the white refrigerator and spraying it. The spray was pink-bloody. The veterinarian was called immediately, the problem diagnosed, and treatment prescribed. As in Pete's case, the treatment included a pill a day for life to control the problem. Padraic has had several recurrences since that day of extremely difficult urination. Each time, he somehow warns his mistress that there is trouble afoot, either by the very graphic method of spraying—always against a white background, though the spray is not always bloody—or by making ridiculously frequent trips to the litter box, for no apparent reason.

Body movements can tell you many things about your cat's well-being. Chip, sprawled frog-legged, like this, with feet poised in mid-air, obviously feeling no pain. All this wonderful relaxation disappears in illness when the cat crouches or hunches tightly in misery.

Your cat may not be so wise. So check the litter box instead of dumping it as fast as you can. And if you even have a hint that there can be a difficulty in urination, get your cat to his doctor quick. There would be far fewer fatalities due to urolithiasis (gravel) if so many owners did not mistake straining to urinate for constipation, thereby delaying treatment which may come too late. Very few cats will show strain in the litter box for long periods of time due to constipation.

Body Movements. The normal healthy cat is fluid in movement. He sleeps with complete relaxation. Some, like my Chip, with the whole tummy side turned up to the sky and feet posed gracefully without support. Some laid out flat so completely limp you wonder if they are alive. Some tucked into a neat ball.

A quick eye sees any changes in normal body movements, and here are a few that are cause for alarm. When puss sits hunched up in an unnaturally tight position, as if holding himself together. When he drags his tail-end across the floor as if it itched. When he walks with the rear end stiff or dragging. When the skin ripples constantly and his ears twitch. When he moves stiffly or as if in pain. When he lacks coordination in walking and particularly in jumping, and sometimes falls. When he claws at things, not just sharpening claws in a routine fashion on your best sofa, but claws frantically as if to destroy. When he switches his tail and can't seem to stop.

Pete's form of total relaxation is slightly different. And your pet will have his very own favorite position of at-easeness. Study your cat's body movements and learn to interpret their meanings.

Even when he plays dead, no cat is completely still. A peeping eye, a twitch of a paw, a flick of a tail says all is well.

Few people seem to watch this interruption of natural, smooth body movements. But it is a fact that any kind of awkwardness in an animal that is never awkward when well and strong may be the very first indication of a health problem.

Constipation and Diarrhea. Detecting either of these symptoms is sometimes difficult. If your cat goes outdoors, the only solution is to follow him periodically and take a good look. Indoors, of course, it is simple to check on the regularity of the bowel movement, its consistency and color. After a good and normal movement, most cats are lively, happy, and ready to play. When my Big Boy bounces lightly into the house, plays madly for a minute or two, and then wants food, I know that his inner mechanisms are working properly.

Especially in older cats, constipation can be a real problem. Ask your doctor's advice on medication you can give at home.

Diarrhea may or may not be alarming. Milk will give many cats diarrhea, and so too will raw liver, if the cat does not get this as a part of daily diet. Many cats will eat all kinds of strange things—bugs, flies, paper, string, plants, and several of these tidbits can produce diarrhea or constipation that is uncomfortable.

When diarrhea is continuous over a period of days, or when the color is strange—very black and tarry or an ugly brownish-yellow, flecked with blood, get the cat and a sample to your doctor quickly. Without the sample, treatment could be delayed for hours, and with dangerous results. In fact, make it a rule that if any intestinal disorder is suspected, samples of excreta go along with you and your cat to the doctor.

Sore Eyes. Sore eyes travel with a number of ailments that attack nose, throat, lungs, and usually clear up when the major illness is conquered.

Badly fed and cared for cats, such as the strays you see on the streets, frequently have sore and crusted eyelids. If you have other pets at home, don't listen to your soft heart. Either walk away if you can do nothing positive, or take the stray to a nearby health center and leave the job to them. Make sure you disinfect yourself rather thoroughly before handling your own pets.

Little kittens seem to have more than a fair share of eye difficulties, even kittens from strong, healthy mothers. A sticky eye of the newborn is one thing, and not worrisome. An infected eye is quite different. If you find a yellowish matter in your kitten's stuck-tight eye, get the kitten to a doctor. Some very nasty things can happen to a little cat's eyeball unless he gets the right treatment quickly.

Some morning you may look at your cat and see a milky veil over the lower portion of the eyeball. This membrane, sometimes referred to as the "third eyelid," helps puss keep his eyes cleaned much as you do by blinking—something a cat can't do. Normally you never see this veil, but when you can, it usually signals some intestinal upset. If the veil continues to show, best check with your doctor.

Tail-Gate Difficulty. A variety of "tail-gate" difficulties show several characteristic signs. When your cat drags his rear over the floor, almost as if skating on his tail, or when he licks constantly at the rectum or the penis, he is trying to relieve himself of discomfort. Several things may be causing such irritation—constipation, diarrhea, urinary gravel, impaction of a small gland near the rectum. All of these ailments can be serious, so best get your pet to your vet, pronto.

Body Pain. Most cats will cry if picked up or handled roughly. These cries of protest are warnings against thoughtless and inconsiderate hands. When your cat cries on gentle touch, something is cooking. My Pink, as she grew older and still insisted on having kittens, came up one night in such pain that she tried to bite every time I went near her. I soon found out she had a raging fever, so hot my hands could feel it, and inflamed and swollen breasts. I tried every number in the book until I found a veterinarian who said he would come. If he had not, Pink might have died before morning. Antibiotics, which I found at the only all-night drugstore in New York, pulled her through and gave her three more years of happy comfortable life.

I have seen another kind of pain that I don't like to remember. A cat brought into a veterinarian's office, so full of pain that he could not be touched on any part of his body. The problem—poor nutrition and vitamin E deficiency. An all-fish diet. I have dealt with this nutrition deficiency in the chapter on Food and Drink, so will not repeat here.

When a cat winces away from a loving hand, on any part of his body, investigate gently but immediately. Puss, unlike man, does not usually make something out of nothing. Even in fear he is brave. If you fear a fight or a bite, wear gloves, but do at least find the point of pain so that you can report it to your veterinarian. Due to fear in the veterinarian's office, a pet may not show the signs of pain that he does in the solitude of his home, so it is especially important for you to pinpoint his problem and to describe it accurately to the veterinarian.

Changes in Color, Markings, Personality. This may sound to you like mumbo jumbo, but truly it is not. Ambrose, my favorite Siamese, lost his sharp seal-and-fawn color, grew thin and plaintive, until a correct diet was found for him—a raw-liver, raw-kidney, raw-fish combination. Then he ate once a day, moderately, and bloomed. Coloration came back, along with bounce and the right kind of voice for a healthy, talkative Siamese.

When my Big Boy had severe rhinotracheitis, the bold, clear markings of this magnificent red tabby were blurred. Indeed, they started to blur before he got seriously sick.

Changes in personality should also alert you. When a normally friendly cat, the best-adjusted cat I have ever known, Chipper, began avoiding people, never jumped up on my bed for a morning love-in, and ran away when he was called, I got him to the doctor. He had no symptoms as such. Nothing in the book. A thorough-going check revealed worms—round worms. Not too difficult to cure, but the burden he was carrying around spoiled his disposition.

To repeat—anything out of the norm should be watched and checked.

Hiding. Perhaps this symptom should have been included in the last discussion of habit changes. All cats hide at some time. One of Chip's great morning games is to hide under a newspaper and wait for me to find him. Pete prefers a shopping bag, out of which he can rush when discovered. All of my three have hidey holes in closets, bureau drawers, and a linen closet with many enticing shelves. Chip loves the file cabinet, where he can move from level to level until I catch up with him.

When people walk into my house, I am sure they label me untidy. All closet doors are slightly ajar. This is easier than checking each closet before I leave for work each day, making sure that I do not have a closet captive. I also let my cats explore shelves and drawers where they do no harm and have a lot of fun—all of us.

But this is not the kind of thing I mean by hiding. A sick cat hides in a different way. If he can get out of the house, he hides in places not normally attractive to him. If he is fastened in, you will have to look under, crawl under, tear apart every possible concealment place. For in his misery, he wants to get away, and getting away from pain or illness often means getting away from the people whom cat loves best.

Licking and Scratching. Most cats lick themselves expertly not once but many times a day. And not only themselves, but their animal friends and the people they love, for licking is an expression of affection as well as a concerted drive for cleanliness. Mother cats police their

Scratching is normal and means nothing unless it becomes excessive. Constant scratching, like constant licking, can aggravate skin problems. This kind of scratching is often a sign of some problem you have not recognized.

young with intensity, and the smallest kitten gets into the act as quickly as possible. This kind of licking is normal. Another kind is abnormal and suggests a physical problem. I have already mentioned the licking of the rectal area when the anal gland is impacted, if there is a urinary problem, or difficult elimination.

If a cat is injured in any fashion by a bite, scratch, or burn, or if he has any kind of skin disease, he instinctively licks the wound. His instinct to clean is sound, but too much licking may keep the wound from healing.

With some cats, licking becomes a habit, a bad habit that can produce bald spots. Since it is easier to prevent licking from starting than to stop it, consult your veterinarian.

Excess scratching, like excess licking, suggests that you examine puss carefully. To rid himself of tormentors, he scratches fleas, ear mites, scabs on half-healed cuts, excessive dandruff, and loose hair that he cannot shed without help. Most of the time scratching is a warning sign only, a request for help. Carried to excess, it can become self-mutilation, for sharp claws digging down into the sensitive underlayers of skin may cause permanent damage and scarring.

Licking is a daily activity. The cat grooms himself by licking. He also licks his friends, human and animal, to express his affection. Unfortunately, this good and pleasant habit can present problems. Poisons on feet and coat can be ingested via licking, and excess licking can keep wounds and skin diseases from healing.

Biting, the next step after scratching, can do deep damage. Or biting can be something that is most intelligent. A cat will often open a festering wound by scratching and biting.

Poor Coat. In good health, your cat's coat positively shines. It shows a richness of color and markings according to the breed. It is soft yet alive to the touch. And it is clean and well groomed by the cat.

It is normal and right for puss to shed. The country cat sheds twice a year, in early summer and fall, usually. By rubbing against plants and trees, excess hair is brushed off in other seasons of the year. The apartment dweller sheds all year round and needs your help, via brushing, to keep combed out and comfortable. Regular brushing, incidentally, discourages hairballs.

A dull coat, all the glisten gone, a coat that looks ragged or tousled, is usually a sign of a generally poor condition.

Change of Voice. No two cats cry or miaow or talk with the same voice. In the early morning, when I hear small inviting cries, soft cries, I know without looking that it is Chip bird-watching and trying to lure in his fascinator. In his dreams Chip moans and again gives small cries, sensuous Chip this time, as if dreaming of special delights. Petey is a conversationalist, and once heard, can never be mistaken. He cries in a dozen voices, not just to signal his wants, but so that he will get an answer. Like many folks, he finds it dull talking to himself.

Every pet lover knows every nuance of his pet's voice. So when it sounds off-key—hoarse, plaintive, angry—listen very carefully. A distinct voice change can tell you of colds and other respiratory diseases. Persistent crying from the cat that rarely cries, pain cries when some sensitive spot is touched—these merit the most watchful attention.

Rapid Breathing. The healthy cat has a respiration rate of 20 to 30 respirations per minute when resting. When puss breathes too rapidly and pants, he has difficulty. Just plain stress, which is not so plain, can produce rapid breathing. As an aftermath of pneumonitis two years ago, Chip will occasionally breathe rapidly and pant in violent play, which I stop immediately when I see the signs. Like other signs, rapid breathing must be evaluated. If it is unusual for your cat, and there is no valid explanation for rapid breathing, call that number in your address book which spells "help," the telephone number of your veterinarian.

Temperature. Elevated temperature (fever) is almost always a sign of trouble, but not always. Remember when your temperature was slightly low or slightly high in times when you were under stress? Or remember when your physician said to you, "Mr. X, you always run a little high and it's just you, nothing to worry about"? Well, cats and people are a lot alike. A trip to the animal hospital may be enough to produce a small rise in your pet's temperature. A skilled doctor won't be worried, may never even mention it.

When puss—whose normal temperature, as you remember, stays around 101.5° F.—shoots up a reading of two, three, four points, then temperature alone says "sick." Above-normal temperature is characteristic of a score of diseases. It demands investigation. If you know how to take a rectal reading, you can quickly learn the score. Anything over 103° F. or under 100° F. should be viewed suspiciously.

Other signs of elevated temperature are dull eyes, a feeling of body heat, misery in every line of the body and in every body movement. Sometimes there is a quickened pulse rate. And this you can check.

The best place to feel the pulsebeat is on the inner hind leg. The average resting heart rate for cats is 110–130 beats per minute. Young animals have a faster heart rate than mature animals. Watch also for changes in breathing. When breathing is rapid, there can well be an elevated temperature.

There is an old saw that when a cat's ears are cool, he has no fever. How cool is cool? I seriously doubt this one. Body heat, either overall or in one place, is a better indicant. When I have sensed fever, I have wrapped my cat in wrung-almost-dry damp cloths, and called the veterinarian. I have been told that this, as in many cases of heat prostration, can do some good.

Stress. The whole complex subject of stress is so large that it cannot be dealt with here. A whole section has been devoted to the many kinds of stress and how to handle them.

Swellings. Normally no bumps or lumps or swellings mar the beautiful lines of the cat's body. When you do see or feel bumps and swellings, you can be reasonably sure that trouble lurks under the skin. Abscesses from bites and wounds may give kitty's face a lopsided and swollen look. Tumors are not uncommon in the cat and can appear in almost any part of the body. The regular examination, a careful and gentle all-over feel, which the cat will accept as petting, is highly recommended, not just to detect this symptom but many others.

Impact Accidents. Most impact accidents result from falls or from hits by moving vehicles. Signs range from shock and almost complete collapse to bleeding, often from the rectum or mouth and nose, which indicates internal damage, and to body distortions, which suggest broken bones. Rapid heartbeat or frighteningly slow beat and uneven breathing, all may be apparent. If you meet any of these symptoms, after an accident, there are just four things to DO:

1. Get the cat to the doctor as fast as possible.
2. Move the animal with the greatest of care—all in one piece—as the ambulance man does with a stretcher in case of any major and unknown injury.
3. Avoid panic in your voice and touch. The confidence you can give by gentle touch and soothing, affectionate voice may keep the cat alive until the doctor can treat him.
4. Keep your pet warm and quiet.

The Home Health-Care Chest. Keep these items and medications on hand at all times and, if you travel your cat, take your Health-Care Chest with you.

Absorbent cotton and gauze
Adhesive tape
Q-Tips
Peroxide (whiskey is an excellent substitute)
Rectal thermometer
Plastic-strip bandages
Eye ointment (prescribed by your veterinarian)
Vaseline
Anesthetic ointment (for relief of pain and itching)
Milk of Magnesia tablets
Universal antidote capsules
Can of evaporated milk
Tannic acid ointment or concentrated tea solution
Flea powder (prescription from your veterinarian)
Tranquilizer pills (prescribed by your veterinarian)
Any envelopes of medication given to your cat regularly, if the effective date has not expired. All envelopes carefully marked by name of cat, when and for what used
Nail clippers
Medicine dropper
Small pair of scissors, blunt-tipped
A pair of leather gloves
Brush and comb
A collar and a leash (even if you don't normally use them)

HEALTH RECORD

Name of Cat __Chip__   Date of Birth __12/1/65__   Name of Mother __Pink__

How Long Did She Live __18½ yrs__   Cause of Mother's Death __Anemia__

VACCINATION RECORD

Date	Distemper	Pneumonitis	Other
2/15/66	✓		
2/25/66	✓		
3/1/67	✓		
3/20/68	✓		
2/11/69	✓		

VISITS TO YOUR VETERINARIAN

Symptoms	Date 1/5/67	Date 7/15/68	Date 10/3/68	Date 2/26/69
1. Loss of appetite	✓	✓	✓	
2. Vomiting	✓	✓	✓	
3. Constipation	✓			

Symptom	Diagnosis Hairballs	Diagnosis Pneumonia	Diagnosis Sore mouth tartar	Diagnosis Anal sac impaction
4. Diarrhea				
5. Urinary difficulty				
6. Sneezing		✓		
7. Coughing		✓		
8. Fever		✓		
9. Scratching				
10. Cuts or wounds				
11. Infection				✓
12. Pain				✓
13. Unusual body movements				
14. Eye problems				
15. Skin irritations				
16. Rapid breathing		✓		
17. Burns				
18. Loss of weight			✓	
19. Depression				

B. HOME CARE FOR CATS

As you have doubtless gathered, I believe in the watchful eye and the listening ear, regular examinations, an ability to recognize a sign (symptom) when you see one, and an ability to describe that sign accurately to the doctor. I do not believe in imagining illnesses at every flick of an ear, or in running hysterically to the veterinarian with tears but no facts. I do not believe in a lot of home medication without expert advice. Through the years, all kinds of simple home medications have been talked about in cat books. Garlic to get rid of worms, sulfur and lard for mange, emetics such as charred toast crumbs mixed with tea and Milk of Magnesia for poisonings. In the days when it was five miles to town by horse and buggy, and when the local "horse" doctor knew very little about small animals, home nostrums were about all we had. That day is gone, so why experiment with horse-and-buggy medications when better and swifter-acting ones are readily available at not too great a cost?

Above all else, don't use human medications on small animals, unless directed by your veterinarian. Many human drugs contain ingredients kitty cannot tolerate, or ingredients in strengths suited to a six-foot man weighing nearly two hundred pounds, but hardly right for a one-foot-high, twelve-pound cat. One very simple human drug, aspirin, is unacceptable for cats, for the most part, and has been known to kill them. For the protection of your pet's health, don't listen to old wives' tales, and don't try to play doctor. There are many good, simple, and effective home-care techniques that you can employ. Hopefully this list of DO'S and DON'TS will guide you and help you do what you can do competently.

DO'S AND DON'TS

Maintaining High Nutrition. *Do* keep nutrition level high and feeding regular. This is the very first law of home care. The properly fed cat may escape even an epidemic. In my country life, when enteritis swept nearby farms, and animals died by the hundreds, my cat family stayed healthy. Top-grade nutrition not only wards off disease, it often keeps the infection mild and speeds recovery. A session of rhinotracheitis which hit us in the city was under control within a week—with proper medication—and ran its course quickly. The health and correct functioning of every part of the body from hair coat to heart depends on a high-quality, consistent food supply.

What you call a symptom, your veterinarian calls a sign, some indication that your pet is out of condition or suffering from an ailment. A careful and regular body check-over often gives an early clue.

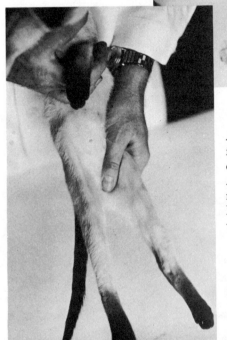

A heartbeat can be felt by placing the fingers, as in this illustration, on one of the big blood vessels in the hind leg. A normal beat is about 110–130 per minute. Fear as well as disease can escalate the heartbeat, so try to check it when your cat is at ease.

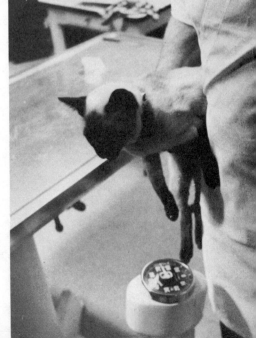

On any bathroom scale you can weigh your cat accurately, and weight can tell you many important things about health. First weigh yourself. Then weigh yourself and your cat. The difference is his weight, which you should report to your veterinarian along with any other vital statistics.

Don't, if you can avoid it, place your cat in a boarding home, even one of the best. Away from their folks, pets eat poorly and all too often come home in bad condition, susceptible to any of a number of diseases. Feeding at home, even by a stranger less careful than you, usually is a better bet than life in a cage next to another cage, strange food, and a whole new world of terrifying sounds.

Giving Medication. *Do* learn how to give medication properly. Speed is imperative. Don't circle your cat as if to attack. Don't tell him what you are going to do. Wait until he is comfortable and at ease. Then move in swiftly and get the job over without turning it into a production.

Have your veterinarian show you how to give medication. If medicine is liquid, do it the safe way with a plastic medicine dropper. Unless given this way, liquids can be dangerous, go into the lungs rather than the stomach. Even a few drops of liquid in the lungs can cause inhalation pneumonia, often a quick killer.

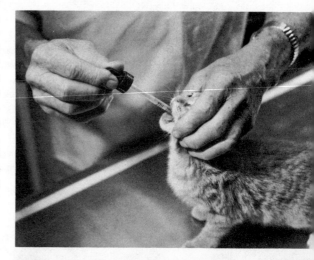

For pills another special technique is needed. Some veterinarians put a firm pressure on the jaw hinge to open and hold open the mouth.

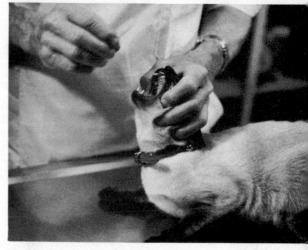

The pill is then dropped on the back of the tongue and pushed swiftly down the throat.

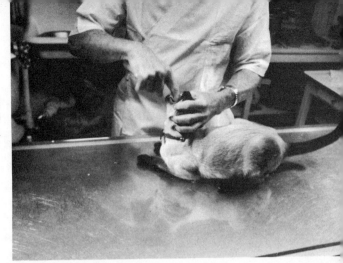

For the amateur it is often simpler to use a slightly different method. Approach your pet when he is quietly at rest. Swiftly tilt back his head. Open the mouth with thumb and forefingers on the lower jaw and drop in the pill and push to back of the tongue. Automatically, the cat will swallow. Try to make this in one movement. Each time you miss and have to try again, the job gets more difficult and triggers more resistance.

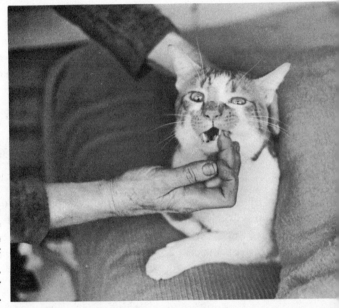

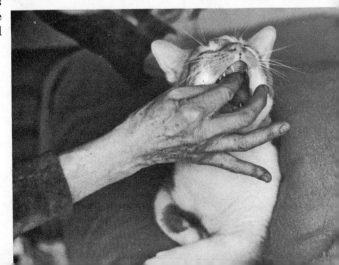

Get the pill in the first time if possible. If you miss and must repeat, and repeat, each repeat will become more difficult. I usually follow a dose with a reward of some favorite food. Just a little bit. Pete knows that he will have a snick of raw liver when the pill goes down, and he counts on this treat for being a good boy.

The expert, your veterinarian, will show you how to hold the jaws of your pet—at the hinge point—how to open the mouth, pop in a pill and push it down over the back of the tongue and into the throat. Getting the pill into position so that it will be automatically swallowed is the real trick, more important than just how you open the jaws. A wily cat can foil you easily; hold the pill in his mouth until your back is turned and then neatly spit it out. Make sure that the medication gets down where it will stay down.

Don't give liquid medications, unless it is essential. In fact, never try to force any liquids into your cat. A few drops of liquid that get into the lungs rather than the stomach may cause inhalation pneumonia, which may prove fatal. If you must give liquids, use a big plastic eyedropper inserted in the side of the mouth.

Quite as important as learning how to give medication is the acceptance of responsibility to give doses exactly as directed by the veterinarian. Pete must have a pill every day to control his urinary difficulty. I ensure this by giving the pill at the same time of the day every day. I just might forget, if I did not work on a schedule. Even devoted pet owners who rush to the animal hospital at the first sign of trouble will often take home an envelope of medicine and then fail to give it as directed. It is an accepted fact that many cats stay sick or never get well because of human failure. Suppose the nurse who was charged with giving you an antibiotic every three hours just forgot to medicate you. "Negligence" is the word for this kind of irresponsible action. Don't be guilty of it.

Temperature Taking. *Do* learn, if possible, how to take rectal temperature with a rectal thermometer, and *do* remember that a cat's normal temperature is higher than your normal temperature, averaging 101.5° F. Most veterinarians recognize a temperature within the range of 100.5° F. to 102.5° F. as perfectly normal. Once again, have your veterinarian show you the best technique and then work out one of your own as nearly perfect as possible. I am told that this can be done single-handed. The left hand and arm are supposed to grasp the cat firmly, while the right hand inserts the thermometer. With twenty pounds of struggling Big Boy to cope with, my good right hand and arm are just not enough. This is a two-man job—two very competent men or women. The great danger lies in trembling hands that fumble

If possible, learn how to take temperature with a rectal thermometer. Sterilize the thermometer and lubricate with something like Vaseline. Lift the tail and very gently insert in the rectum. It takes two people for this handling. Unless you have steady hands, don't try. A thermometer broken in fumbling can do damage.

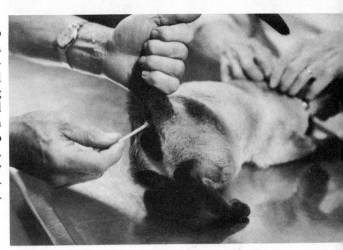

with the insertion. A broken thermometer can tell you nothing and can seriously hurt the cat.

Make sure you have shaken down the thermometer before inserting it into the rectum. Before insertion, smear the sterilized thermometer with Vaseline or some other nonirritating lubricant and gently push it into the cat's rectum. You may have to rotate the thermometer back and forth gently to insert it, for it can become temporarily blocked by one of the mucous folds in the rectum. Pet your cat through the operation and calm his fears. Leave the thermometer in for a good three minutes.

Don't attempt this, if you do not feel competent; leave it to the doctor.

Restricting a Cat. *Do* remember that there comes a time when you must restrict the movements of a sick cat. Usually, restriction means confinement, for above all else you do not want your pet to hide away where it is difficult to find him or to treat him. Often the bathroom provides the best confinement quarters. It is likely to be the coolest room in the house in summer and the warmest in winter. It is also the easiest to clean up if there are accidents. Resisting all pleas for freedom, firmly

When your pet's movement must be restricted for rest or because of illness, the bathroom is the best place. Make him comfortable with easily available food, water, and litter box. Visit him frequently so that he does not feel deserted.

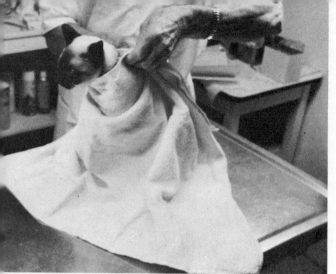

Sometimes the most loving and affectionate cat must be restrained for examination and treatment. If you must protect yourself against tooth and claw, do what the doctor would do. Take a square of soft material, the size determined by the size of your cat. On the triangular end, pull it under his chin . . .

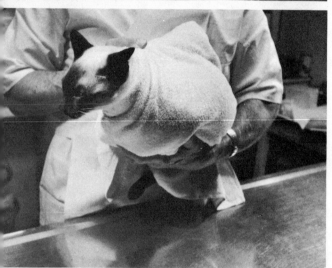

. . . slip the other triangular end under his feet . . .

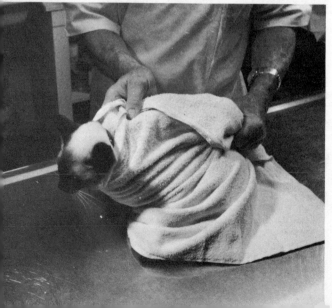

. . . then secure four ends of the cloth at the back. Now you have the situation under control for medication or to lift and move even a struggling cat. The wrapping will divert his attention.

shut puss in. Give him a soft warm bed, a litter box so that he can function normally, small bowls of water, and dry food just in case his appetite rouses. Give him light, not a glaring light but a small one. And check on him frequently so that he does not feel deserted.

Sometimes, other forms of restraint are needed. Angry or difficult-to-handle cats can be dangerous to handle and to medicate. Wrapped firmly but gently in a large towel they can be controlled without a disturbing fight.

Most cats can be restrained for examination and treatment by simple handholds.

Cleaning Up a Sick Cat. *Do* help to keep your cat clean if he is too sick to do the job. Normally, puss works diligently to remain spotless. When he is very sick, his coat may be sticky and stained with discharges from sore eyes, a runny and sneezy nose, or from food particles that stick to his fur as you force-feed him. Sometimes he will mess up his bed with urine and involuntary bowel movements, and he hates himself when he is filthy and smelly. Remember how you felt in a hospital bed, a soiled hospital bed, when you had been very sick? Remember how much more like living you have felt after a gentle nurse cleaned you up and gave you fresh linen? This is something very positive that you can do for your cat.

Don't keep annoying a sick cat all day long even with clean-ups and loving attention. Did you hate the nurse who got you out of a sound sleep at six o'clock in the morning to give you a bath and breakfast? Yes, you did. Rest for the sick little animal is part of the cure.

Scratches, Cuts, Wounds and Bites. *Do* clean and medicate all injuries to the skin, and as quickly as possible. Wash them out with warm water and a mild soap. An antibacterial soap such as Phisohex may be used. An antiseptic such as 3 percent hydrogen peroxide (not stronger) diluted in warm water to one-half strength is also satisfactory. Peroxide does sting, however, and if the wound is extensive, it may cause irritation that can turn your ordinarily docile cat into a fighting tiger. Most minor cuts and wounds heal more quickly if they are kept open, and puss will try to do his share of the job by licking. Since too much licking keeps a sore from healing, bandaging with a soothing ointment may be necessary. Cutting the hair away from around the wound will make all treatment easier.

If the cut or bite is deep and vicious, get the cat to the veterinarian. In the case of spurting-type bleeding, you can try to stop the flow by applying pressure on some of the main blood vessels. Remember that

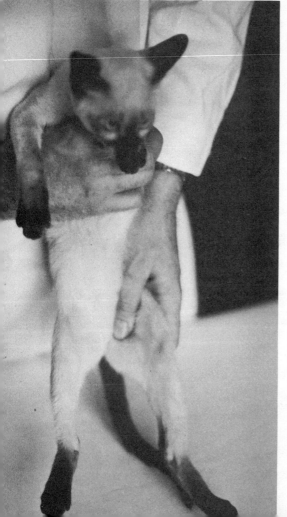

Assemble a feline medicine chest. Include simple medications: Vaseline, Milk of Magnesia tablets, an antiseptic, absorbent cotton, cotton-tipped swabs, a flea powder recommended by your veterinarian, a deodorant, plastic-strip bandages, scissors, tweezers, a magnifying glass, medications still potent for ailments which can recur. And be sure to mark the date of the issue on medication, the name of the cat, the recommended dosage. Carry such a medicine chest with you if you travel and keep it up to date at home.

When injury is serious, and profuse bleeding is of the spurting type, pressure at an artery point may give some control, lessen blood loss until you can rush your cat to the animal hospital. Don't use a tourniquet. Left on too long by a novice owner, a tourniquet can cut off circulation and seriously injure the portion of the body that is cut off from a normal supply of blood.

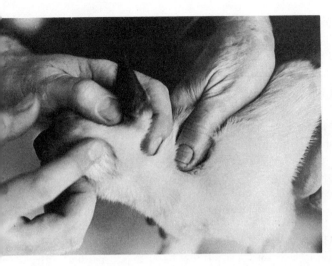

Salves and medications that need to be rubbed in should be thoroughly rubbed in. Left on the surface of the coat, salves invite and encourage licking which negates the treatment.

even critical wounds can be healed if action is fast. Years ago one of my cats, Kitten, was caught in the hayfield by the knife of a mowing machine. She got home somehow, dragging the nearly severed leg. I used a tourniquet and raced to the vet. After one look, he shook his head and said, "I'll bet she is a special one, and you want to save her. But she will never walk again." At my request he went ahead and skillfully put her together. For a long time she hobbled three-legged. Then, one day, I watched her jump and make it. She lived many years, had scores of kittens, and showed only a slight sign of stiffness as she grew older. All of which says that even impossible wounds are worth treating —immediately. If the injuries are so extensive that a satisfactory recovery appears unlikely and pain is severe, you may have to consider euthanasia.

Don't use salves or ointments, with the exception of plain white petroleum jelly, unless you have medications approved by your veterinarian. Your cat will most assuredly lick the stuff off, so the medication must be harmless to him, but effective on the wound. Petroleum jelly will soothe, and later, as the wound heals, it will help to keep scabs from causing discomfort which in turn causes scratching or excessive licking.

Don't overlook the puncture wounds that can be made by claws, barbs from a number of thorny plants, tacks and nails, and such. Punctures, untreated, may become infected, even cause abscesses that can lead to more widespread systemic infection.

Don't try to bandage wounds, unless advised to by your veterinarian, for kitty knows how to shred and strip off any bandage made by an amateur. Some veterinarians have mastered the technique so that the cat will lick the bandage as if it were his own skin.

Sore Eyes and Stuffed-up Nose. *Do* wash out sticky and weepy eyes with a sterile cotton swab dipped into warm water. If you have time, it is a good idea to boil the water first and let it cool. If discharges from the eyes are profuse and thick, chances are that the nose may be stuffed up thoroughly as well. Often the cat can sneeze out the matter that collects in the nostrils, but sometimes he cannot. Gently, very gently, with a cotton swab, you may be able to dislodge nose plugs so that the cat can do the rest of the job himself.

Certain of the antihistamines work well to relieve both weeping eyes and stuffed-up nose. Here is one place where a human medication can be used—if recommended by your veterinarian. As with all medications, however, there may be unwanted reactions, so antihistamines should not be used without proper authorization and dosage information.

Do wash out the sticky eyes of small kittens—just warm water, again, and a cotton swab. And *do* clean out the corners of your pet's eyes if a small drop of mucus-like material collects there. Some cats have this minor eye discharge even when they are in the best of health.

Don't fool around with your cat's eyes or manhandle them as you

Treat your cat's eyes with a gentle hand. Even a healthy cat may tear or sometimes have small collections of matter in the eye corners. Clean eyes every day, if need be, with cotton dipped in warm water.

often do your own. I once watched a child try to trim a little cat's eye-lashes with a pair of sharp nail scissors. Fortunately injuries of the cats' eyeballs are not too frequent, thanks to those radar-warning whiskers and eyebrows.

Don't use salves or ointments for reasons already defined, unless instructed to do so.

Constipation and/or Diarrhea. *Do* make constant checks to find out whether your cat has either of these ailments. Often a simple change in diet will correct the problem. Remember that milk and raw liver often cause simple diarrhea in some cats. And a diet without bulk can cause constipation. Any repetitive or very persistent constipation is a problem for the veterinarian—and this is much more frequent in aging or old cats.

Do above all else try to prevent both of these disorders, not just with food, but by giving regular doses of such things as butter, vegetable or mineral oil, or my very favorite, Vaseline. These lubricants help to keep intestines working normally and smoothly.

Don't fail to give enough of these lubricants and to give them regularly once or twice a week, not just when you remember. As to dosage —a teaspoonful of Vaseline or butter or oil is usually necessary to accomplish the purpose; smaller doses may be just a waste of time.

At least once or twice a week give your cat a lubricant that will aid elimination and discourage trouble-some hairballs. Vaseline is excellent and my cats eat it like candy from my fingers.

The "so-called" flea collar, relatively new, seems to be effective in controlling parasites that add up to a lot of trouble for puss—if used according to directions. Some cats are allergic to the chemicals used in the collar. Some will refuse to wear the collar. Best check with your veterinarian. A number of manufacturers make such a collar.

Defleaing. *Do* have your veterinarian recommend a good flea powder that has no ingredients harmful to cats. If you have failed to do this, check the label on a standard product made by a good manufacturer and make sure that it is guaranteed safe for cats.

The idea is to get the powder down to the base of the hair, not sprinkled lightly on top. Brush off as much of the top-of-the-hair powder as possible, for you can be sure it will be licked off immediately. Protect the cat's eyes, ears and nostrils. The modern flea collar does away with dusting, and is efficient in preventing but not always in curing a heavy flea infestation.

Little kittens and badly nourished cats usually attract fleas much more than strong, healthy, adult cats. Kittens are often invaded by a flea army that settles in all over the body, but with special concentrations around the rectum and the ears. Scores of small, black dots, the ones that don't move, are flea excreta. The kitten can be washed with a mild flea shampoo. Keeping eyes and nose out of the water, dunk the kitten in the bath, rinsing clear in clean, warm water. Dry thoroughly and place in clean quarters.

Don't forget to dust bedding and carpets and any favorite places of your cat family. Dust the powder deep into the nap of pile fabrics. Incidentally, you are more apt to have a flea invasion in warm weather months and climates than in cold temperatures.

Poisoning. *Do* make every possible effort to identify the type or brand name of poison. This kind of information may save your cat's life. Usually the first thing to attempt is an emetic that will get the poison out of the stomach before it has a chance to start moving through the body. In some cases where vomiting is not desirable, a drug to neutralize the poison, rather than an emetic, is needed. Only your veterinarian can decide which is best.

Ask your doctor for an emergency emetic which you can keep in your medicine chest and give without danger for poisons that demand an emetic. In recent research material, evaporated milk is mentioned as a good specific for poisonings. It has as one advantage its almost immediate availability in most households.

Remember that most cats, if poisoned, are poisoned by something you have used in your house or around your grounds. Avoid these chemicals at all costs if you want a home safe for cats. There are a few, a very few, pet poisoners and killers around—twisted, sick people, like the man who used my Big Boy for rifle practice and left rat poison in Big Boy's favorite hunting areas. It is impossible to spot them or their favorite brand of death, so at times you can only do your best and pray. I may say that in thirty years I have never had a poisoned cat.

Heat and Cold Reactions. *Do* watch the temperature. Your cat's skin and coat cover help him to regulate body temperature. When the temperature climbs over 90 and when the humidity is high, discomfort can be great. Let the temperature rise into the hundreds, and heatstroke may occur. This may be hard to believe as you watch your pet bask in hot and brilliant sun you cannot stand. But don't discount the bad things that high heat and high humidity can do, especially if your pet is overweight or not in the best of health.

By extra licking and washing, your cat tries to take care of the heat problem in his own way—much as you would do with a series of tepid baths. Nature has provided a heavier-than-usual flow of saliva when the

Your doctor can show you how to clean your cat's outer ear with a cotton swab. Never push this swab into the inner ear. Deep cleaning and treatment calls for the experienced hand of your veterinarian.

thermometer climbs. If there are signs of collapse from heat, a towel wrung nearly dry of cold water, or even ice packs, will provide first-aid relief.

Don't, if you live in a house with air conditioning, turn off the machine while you are away. Give kitty a break. The cost is apt to be less than a turn-off-turn-on system.

Sore Mouth. *Do* watch for any signs that say your cat is having difficulty in eating or chewing. Examine his mouth and look for tartar on the teeth, irritated gums or tongue, a bone or some other foreign object caught in teeth, mouth, or throat. Remove any foreign object if you can. If you cannot chip off the tartar—with a well-cleaned fingernail—make a point of having your doctor do this job for you periodically. Cats who get very soft food that requires little or no chewing are more likely to build up tartar, as are those in advanced age.

Don't ignore any smears around the mouth. Little kittens sometimes try to eat cat litter, which can choke them. And some poisons leave stains on lips and fur.

Sore Ears. *Do* try to determine whether the soreness is external or internal. Scratches, bites, wounds, skin disorders like ringworm and ear mites—any or a combination can produce sore ears.

Don't fool around with the inside of the ears. This is no place for the amateur hand. Have your veterinarian demonstrate the safe and proper method of cleaning kitty's ears.

Burns. *Do* remember that a large majority of burn injuries suffered by cats are caused by boiling water or other hot liquids that are spilled. Get a burn case to your veterinarian quickly so that damage can be assessed. If the area of burn is small, a thick coat of Vaseline may give temporary pain relief. Home medication of burns is not recommended.

Electric Shock. *Do* remember that cats will chew electric cords. If you find puss with teeth stuck in an electric cord, protect yourself from shock. Use a rubber glove or hot-plate holder to pull the plug from the socket. Then call the doctor.

Don't grab hold of the cat unless you want to join him on the hot line.

Overexposure to Cold and Frostbite. *Do* examine a cat that has had long or severe exposure to intense cold. With his particular temperature-regulating mechanism, the cat can stand an amazing amount of cold. However, frostbitten ears and even feet are not uncommon. As in human home care, cool or tepid water is the best immediate specific. Sometimes the tips of ears slough off, leaving the cat with a rounded rather than pointed look.

Body Cold Induced by Medication or Shock. *Do* understand that certain medications commonly used in treating cats may produce a drop in body temperature—medications such as sedatives, tranquilizers, and anesthetics. In such a case, keeping your pet warm is highly desirable, *but* . . . *Don't* put him on top of a hot-water bottle or a heating pad or under a heat lamp. Too rapid recovery from lowered body temperature before his central nervous system is in control may have disastrous results. This is one of the many forms of "killing with kindness" that distracted cat lovers perpetrate, and all too frequently. A thick towel or blanket to lie on and to be covered up with usually solves the problem nicely.

10

Comfort

There are few nicer words in our language. All wrapped up in the concept of comfort is relaxation, freedom from irritation, an at-ease body and mind, companionship, security. And having said this, I have spelled out the good life for cats. They luxuriate in comfort, and in comfort their personalities flourish and develop to the peak. Giving your cat comfort is so very easy, and it pays high dividends.

A. GROOMING – BRUSHING

One of the first contributions to comfort is regular grooming. Puss loves to be brushed, and if he is a city cat or a longhair, he needs brushing to clean out the loose hair that even his constant washing cannot remove, to polish up his coat and make it shine, to protect him from the annoyance of hairballs.

One of my veterinarian friends tells me that a comb, not a brush, is the best grooming instrument. This gets down through the thick outer coat and into the wool coat, which has a tendency to mat. The comb this veterinarian uses is a small steel comb with blunt teeth that cannot injure tender skin. Brushing the longhair cat is not just a matter of good grooming; it can be a matter of good health. Hannibal, a magnificent blue

Comfort is not costly, but it pays huge dividends. For example, freedom of movement is highly prized by a pet, and he hates to be put in his place. If you both like the same chair, let him have it when possible, and without an argument.

Cleanest of animals, the cat grooms himself constantly and meticulously. To him cleanliness and comfort are synonymous.

For most cats brushing is sheer bliss.

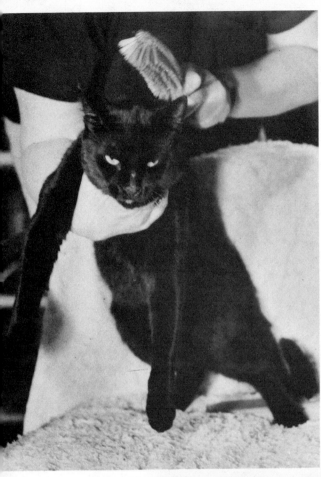

And some cats do not like to be brushed.

To get down into the wool coat, a small blunt-toothed comb is more efficient than a brush.

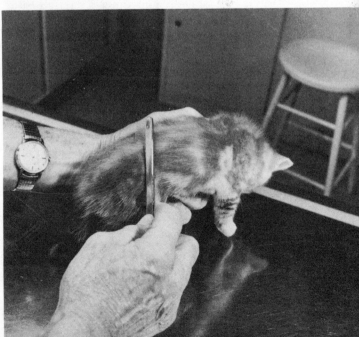

Persian, was left in the hands of a baby sitter who failed to brush him. At the end of a week, when his mistress came home, she had a very sick cat. Matted and tangled hair was pasted over the anus; Hannibal literally could not eliminate. It took days of painstaking and painful treatment to correct this problem.

Unlike the brushing technique for the shorthair—brushing with the lay of the hair—brushing the longhair is a one-two routine; first against the lay of the hair with both brush and comb, and then in reverse, to sleek the coat down. And be sure to do this once a day, for both kittens and cats. Brushing has overtones of value for you—less hair on your rugs, furniture, clothes.

It is said that cats enjoy being vacuumed. This I cannot substantiate. Perhaps my cat family is completely old-fashioned. To them a vacuum is a strange modern device to be avoided or attacked as an invader.

Nail Clipping. In the country, I never clipped a cat's nails. He needed all of them in the active indoor-outdoor life he lived. Claws were his weapons of defense, his tree-climbing and jumping hooks. In the city, where nails have few opportunities to wear down, a regular clipping is desirable. Country cats also keep their nails in trim by scratching against the bark of handy trees.

Some cats, Chip among them, clip their own nails, neatly biting them off when they get too long for comfort. Most cats do not.

Clipping is most necessary if the cat has any skin ailment. A small scratch on Big Boy's throat almost became a dangerous infection as the result of scratching. It took four weeks, a visit to the veterinarian, and application of ointments four times a day to heal a simple skin abrasion that ceased to be simple when aggravated by scratching.

Nail clipping has to be done very carefully so as not to injure the "quick" of the nail. Use animal clippers, not your own. The animal clippers are made to fit the rounded contour of dogs' and cats' nails, whereas your own were made to fit the flat human nail. Using the wrong kind will pinch and may scare puss away the next time you try to trim his nails. It is, of course, easier to clip kitty's claws if there are two people, but this is not always possible. If your cat is too frisky or uncooperative or jerks his paws, better turn the clipping job over to your veterinarian rather than risk damaging the tender "quick."

The Scratching Post. While we are talking about claws, we might just as well discuss scratching posts. These devices have made a nice piece of money for manufacturer and retailer. Kittens, as they learn

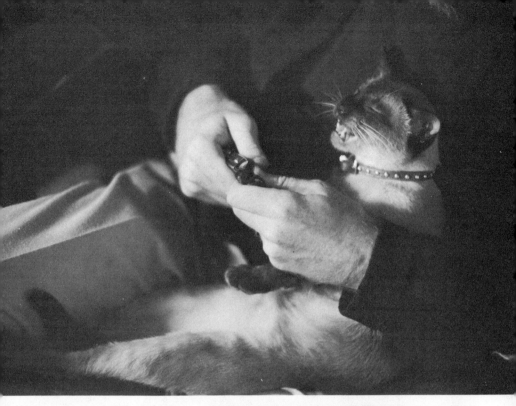

Every cat is more comfortable if his nails are not too long. The country cat wears nails down naturally. For the city cat regular clipping is indicated. You can clip the tips in safety, but for a thorough job, turn to your veterinarian.

Some cats, like my Chip, do their own nail clipping . . . and expertly.

Here is a scratching post that will be used and it costs little. A cedar slab from the five - and - dime — the kind sold for climbing plants—fastened to the end of an old couch.

to climb, will explore them and have fun. But I have never had an adult cat who would give them the time of day. The post I have sits lonely as a cloud. No one approaches it. An invention of my own, which cost very little, is a great success. A cedar slab, sold in the five-and-dime as a climbing post for plants, has been fastened to the end of an old couch. Claws are sharpened on this post every day, but the upholstery of the couch is not touched. One well-known breeder has developed a scratching post made of big nautical corks threaded on a rod. This fastens easily to a door jamb or a cabinet that you don't consider priceless. It is the breeder's theory that he can train his cats never to scratch on anything but this cork post. You can make it simply at home by threading corks on a towel bar. I cannot guarantee results, but cats love the feel of cork and will use the post.

Shampooing. Very few house cats ever need to be shampooed. The kitten or cat with fleas or some skin ailment—perhaps yes. For him, warm water and a mild soap or a safe insecticidal shampoo may be desirable. For the cat who has met a skunk or emerged from a cat fight or who is otherwise injured, gentle bathing and cleaning with a mild or castile soap adds to comfort. The show cat, like the actor, is a candidate for intensive cosmetic care, but unless your cat is in show biz, forget it; don't invest in expensive beauty aids.

Another very successful scratching post is made from big corks, threaded on a metal bar and attached to a bathroom cabinet.

B. SLEEPING EQUIPMENT

Judging from the number of rather expensive baskets in pet shops and department stores, people do buy these things. Why, I will never know. Once a very dear friend of mine gave me one of these contrivances. Wicker, double cushioned and—a canopy with tassels. My cats eyed this with astonishment. Assuming that it must be a playtoy, they promptly

Don't waste money on expensive sleeping baskets. There is nothing so popular as a small-small corrugated box that is just cat size.

tore off the tassels and kept me busy keeping them from swallowing same. Then they attacked the wicker, chewed it off in little pieces or used it for claw sharpening. Finally they climbed up on the canopy and bounced until they destroyed it.

No cat, not even the most aristocratic purebred, needs this kind of sleeping equipment. Most cats would prefer to sleep on your bed and with you. I don't happen to mind Big Boy and Pete down by my feet or moving in closer in the morning to nip my fingers and advise me that it is time to get up. If you object to this, try shutting them out, and try living through the rumpus they can create as they skillfully learn how to open your door.

Most doctors and veterinarians object to cats sharing sleeping quarters with the owners, for through close contact, diseases such as ringworm and other fungal infections can be transmitted. So make your own decision.

Being simple, natural folk, cats just want to be comfortable. They will fight for your favorite chair, or share it with you if you insist. If your cat must have a bed, I highly recommend a corrugated, cat-size, low box from the supermarket. As you look at the box, you will be sure no cat will

If he has his druthers, your cat would much prefer to sleep with you. And there is much to be said in favor of this closeness—and on both sides. Veterinarians discourage the practice, pointing out that humans can catch certain cat diseases, among them the skin ailment ringworm.　　*Photo by Frank Bear*

Cats love hidey-holes just like children. Both Chip and Pete dote on the top shelf of a linen chest . . .

. . . or a drawer full of clothes that smell like someone they love . . .

fit in, but even twenty-pound Chip makes it with a squeeze, and this is his most favorite sleeping place. A hooded box in which kitty can hide, warm and draft-free, is also on the preferred list. A fiber transfer file is perfect.

Every cat I know or ever had, loves to sleep in or on a bag. Older cats, particularly, like to sleep under the warmth of a table lamp. Very few will ever break the lamp or disturb whatever you may have on chest, desk, table. So why object? The cat who has free range of his house is almost never destructive, usually destroys or creates a fuss only by accident or if he is thwarted. In my thirty-some years of cats, I have had only two valuable things broken.

. . . or a snug shopping bag. For safety's sake, best tear the handles loose. A small head can so easily get caught.

Free range of the house includes the high places—even the top closet shelf. Why not? Don't you like to explore every part of your environment?

C. HOUSEBREAKING

The cat is much easier to housebreak than the dog. All he really needs is a litter box in a convenient location, a box to which he always has access. There is one other vital element: The box must be clean. Even tiny kittens, without any help from you, will find their way to a box rather than mess up the floor. To help kittens get the idea, just keep dropping them into a junior-size box placed close to their nest. If you plan to place kittens for adoption, your assurance that they are house-broken will add immensely to their desirability.

The Litter Box. Personally, I prefer a baby's plastic bathtub. It is deep enough to hold three or more inches of litter, and also deep enough to prevent litter from being kicked out on the floor. It has a rim on which the cat can rest his paws, and many cats prefer this sitting-up position. The bathtub is also big enough for comfort—cats hate little boxes—and it is easy to clean and deodorize. There is, by the way, a new deodorizer now available in pet shops. One drop or two of this chemical will destroy all odor for a day or more. This new product was originally

A clean litter pan is tops on the comfort list, especially if placed where always available. On fresh, clean litter, many cats will catch a short snooze. A baby's plastic bathtub makes the best box. Big enough for comfortable use. Deep enough so that litter will not be spilled out. Easy to clean and disinfect.

developed for hospitals, cancer hospitals to be exact, where the problem of keeping the odors of illness under control is a major one.

Some cat litters are better than others, and the best are slightly more expensive. Cheap litters have a claylike quality and tend to pack and stay wet. A new litter on the market recently is very light and supposedly can be flushed down the toilet. This litter is a bit dusty and can provoke a sneezing attack. My cats practically refuse to use it. Whatever litter you select, follow the directions on the bag.

One small suggestion—place the box firmly against a wall and preferably in a corner, so that it cannot be readily overturned. This small suggestion goes for all boxes or baskets that cats use. If possible, place the litter box where it can get fresh air and sunshine.

Other Housebreaking Techniques. Some pet owners have trained their cats to use the bathtub, on the theory that washing away waste is easier than cleaning boxes. If this works for you, fine. Most cats, if given their druthers, like to use litter as they would dirt and "cover it up" with diligent scratching. I have even heard of an owner or two who trained the cat to use a toilet seat. More power to you, if you can bring it off, but you will be fighting the cat's natural instincts.

I have known only a few dirty cats. Sick cats and young kittens can make an understandable mistake. Cats who have access to a fireplace can mistake ashes for litter. A dirty box can force a cat into becoming what you call dirty and what he thinks of as being clean. Loneliness and fear can sometimes turn a clean cat into a dirty one. This kind of dirtiness is a psychological protest. Don't punish the cat, but rather examine what you have done wrong.

D. COLLARS, BELLS, LEASHES

I have known few cats who really like a collar. All cats detest bells. And as for parading on the end of a leash, there are a only couple of Siamese in my acquaintance who seem to find this acceptable.

The main reasons cats dislike collars is because they are confining, and no cat wants to be confined. I dislike collars because they can catch and snag on furniture in the house, on fences and plants in the outdoors, occasionally causing death by strangulation. Some new stretchable collars seem to have overcome much of the hazard. If you move into a new neighborhood where the cat lives an indoor-outdoor life, a collar has very positive virtues—provided it bears your name, not the cat's name, plus

For the in-and-out cat, a cat hole or entry door is a great confidence builder. He never feels shut out—and you save the bother of waiting on your pet. In a low garden window, a simple and inexpensive window screen does the trick.

The open-door policy also spells comfort and security to a cat. Any intelligent cat —and most are—knows how to open the doors he has seen you open.

your address or telephone number. Collars also express the concern of a pet owner, and the lost animal who wears a collar may get better treatment from those who find him than the unidentified stray who seems to belong to no one. Depending on where you live, you and you alone can weigh the advantages against the disadvantages of that strap around your pet's neck. Recently, at a pet show, I found one great section of displays devoted to decorative collars, many with rhinestone settings. Face it: This kind of beauty bit is for you and not for the cat, and certainly is unjustified if it makes puss uncomfortable. In this same display area were jeweled pin-on ornaments, coats, raincoats, bootees, and the final ridiculum, an umbrella that could be strapped on the back of cat or dog. No cat needs an umbrella. They actually like to dash out and in through rain or snow. The hair coat sheds water and can be licked dry in minutes. It is only the stray with no place to escape the elements that can suffer from long hours of exposure.

Leashes have their place. Not on parade to invite the comments of the curious, but as restrainers when you take a pet to the veterinarian or travel him in your car. I once refused a kitten for adoption to a woman who told me she wanted a cat so that she could walk him in the park. I own both a collar and a leash, and I have never used either.

E. MOVING INTO A NEW HOME

Moving and traveling are two different things, and it is moving we are concerned with here. Even if you simply move across the street, there are certain comforts you can and should give your pet. Let him participate in the packing, by all means. He will love the collection of boxes and packing paper. The day the movers arrive, put him quietly away in your bathroom—with a litter box, a water bowl, something soft to sleep on and food, preferably the dry pelleted kind. When all the furniture is gone, get him into a carrying case and transfer him to the bathroom of your new home—with a litter box, a water bowl, a dish of dry pelleted food and something soft and warm to lie on. In short, replace the ingredients of the old environment with the same ingredients in the new environment. If you must wait for days for the furniture, give your pet free run to case the joint as any good cat will do, examining every nook and cranny, smelling every corner and closet. Recently I moved, just across the city. My furniture was in California and did not reach me for more than two weeks. I had a bed, of sorts, a kitchen table, a couple of old garden chairs, no rugs, no drapes, and a mound of boxes. Once my cats recovered from their taxi ride—something they had never taken and did not want to take again—they thoroughly enjoyed life. We shared our limited facilities. The uncarpeted floor became a great game room with nothing to block or hide the movement of playtoys. I really think it was their finest moment. One of the things I love most about cats is their instant recognition of what is essential and what is unessential.

Instead of the traditional catnip mouse, keep a box on hand and give puss an occasional treat. Chip has a passion for catnip, likes a bit on his food now and then, and acts like an idiot at the very smell.

11

To Alter or Not to Alter

Alteration—interruption of reproduction by operation—seems to present some puzzling problems. Surgically, it is both successful and safe. Psychologically and emotionally, it seems to disturb pet owners far more than it does their pets. There are many questions. At what age should a cat be altered? Is it a painful operation, and should the cat be given anesthesia? Should the cat be hospitalized for the operation? Will altering change the cat's personality? Do altered cats grow fat and lazy? Have we any right to interfere with nature, especially in the female cat who so enjoys motherhood? Does the cat, male or female, develop any bad habits if not altered and mated? These are all logical questions to which there are logical answers.

Just What Is Alteration? Alteration in the male, commonly called "castration," means that the cat's testicles are removed. In the female, the ovaries and uterus are removed by an operation called "spaying." Without these vital organs the male cannot sire a litter, and a female cannot have kittens. In human medical language, the female cat has an ovario-hysterectomy. The castrated male is made into a eunuch.

The Age for Alteration. Opinions differ on this date. Unles you want your young queen to have kittens, most veterinarians recommend

Does alteration change a cat? Yes, but usually for the better. My altered three have grown tremendously since castration. But they are active, alert, full of play, delightfully clean, and wonderful companions. Discuss with your veterinarian the best techniques and timing for alteration.

spaying at about five to six months, for the female develops to sexual maturity rapidly, more rapidly than the male. On the right age for castration of the male there is a real argument. Some veterinarians say five to six months. Others recommend waiting until nine or ten months, when the urogenital system of the male has had a chance for fuller and more complete development. At maturity, so the thinking goes, the small urethral tube leading out from the bladder has reached full size and is less likely to be clogged by the gravelly material (calculi) which can so seriously interfere with urination. Not all males develop this gravel, but since many do, the argument for delayed castration until nine or ten months makes sense. New research now in progress at several universities may negate this recommendation and place the blame and the solution for urinary problems on nutrition and/or control of infectious agents.

There is one other argument for delayed castration. A characteristic and good male aggressiveness does not manifest itself if the tom is altered quite young.

Is the Operation Painful? Does It Demand Hospitalization and Anesthesia? Any operation is painful, and your cat is very sensitive to pain. In a healthy cat, altering is not dangerous, but it is much more difficult in the female than in the male, since spaying necessitates abdominal incision. I have seen country male cats rolled into a rug and castrated in a few swift minutes. On the farm, where pennies are counted and animal discomfort somewhat discounted, castration is accepted as normal, and a simple household lubricant, lard, is often the only wound dressing used. Many veterinarians insist on the use of anesthesia and overnight hospitalization, and these I do approve of. But I object strenuously to another practice often encountered in the city: the combination of castration and distemper shots or some other treatment that is on the list of routine health care. Castration produces stress. So do distemper shots; and adding stress to stress multiplies the insult to body tissues. Don't try to avoid the cost of a second visit to the animal hospital by asking or letting your veterinarian combine castration with another important treatment.

Spaying of the female is a sensitive operation. Hospitalization and, of course, anesthesia are both essential. Be sure to leave your queen in the hospital until she is well healed, especially if you have other cats in the house. Even a play attack from another member of your cat family can injure a tender scar.

Spaying the older female who has had many litters should be fully discussed with your veterinarian. The shock to a mature animal is much greater than to a five-month-old kitten. My Pink had to be spayed at the age of fifteen—to save her life. It took her a year to make a recovery of sorts.

Does Alteration Change the Cat's Personality? Yes and no. Usually alteration changes the cat's personality for the better. This is especially true of the vigorous young tom almost at full tide of sexual maturity. Anxiety, stress, aggressiveness, howling—all signs of growing up —will be tempered by alteration. Recently I helped to photograph a young tom who was in the veterinarian's office for castration. He never stopped snarling, spitting, or wailing as the doctor put him through an examination. I understand that a month after we met Michael, he was a completely changed cat who turned his vitality to play rather than hostility. Most cats, both male and female, become more pleasant house pets, more even of disposition, less noisy, more loving and relaxed after alteration. Castration and spaying do not—*do not*—change the basic and charming personalities of cats or affect playfulness and smartness. If anything, your altered pet will be more fun when he or she does not have sex on his or her mind. Alteration does not turn your pet into a fat, stupid fool unless you overfeed him. Many altered cats will put on weight and size. My three boys have grown to be the size of small dogs, but they are all bone and muscle, alert, immensely active, bright as a dollar. I have met altered cats who sit all day and eat all day and grow to be nuisances, but that depends on you and your permissiveness.

What About a Pill for Puss? Instead of surgical alteration, there has been some talk of controlling the reproductive urge by pills and injections. Although these methods were utilized for a time by some veterinarians, the practice has been discontinued because of too many adverse side effects. The pills were not too effective in many cases, anyway.

Should We Interfere with Nature? This is a question that seems most to bother the pet owners with females. Castration of the male is sometimes more readily accepted than the thought of robbing the female of her motherhood. This stirs all kinds of emotional thinking not unrelated to the arguments about abortion and the use of "The Pill" by human females. There is probably nothing more delightful to watch than a mother cat and her litter. She has no interest in birth control, just in more kittens. But how are you going to place all those endless youngsters in satisfactory homes? The inevitable answer is to alter your pet.

There are still other major problems to meet in the unaltered male or female. Given no opportunity to mate, as they would naturally, leads to the development of undesirable conditions for both you and your cat. The female can go into almost constant heat. Not a few times a year as nature planned it, but every three or four weeks, sometimes more often. This repeated and exhausting rolling and crying keeps the female cat nervous, anxious, distressed. Whatever your ideology of nature may be, don't put your pet through this. Spaying a female when she is young (six to twelve months) is likely to lengthen her life, for she is less likely to develop female health problems. If spayed, she cannot develop pyometritis (uterine infection), which is not uncommon in unspayed middle-aged and older females and which requires surgical treatment at a time when the animal is quite ill. Furthermore, a female spayed young is less likely to develop breast tumors, especially malignancies (cancer), when she grows older.

The male, unaltered, often establishes a habit bad for him and unendurable for you—the spraying habit, in which he decorates the floor, the litter box, the walls with a musky urine impossible to live with and almost impossible to eradicate. Obviously, the unmated male does not find this smell objectionable, but you and your neighbors will. If alteration is delayed too long, this spraying habit can continue even after castration, although the odor won't be as objectionable. If you love your pet, don't put off a simple surgical treatment that will make both of you able to live together in comfort.

The Cost of Alteration. There is a price tag on everything, including alteration of the cat. That price will vary from country to city. Castration in most country and semirural areas may not run over five dollars. In good animal hospitals in the city, with anesthesia and overnight hospitalization, expect a bill of ten dollars or more. Spaying is more costly, for obvious reasons. Country females can be spayed properly for twenty to twenty-five dollars, or a bit less. In city communities, the price rises to thirty-five dollars and up, depending on the difficulty of the operation and the age of the cat. Veterinarians who cater to an affluent clientele may double and triple these prices without improving the quality of care. Price, as you know, is relative. What you consider cheap may be exorbitant to someone with a lesser income.

12

The Sex Life of Your Cat

The cat family is not only prolific; it thoroughly enjoys its sex life, and both male and female continue to breed until they are senior citizens. Pink had her last litter when she was over fifteen and bitterly resented the operation that robbed her of the delights of rearing a family.

Breeding. Somewhat like the human mother, the lady cat has periodic "heat" periods—sometimes every fifteen to twenty days, frequently less often. Unlike the human mother, she has only a few peak periods in which pregnancy can occur—periods called "estrus."

Traditionally there are two, sometimes three, major estrus or breeding periods, one in late fall or early winter, one as winter turns into spring. Many cats happily break this tradition. Kitten, one of my jet-black queens, was so enamoured of the whole business that she never stopped milking, and between litters of her own—at least four a year—she borrowed kittens from any other nursing family on the place.

Again traditionally, the female reaches breeding age at about seven months, but many is the watchful pet owner who has been astonished to discover a five-month-old youngster with kitten. The male, often slower to develop in many ways, rarely breeds before the seventh or eighth month, but—and in cats there always is a but—the well-fed, rapid-grow-

"Making bread" is one of the familiar signs of sexual excitement. When emotionally aroused by another cat, by a favorite person, by inviting smells or fabric textures, almost all cats will knead with claws outstretched. This seems to be a carryover of the kneading done by the newborn who instinctively invites the flow of milk by the rhythmic pressure of small paws.

ing male ignores the rule book and may sire a litter as early as six months. Just remember this when you leave a lot of youngsters together, secure in the theory that "nothing can happen." It can and does.

A normal gestation period is about sixty to sixty-three days. It, too, can vary from fifty-six to sixty-five, or up to sixty-nine days in the case of the Siamese breed. It is difficult to pinpoint the exact moment of impregnation. During the eight to ten days of estrus the female may mate four or five times a day, to say nothing of what she may do at night, when you are asleep. In the interests of accuracy, write down the estimated dates of mating so that you have some reasonable idea of when to expect your new family.

In a first mating, and depending on the age of the mother, get ready for three to four kittens. I have had older cats who have given me eight at a time, all strong and healthy, but this is not the usual case. As the lady cat begins to feel her years, her litter size may drop back to four, three, two. Or sometimes her litters are not vigorous. Some can be born dead or too weak to live.

It was once thought that cats never rebred while nursing kittens. Forget this old wives' tale. Some very ardent mothers will not leave their kittens, some are prevented from leaving by watchful owners, some thoroughly sexy felines consistently try to rebreed when the kittens have reached the three- or four-week-old mark. Whether or not there is any connection I am not sure, but at about this time, the mother cat starts to wean her little ones. The weaning process is usually completed by the seventh or eighth week. Many queens who enjoy nursing will permit it for many weeks longer. Big kittens, almost full-grown cats, who also enjoy nursing will sneak back to suckle, and frequently, if mother is permissive.

The cat family has its shy breeders, those who literally refuse to accept a male, fight so hard that they discourage even the most ardent tom. And there are those who, amazingly, are monogamous, and will accept only one male. I had one of these faithful ladies, Angel, who resisted all suitors until a certain ragged bum of a Maltese got around to visiting her. To his charms she always succumbed.

The Mating Game. Between cats, this is a strange and rather wonderful thing. The seeking female, not too unlike her human counterpart, raises her voice and calls in what she imagines to be sweet tones. To the human ear these are shattering noises, hardly bearable, but such is the sound differential of cats, that eager toms, sometimes miles way, find the tones dulcet and inviting, and answer with howls of equally ear-shattering intensity. When I brought my cat family into New York and let them run free in the back court of a city complex, I misjudged how far and how effectively these vocal invitations could carry. A resolute female who knows her intentions cannot be stopped or muffled by walls and gardens and tall buildings that tower above her. If the visitors were slow to approach, my queens traveled the block-long court and hunted out the males. One thing that used to astound me was the reaction of my total cat family, those who were not in heat. They all went along for the fun. Insisted on being witnesses. And they all escorted the satisfied lady back home.

The young and inexperienced tom often presses his luck, and so gets a healthy bite or scratch for his efforts. The older male bides his time and uses blandishments. Instead of rushing the issue, he makes friends with his intended. Purrs to her. Makes affectionate advances, if she will permit. Lies down beside her or touches her. In the final moment of mating the female crouches on her belly, elevates her rear quarters, kneads with her front paws, as the male mounts and grasps her firmly with his teeth in her loose neck skin. Instinct born of thousands of years has told these two that this is the correct technique, the mating position for successful insemination.

The mating game of cats is a sort of animal ballet. Advance and retreat, rejection and acceptance, done to a rhythm that changes its pace as the dance approaches its climax. And the ballet team has a fantastic footwork, as they whirl and leap or roll in invitation. Curiously enough, there is nothing ugly or offensive about this mating game. It is natural sensuousness, not postured sexiness.

Many new pet owners do not recognize heat or its body movements. A young city neighbor of mine is typical. She called me frantically to say that her cat was sick. The cat was crouching on the floor, crying, making strange movements, and must be dangerously ill (so the owner thought). I climbed up five flights of stairs to watch a very familiar performance. When this was repeated every ten days, I urged my neighbor to take the cat to the veterinarian. I suspected that this female was in constant heat and needed attention. Because of her owner's deep-seated conviction that nature must not be interfered with, this poor cat was not altered, as she should have been, for nearly a year.

As a part of the mating game, male cats frequently spray a very musky and foul-smelling urine, usually near the door and window areas of a house or apartment. In the cat world, this is perfume of the highest quality. In today's lingo, Numero Uno. Since you are not a cat, you will find this musky odor most offensive, and so will your neighbors. As a home-type pet owner, not a breeder, solve this spraying problem as quickly as possible by castration.

Contrary to what you may have heard, the tom's interest in the queen does not end with the mating. On the birthday of litters he sired, I have seen Chip lie close to the birthing box and keep his lady company all through her labor. And I have seen many a tom play gently with small kittens, help in the discipline and training of the youngsters.

Birth. The period of birth and labor varies from cat to cat. With some queens, the whole business is over in a few hours, or it may last a full day. Often a mother cat will have a first kitten, and then take a breather before she produces the next one—that breather may range from ten to sixty minutes. Nervous young females may leave their nest and drop kittens around the house in odd places. The whole subject of birth is discussed in the following chapter.

Disorders of the Female Reproductive System. Normal, strong young females have some problems in the reproductive system, but more disorders and diseases come with age.

Mastitis. Shortly after delivery, some older cats may develop mastitis, what humans once called "milk fever." The breasts swell, are an angry red, and the flow of milk ceases. The pain of the swollen breasts is intense, and the queen rapidly runs up a high fever. Antibiotics administered as quickly as possible are the answer and usually solve the problem most effectively. Without relief, the mother cat and her litter can die—also quickly.

Pink, after years of normal delivery, suddenly developed mastitis and repeated this dangerous condition on all subsequent deliveries. In the interests of her health and life it became necessary to spay her, even at her advanced age.

Infections of the Uterus. In older cats with a repeat history of breast and other female problems, uterine infections may occur. Here again antibiotics may seem to check the ailment, but spaying is usually the only true answer.

Ovarian Cysts. These can occur in queens of any age, young or old. Such cysts will often keep a cat in constant heat and also prevent breeding. Sometimes the cysts can be removed through surgery. Usually, spaying is necessary and desirable.

Cancer. A history of mastitis, infection, and cysts sometimes suggests the development of cancerous growths. Decisive action should be taken before cancer has a chance to move in.

Disorders of the Male Reproductive System. These are said to be uncommon except for urolithiasis, a urinary-system disease but one that very frequently involves mechanical obstruction of the penis. Actually, no one really knows what is the true incidence of disease involving genitals. Except for breeder males, the veterinarian usually sees only the castrated males or males about to be castrated. Since castration lessens or eliminates the possibility of disease in some parts of the reproductive mechanism, anyway, there is little statistical data to lean on. Judging from the twenty to thirty million pet cats believed to be living in American homes, the male cat population has stamina.

13

"Kittens, Kittens, What Kittens?"

The nonchalant Mehitabel was apparently able to flirt her tail and disown her own, yet even strong two-fisted men are putty in the paws of a gay and confident kitten. All baby animals pluck at the heartstrings—the leggy colt, the nuzzling calf, the roly-poly puppy—but kittens seem to have a special and transcendent charm.

If you have not had a kitten recently, you will be amazed at its size. You can hold one in the palm of your hand and have room to appreciate a minute body, the smallest of ears close-hugged to a little round head, a wisp of a tail. As you look at this tiny one in something of awe, remember that it is not an hour old, but some sixty days old, and that you, quite as much as its mother, have already contributed to its health, vitality, and chances for a long life. As with the human baby, prenatal care of the mother—with a strong root in good nutrition—is a master key to little cat's future well-being.

The responsibilities of a pet owner are numerous and some may be burdensome, but if you love cats and kittens, you will take the necessary daily chores in your stride.

Getting Ready for Kittens. Millions of small cats have been born without the help of humans. Although the mortality rate is higher in the unattended, a goodly percent survives. If the mother cat is

So tiny he is, the blind newborn, that he can rest in the palm of your hand and with room to spare. The miniature perfection of these small ones will never cease to astound you.
Photo by Henry Briggs

your cat, you will want to prepare for the event and supervise it.

Long before the birth day, introduce your queen to a birthing box or basket. Put it in one of her favorite hiding places, and persuade her to accept it. If she seems hesitant, change the location until you find one that suits her. Remember that when she gives birth, she will want quiet, a sense of security, and often darkness. A closet where the door can be kept constantly cracked open is often a chosen place. Select a box that is big enough for comfort. As your expectant mother grows heavy, and after the litter comes, she should not be cramped, should be able to lie out at full length, relaxed. Pick a box with reasonably high sides, walls of security, but low enough for easy jumping in and out. Cushion the bottom of the box with newspapers and some soft materials, such as old towels, that you are prepared to discard. Don't crumple them too much or the newborn may smother. If your choice of location is right, you will soon find your pet sleeping in her box part of every day.

As Birth Begins. The mother cat will usually show signs of anxiety at this time. She may cry, get in and out of her box, demand special affection. When nature strikes the clock, the first sign of impending birth may be what seems bleeding, but in reality is the breaking of the water sac—a pinkish, wettish serum that stains the cushioning of the box.

Soon, very soon, the muscular contractions of birth will start, and since it is these contractions that will push the kittens out into their new world, encourage them. I once had a wonderful old man who cared for all my country animals. Whatever hour of the day or night we expected a little one or a litter, he was always on deck. With gentle and soothing hands he would stroke the laboring female, and with firm but affectionate voice he would reassure her. I watched him one night with a sow who had turned ugly, and dangerous. I will never forget his voice as he said over and over again, "It's all right, baby. Push a little harder, push a little harder." I recommend this kind of close personal contact with the laboring cat. And pushing a little harder is exactly what your queen must do. Occasionally you can even help your pet by giving her your firm hand to push against, and by massaging her spinal area with tender fingers.

The first kitten, from a young or older mother, may cause distinct pain. Many kittens come feet first instead of head first. This presentation may be more difficult and more painful. You can sometimes hasten such a presentation by what is called "traction," a gentle pulling on the emerging legs of the kitten. This pulling must be very gentle indeed, and it should be synchronized with the pushing contractions of the mother. Don't attempt this unless you work with the greatest of caution.

In normal birth, the mother cat cuts the umbilical cord with her teeth. Some kittens are born in a sac, a membrane which encloses them. Most cat mothers know how to break the sac and get air quickly to the baby. Occasionally the mother cat is too tired or too inexperienced to bite the sac open, or the sac may be too tough. At times I have had to tear this sac, and apply mouth-to-mouth breathing to the kitten. If mouth-to-mouth breathing does not work, run your small finger inside the mouth of the kitten, cleaning out the sticky material which may stop air from entering. And as the doctor does with a human baby, swing the little kitten gently by the back legs and pat his back or belly until he sputters and coughs.

As the queen washes, cleans, and dries off the babies, they move swiftly and instinctively to her warm breast and start the milk flowing by sucking and kneading with tiny but strong paws.

Afterbirth (Placenta). Many new pet owners are horrified when they discover a bloody mass of material in the birthing box. And equally horrified when they see their mother cat trying to eat this nasty-looking stuff. Nature told her to do this—to remove the signs of birth so that marauding enemies will not be attracted, and to use the afterbirth as a kind of vitality food. If the litter is a large one, don't let your queen eat more than a few placentae. Too many will cause intestinal disorders.

In a warm nest the mother cat hovers over her litter. During the early weeks, when baby cats concentrate on suckling and growing at a fantastic rate, the mother cat rarely leaves her box and her brood.

The First Two or Three Weeks. Two things must be done immediately after the last of the litter is born, and neither of these jobs is fun.

Let's take the worst first. Unless you are a breeder, and sometimes even then, you may not wish to or cannot keep the whole litter. Good adoption homes are hard to come by. It is kinder to the mother cat, the kittens, and yourself to limit the litter immediately. In the first few hours after birth, the mother cat has not yet learned to count her young. She will not miss the ones you take away. Putting newborns to sleep is infinitely better than allowing them to grow into delightful individuals that you could not destroy. As coldly as possible, you must turn from life to death. Select the babies that have the best colorings and markings, the males rather than the females, the strong instead of the weak. Do not hesitate. Limit the litter to the number you can keep yourself or give to people you can trust. I have found that chloroform, administered in a tightly sealed container, is quick and almost painless.

Your second chore is cleaning up the birthing box. Remove the wet and stained cushioning at the bottom of the box, and make your new family warm and dry.

In the next few weeks there will be peace in your house. The new mother is fiercely protective and leaves her nest only for trips to the litter box and to get her meals. She blissfully enjoys her kids, purring loudly as they disentangle from their furry heap to nurse and nurse again. The very overprotective mother can fail to get sufficient food.

All of the queen's reserves have been drained in pregnancy and birth. For her good and the good of the kittens, she must have better food and better care than you have ever given her before. Remember, she is not only eating for two, more probably for five to eight.

Three litters at a time were not uncommon in my country days. One night I came home to discover old Kitten, who purely loved kittens, stuffed into her box with twenty-four babies around her, varying from newborns to ten-day-old youngsters with their eyes open. Two frustrated mothers circled the box, but there was no room in the inn. Quickly I lengthened the compartment, built on a corrugated box addition, and within minutes all three families were snug as a bug in a rug. The community nest had vast advantages. One mother would baby-sit while the others took time out or went for a prowl. Nobody knew whose kittens were whose, and no one cared. My queens found this much to their liking, and so it became a family tradition, repeated by the mothers themselves.

Somewhere around the tenth day, as you know, the little cat's eyes will open, and then the personalities of the youngsters will explode. Don't be surprised if you find yourself playing favorites. In every litter there is a special one who begins to respond to your voice and your hand, a clever kid who has started a campaign he will probably win—a strategic campaign to become one of your best-loved cats.

There is a theory that if you touch a kitten, the mother will move the whole litter to a safe place. This depends on whether the reaching hands are strange or familiar. I have consistently handled baby kittens to make them sure of my hands, and to convince the mother cat that she can trust me. She will be suspicious of strangers, and suddenly you may find yourself hunting for your litter.

In time, the familiar box may lose its charm. As the mother cat watches her young scrambling over the box edge, she knows instinctively that a move of location is in the cards. And one day the old box will be empty. Just look around. On a comfortable couch or in your favorite chair, or perhaps in a closet, your family has taken up new residence, a place where

There then comes a day when instinct tells her it is time for a flitting. The box is too small for the movement a kitten needs to find his feed and walk into his world. There will be many moves until the youngsters are competent to take off under their own steam.

kittens can begin to move more freely, to learn to use their legs. There may be several such moves as the children grow older and more competent, each triggered by the mother's knowledge of what is best. Don't argue the issue, for if you do, you will lose.

Policing. In the early nursing days, when little cats get only mother's milk, the lady cat very carefully polices her young. Not just licking coat and eyes and ears, but cleaning up the excreta. Newborn kittens can neither urinate nor defecate without a stimulating massage done by mother's tongue on the anal and genital regions. This may not sound fastidious, but it is as nature intended it, and the technique keeps both babies and box sweet and clean.

As quickly as possible the baby cat should be introduced to a litter box. So basically clean is the cat that even tiny kittens will get to a box quickly if it is in easy reach.

Weaning and Box Training. Good mothers begin to wean their kittens around the third or fourth week, and, as you already know, the major weaning process is over by the seventh or eighth week. Weaning is done gradually. The queen leaves her box for longer and longer intervals. As the kittens begin in earnest to explore the world outside the box, I make it a practice to put a small litter box close by. A disposable aluminum broiler pan filled with a small amount of cat litter is just right. At first the kittens play with the litter or sleep in the pan. As more and more solid food is introduced into their diet, they start scratching in this shallow container, and finally, one day, will begin to pass some rather hard stools. You can encourage the use of litter by placing the kittens into this junior-size litter box and manipulating little paws to scratch. The earlier you help the kittens to establish this pattern, the lesser your problems. They may make an occasional mistake, but so clean is the cat that, once he gets the idea, he is firmly box-trained. I have had a few, a very few, dirty kittens who could not be box-trained. The number is so small it is hardly worth mentioning.

Teaching the Kitten to Eat. Left to his own devices, any smart kitten will find his way to food not supplied by mother. You can help this development by periodically dipping the little cat's lips into a shallow dish of milk. Lips, not nostrils. After a sputter he soon settles down to lapping. In the solid-food department, even tiny cats will attack a small bit of raw meat, often growling ferociously and pinning down the morsel with a quick paw. In general, little cats and big ones do not like the texture of chopped meat but prefer the solid morsels. Some feline babies delight in the human-baby food Pablum, and this is fine for them. With some fussy and particular kittens, I have found that human-baby foods are the most acceptable. Soon the small cat will move to the communal plate with any adults in the family, often chasing the big ones away. Now all you have to make sure of is the three to five feedings a day required by the growing kitten.

Discipline and Grooming. Once the kittens are tumbling about, darting everywhere, the mother cat has the best time of her life. She plays with her youngsters, and with delight. This play has a purpose. As she rolls them around, catches them in her paws, bites them, sometimes until they squeal, she is teaching them a feline form of self-defense. As a part of this mock fighting, she often introduces that great prize, a mouse, and joins her kids in the chase. When mice are scarce, she may bring in a piece of meat, such a delicacy as a bug, or even a bit of sweet corn on the cob. This hunting game is as old as the cat family, and was invented for survival long before food manufacturers dreamed up succulent, well-balanced diet foods in cans. It is really extraordinary how the instinct has lasted for centuries, during which the need for hunting by the domesticated cat has practically vanished.

Good Manners. Your mother cat will go as far as she is able in teaching her kittens good manners. Then you must take over. If you have a badly behaved cat, it is usually your fault. The chapter on "Discipline" will suggest simple techniques that will make your pet pleasant to live with.

Keep the baby cat's feeding equipment small and low, kitten-size. At some point, about eight weeks, mother will wean them. They will nurse only occasionally, and seek their food—supplied generously by you—with eagerness.

The Adopted Kitten. This youngster poses some different problems. Whether you get him from breeder, pet shop, or friend, you would do well to take him immediately to your veterinarian and have him thoroughly examined. It is best not to adopt a kitten until he is seven or eight weeks old, when he should be completely weaned, already on solid food, and already box-trained.

If you succumb to your children's pleas for a small one who is too young to leave his mother, you may have a series of problems, the kind which can well sell you permanently off the idea of having a cat. This too-young one is still in the nursing stage, not ready to eat on his own, and so must

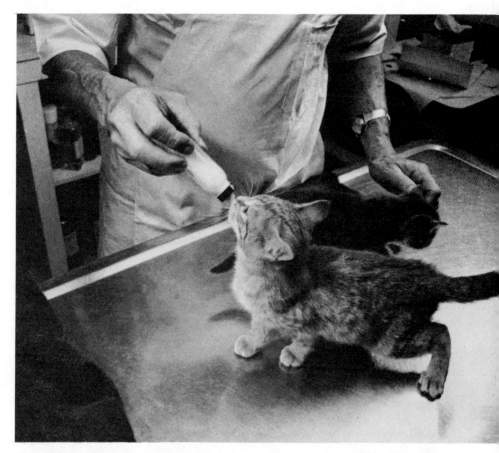

For orphan kittens your veterinarian can provide a nursing bottle or you can buy a doll's bottle in the five-and-dime.

Little cat takes a trip, climbs that highest mountain, and discovers that he has working claws and strong healthy muscles. A scratching post is more important in kitten days than ever again. *Photos by Sue Meyers*

be bottle-fed and burped like the baby he is. With lots of patience you can handle the situation, using a doll's nursing bottle. But some of the immediate fun you expected from your new pet will be clouded by the absolute necessity of daily feeding—many times a day—by the necessity of teaching the little cat to eliminate, and by the kitten's natural loneli--ness, his great sense of loss, the loss of mother. You, and not your children, who really just wanted a live toy, must now become the kitten's mother. All kittens need constant love, affection, and attention, but the very young kitten needs twice as much.

If your new pet comes into your home at eight weeks, the picture is completely different. He is now on his way to being his own competent self. You and your family can enjoy him, not just worry about him. By the way, many of the adoption agencies will not give even an eight-week-old kitten to a family who all have to leave home every day—to school, to office or community duties. To such a home, if it is otherwise a good home for pets, they may give two cats. A pair will keep each other company May I say that two cats are not just twice as much fun as one, they are ten times as much fun.

Children and Kittens. Among the old wives' tales there is one to the effect that cats suck a child's breath. This is the sheerest nonsense. Then there are those highly antiseptic parents who are sure that a cat, or any pet for that matter, will carry "germs" and endanger the child's health. If the kitten is healthy, this need not be a great worry. Generations of babies have survived sleeping close to warm little cats who are delighted to cuddle with someone their own age.

Toddlers and children between three and ten sometimes resent a cat. Some of this resentment grows out of jealousy. As the child watches a little cat steal the center of the stage, he or she may come to think of the new pet as an enemy, a feeling quite akin to that emotion children have when a new brother or sister arrives to share affection. Some children like to make the cat cry or fight, then complain loudly if kitty strikes back. By this ploy, children draw attention to themselves and try to point the finger of blame at that villain, the cat.

No one but you yourself can decide when and whether to combine children and pets. Avoid the situation entirely unless you can be sure that both children and pets will be wholly happy, and for many years.

Have a Kitten. Somewhere in your pet owning life, do have a kitten and watch him grow up. At the moment, I have no kittens, and believe me, I miss them.

14

Health and Disease

There is a fine old line in our marriage vows to which every cat owner should say a hearty "I do"—the line that ends "in sickness and in health, until death do us part."

Your cat's health is one of your prime concerns, but you can only assure it if you fully understand the nature of the cat, his physical makeup, and the meaning of feline health.

For the proud owner who boasts of his pet that "he is almost human," there is more truth than fancy in the statement. Your cat is very like you organically and psychologically. Both he and you are considered sophisticated mechanisms.

Read any simple text on human anatomy and you will know a lot about your cat. You have similar bony structure—about twenty-four more bones to the cat's score than to yours. You have the same vital organs, only slightly different. Your skin coat is remarkably like his, except for the fur you lost as your environment changed. Your ailments and diseases are much the same and stem from the same basic causes. Just name a health problem from asthma to worms, and both of you are candidates. And you can even "catch" certain ailments from each other.

With all these similarities, there are some extraordinary differences, and in the cat's favor. Have you ever wished you had a tail? A tail you could wave graciously, wag like a dog, lash in furious anger, move gently just at the tip end to express interest or affection? I have wished many times for a tail. I can think how a beautiful and provocative or demanding-attention tail might have served me in many a business conference. Or perhaps you would prefer eyes like the cat—eyes that let you see in the night? Or a set of muscles that give effortless ability to roll, tumble grace-fully, bite your toe as easily as you bite a finger, jump fifteen feet straight up without advance training for the Olympics? Or a pair of ears that can hear the faint sound of a butterfly's wings and all those minuscule noises as tiny things climb up a grass blade? Have you ever considered the ad-vantages of a defensive set of claws that would provide superior protec-tion in a world where physical defense becomes a necessity? Chances are you have never wished for eight children all at once. But the queen, with a dual uterine arrangement, gives birth much as you do, loves eight as deeply as you love your one.

In this health-and-disease section we will try to explain the similarities and differences between you and your cat, to set up some feline physical fitness standards, to analyze the major health problems cats face, and to report how well modern research is solving those problems, just as it is solving yours.

A. HEART AND BLOOD

Middle-aged citizens, who are busy taking their pulses or rushing to the doctor for EKGs and blood-pressure checkups, might do well to look to their feline friends. The cat has relatively few heart problems, and most of these never occur until old age. Part of this heart vitality undoubtedly stems from the sensible life a well-cared-for cat lives. He eats enough to satisfy a keen appetite, but he rarely overstuffs himself. When he has eaten well and fully, he does not dash off to a business appointment, or work fifteen hours a day, or try to prove in violent sport that he is younger than he is. Instead, he lies down and sleeps while his food digests in peace. He drinks plenty of liquids—the right kind, not the wrong kind. Instead of sitting glued to a television set, he exercises daily, running and jump-ing, playing for the sheer fun of play, not for competition or trophies. It is we, not he and his tribe, who are the dumb animals.

A husky heart, a network of blood vessels that carry essential nutrients to every part of his body, another set of vessels that carry waste products to organs that dispose of them, plus the blood-forming centers—bone marrow and spleen—make up the cat's vascular system, which is much the same as yours.

Like you in good health, the cat's bloodstream maintains a fine balance

Because he leads a sane and sensible life, the cat has few heart difficulties. Much of his life is spent in sleep and rest with always a nap after a hearty meal.

of red and white blood cells, a balance that can be changed by disease. If there has been a serious illness in your family—say pneumonia or a bad appendix—your doctor may have said to you, "The white cell count is too high." This warning rise in "white count" tells your veterinarian, as it tells your doctor, that danger lurks. Excitement, stress, high altitudes, dehydration—all can upset the balance between white and red blood cells. Such an upset is usually temporary and usually correctible, with dehydration spelling the greatest threat.

Actually, there is not too much that you can or should know about your cat's circulatory system. But since the heart can pump life—or death— through the bloodstream, there are times when you must be prepared to act intelligently.

Injuries. Serious cuts and wounds can cause profuse bleeding. This kind of excessive bleeding must be stopped as quickly as possible.

Infections. Any break in the skin—a simple scratch, which your cat in turn scratches, a puncture wound that is hard to detect without regular examination, a skin disease—if unchecked, can become infected and set off a bloodstream infection. Before the time of antibiotics, infections claimed the lives of thousands of cats. Today, with prompt treatment from your veterinarian, infection can be controlled.

Anemia. There are a number of types of anemia to which your pet is prone, one of them contagious and apparently carried by fleas. The signs of anemia are loud and clear. The pink tissues which you can see clearly—the mouth and gums, the inner lining of the eyelids, the nose—grow strangely white. There may be a tarry black diarrhea. Your cat shows lessening vigor and activity. Only your veterinarian can diagnose and treat. I have lost one cat, my old lady Pink, to an anemia which could not be stopped. Hers was an ailment of old age, which in one short month and despite every possible treatment drained her life away.

B. MUSCLE AND BONE

Ever since the animal family firmly established itself on this planet many eons ago, there have probably been wild cat creatures. But *Felis catus* or *Felis domestica*, whichever you prefer, appears first in recorded history only five thousand years back, when Egypt was in her glory. And, interestingly enough, the basic body of the cat has not altered in fifty centuries. The reason for this maintenance of structure is a very simple one. In most cultures the cat was a decorative, somewhat mysterious pet, not primarily a working animal. Even the early breeders were most interested in coloring and markings and length of coat, less interested in tinkering with nature. Fortunately for the cat, and most unfortunately for the dog, man concentrated on the canine population, breeding for toy or giant types, shortening legs to produce hunters who could squirm into low brush and flush out game. Drastic changes like these in the dog's bony parts are responsible for many canine bone disorders from which most cats are singularly free.

There are a few exceptions, rather nonessential exceptions. The Manx cat from the Isle of Man was inbred to be tailless. Without a tail, a switching tail that triggered his intent to attack, the Manx proved to be a better hunter. Then, somewhere in time, the Peke-face or dish-face caught the fancy of Persian breeders, and this characteristic has been maintained by line breeding. Just when someone decided that extra toes brought good luck to the house, no one knows, but this feature is also fixed by breeding. Short-haired cats of many colors turn up with extra toes, usually on forepaws only, rarely on the rear paws.

If you could place, side by side, an X ray of man and cat, both bodies in an erect position, you would see many striking similarities. There is a

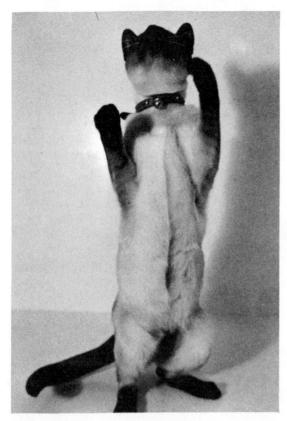

Physically you and your cat are much alike. If an X ray could be taken of you both in an identical upright position, it might be hard to tell who was who. Thanks to a tail and a few extra ribs, your cat's bone count is slightly more than yours.

slight difference in number of bones. Since man lost his tail long ago, he lacks some twenty-three or more vertebrae that appear in this part of the cat's body. And the cat also boasts some extra ribs that are relatively unimportant.

Bones that do make an enormous difference in the cat's mobility are those found in the hip and the neck. Watch your pet as he twists himself into impossible shapes. Hipbones that move freely, almost like a swivel, give him a freedom of movement beyond your wildest dreams. And watch too as he moves his head with incredible speed. Lacking a collarbone like yours, his neck movement has been carefully designed to compensate for a rather faulty eye-focusing ability.

Better than five hundred muscles help the cat achieve that very beautiful fluid motion which is one of his great charms. And, very unlike you, he keeps these muscles in top form by constant exercise. From the moment he can crawl over the edge of his kitten box until the day he dies, kitty does daily exercises that put you to shame.

Disorders of Bone and Muscle. Faulty nutrition, injuries, and old age can and do cause bone and muscle problems.

Injuries. Falls and impact accidents can break or fracture bone, as you know. One not-too-uncommon injury is a broken tail. Caught by the tire of a moving vehicle or pulled too hard by a strong hand or caught by a closing door, vertebrae in the tail can be pulled apart. Surgery is usually the only answer to a broken tail. The cat may miss this appendage as the ancient Chinese missed a pigtail, but he can live well and comfortably without it.

Constriction of Circulation. Traps, tourniquets applied by inexperienced people who forget how long the tourniquet has been left on, and things like rubber bands which children will fasten on necks, tails, and legs—all these interrupt circulation. Cut off the blood supply from an important member, cut it off too long, and body tissue will begin to die. Rubber bands are the most insidious. They can be buried in fur and lost from sight. A simple daily check on your pet will avoid this hazard.

Faulty Nutrition. Few people understand that the bone must be fed like the rest of the body, and that bone is not a concretelike solid. The bloodstream carries nutrients in and out of the bony structure. When the flow of nutrients is adequate, bones grow, are strong and sturdy. When vital minerals are not available in sufficient quantity, or may be depleted, as in pregnancy and disease, bones can grow thin and fragile.

Important worldwide research has focused attention on the depletion of bone resulting from faulty nutrition, and this research has been spearheaded by one of the greatest of experts in feline nutrition, Dr. Patricia Scott, University of London, Royal Free Hospital, School of Medicine. This remarkable woman writes about cats and primarily cat nutrition as does no other research person in the feline field, with a rare combination of technical skill and warm understanding that makes the most scientific information come alive. It was she who first reported to an international congress on small animals that a deficiency in calcium and an imbalance of calcium and phosphorus could spell bone damage, particularly for the city cat shut off from the natural mineral source that country cats find in the bones of rodents and birds.

American university animal research teams have picked up Dr. Scott's findings and studied them with great interest. The city cat or the house-confined cat may well be short of an essential bone ingredient—calcium. On a high-meat diet, and without milk, which many cats refuse, calcium intake is minimal. Calcium shortage results in depleted bony tissues and easy-to-break bones, especially in pregnancy and in old age.

Lack of calcium is apparently not the only factor in this complex diet deficiency. In meats commonly fed to confined cats—beef, liver, kidney—

not only is calcium low but phosphorus is high, and vitamin A is very high in the organ meats. One expert at the University of Pennsylvania says that diets with such mineral and vitamin imbalances are actually "toxic."

Just how might you suspect that your cat lacked calcium in the proper ratio to other nutrients? Lameness is a common sign, and it can occur in growing kittens as well as older cats. If you see signs of lameness, check with your veterinarian and do not be misled by the outdated belief that lameness is usually an inherited problem.

Other Bone and Muscle Disorders. One problem, most frequently met in the Siamese, is hip dislocation. Although this seems to be a breed characteristic, it may also be calcium-related.

In older dogs, a slipped disc is not uncommon. It is far less frequent in cats and much less disabling.

It is safe to say that the well-fed cat who is also well protected against injury lives out his days without many bone and muscle problems and very few aches and pains from arthritis, an ailment which your own medical doctor will tell you every human will have if he lives long enough.

Declawing. Some pet owners, worried about furniture damage, often insist on declawing. Correctly, this "cosmetic" surgery is performed by the veterinarian and usually on the forepaws only.

There is considerable medical opinion that says declawing spoils the cat's balance in jumping, puts him off balance so that he is apt to fall. Even in an apartment, your cat needs his claws as he jumps and grabs. And at times he needs them for protection against a newcomer cat who tries to become boss, against your own children before they have learned that tails were not made to be pulled, or for possible life-saving protection in case your apartment pet sneaks out an open door or window.

Also, today, when cats travel so much, have summer and winter homes, the declawed cat may be at a serious disadvantage in the summertime outdoor environment.

C. EYES AND EARS

The Cat's Eye. There is perhaps nothing about the cat so unique as his eye. Contradictions and compensations in its physical makeup give the cat rather extraordinary vision and equip him to operate very successfully in his environment. In hunting, for example, once a survival activity, the cat, unlike the dog, depends on his vision more than his sense of smell to locate his game and attack it accurately.

Your cat has camera eyes. Although his focusing is neither as quick nor as sharp as yours, he can, like a camera, "shut down" the pupil to adjust to different light intensities. Or with pupil wide he can look through the night and see competently.

Highly sensitive and easily injured is the cat's ear. It is the edge of the outer ear that often suffers from small cuts, scratches, or skin ailments which spread to the ear from the body.

The beauty and expressions of the cat's eyes have inspired artists, poets, and designers of fine jewelry. Folklore and myth are filled with reference to the cat's eye. Indeed, the "evil eye," the eye that can kill, is a cat eye, possessed, so legend says, by humans who are really savage animals.

If you compare your eye with the eye of your cat, you will discover some interesting dissimilarities. Your eye is smaller for body size than the eye of your pet. You move your eye, even in sleep, very rapidly. The cat's eye movement is slow. But his neck movement is so fantastically fast that he shifts his vision almost instantly. You blink frequently. Cats almost never blink.

Think of your cat as having camera eyes. When activated by a set of muscle bands in the iris, a mobile pupil "shuts down" much like the lens of a camera, lets in more or less light, as the situation demands. In intense and blinding sunlight, the pupil pulls down to a mere slit, cutting out light rays that could be destructive. Or the pupil can open into the round-eyed look for full vision at night. So does your camera function when you shift to a low *f*-stop, letting in the maximum amount of light to get a correctly exposed picture on a dark day. This sensitive and instinctive pupil change gives your cat the ability to see well both in the dark and in daylight.

When you "get something in your eye," your eyes blink and tear, and often wash out with tears the intruding bit of dust or splinter or whatever it is. Your cat does not need to blink, for he has something you do not have, a so-called "third eyelid" or in medical terms the "nictitating membrane." This filmy white membrane you may never see unless your cat has some nutritional disorder. Then, like a milky veil, it may partly cover the eyeball. The third eyelid does what you do with just two eyelids. It distributes tears, clears out such foreign things as dust and dirt, and helps to protect the eyeball.

There is another unusual membrane in your cat's eyes, a reflector membrane, which, in photographic terms, "bounces" an extra amount of light back into the light-sensitive areas of the retina. This membrane plays a part in your pet's night vision.

Presumably, a cat has little or no color perception. I am not sure of this. Quite probably the experts will confound me, but it is my considered observation that cats have a kind of color response. This may be just a response to gradations or tonal qualities of gray, but hear me. Pete, a plant eater, will eat first the brilliant blossoms. Chip will not touch food if it is served on a translucent Pyrex plate, or a deep-toned plate, but will eat eagerly from a newspaper—black and white—a linoleum floor, gold, or any pastel-colored dish. This may mean something or nothing.

Whether or not puss is color sensitive, he captures in his own eyes some of the beauty colorings. Chip has that wonderful hazel green, his mother's eyes, slightly tinted. Big Boy repeats the gold, the red-gold of his coat in the liquid gold of his eyes. Pete coordinates lemon-gold eyes with the lightest stripe of his coat. Billy, one of my white ones, had one brilliant blue eye and one golden. Ambrose, a Siamese friend, has color-flecked eyes, with blue and gold intermingled. Would that fashion experts could make such matches and blends!

The next time you watch your cat jump ten feet into the air and land with precise accuracy on a six-inch square of fence, envy him his vision. The incredible speed with which kitty can snag a fly, pounce on a mouse, swipe at and hit a moving play-toy will give you repeated evidence that your cat's eyesight is very much all right, along with his nerve-muscle coordinator.

Diseases of the Cat's Eye. Very few of the cat's eye problems can be detected or diagnosed by the pet owner, or even by the breeder, who must be knowledgeable. Some of the disorders are rare and may be congenital. Some are characteristic of the breed. Persians, for example, may be weepy, with the fur around the head soiled by discharges from the eyes. This results from a special construction of the Persian's eyeball, slightly bulging in front, somewhat shallow in the back, a rather shallow "tear lake" toward the back of the eye that allows tears to spill over.

Many eye difficulties are secondary to other health problems. If kitty has a cold, rhinitis, eczema, or mange, he very probably will end up with sore eyes, eyes that will be well again when the major ailment is conquered.

Conjunctivitis. This common and annoying complaint can have many causes. Injuries to the eye, foreign matter such as cinders, dust, small barbs from plants, chemical sprays used around the house and grounds, a respiratory disease—any and all may produce a type of conjunctivitis. Which means that your cat has red, weepy, and very sore eyes, which may finally be filled with a yellowish and infectious discharge.

The catarrhal form of conjunctivitis is probably most frequently seen as a corollary to the respiratory ailments pneumonitis and rhinotracheitis. Although stubborn and persistent, this type of conjunctivitis can be controlled and cured.

Conjunctivitis demands special medications which only your veterinarian can provide, but which you can administer successfully.

Mange. Mange mites can find a happy home in the eyelids and surrounding flesh. Indeed, any skin ailment can spread to the eye rims or the surrounding skin. Mange of the eyelid looks much like mange on any other part of the body. It may be seeping and crusty, dry and scaly. In any case, painfully sore.

Infections in Kittens' Eyes. Eye infections in the newly born are quite common. The kitten is born "blind," or to be exact, with eyes sealed tight. Normally these lids open in a week to ten days. Occasionally they are very sticky, half open, then pasted shut again. When this open-shut business repeats and a pus-filled matter oozes through peepholes in the sealed lids, you may well have trouble. It is thought that the source of such infection may lie in the mother cat, in the secretions that are a part of the birth process. Whatever the cause, if you see this symptom in the newborn, recognize it as serious. Simple cleaning will not solve the problem. Antibiotics are needed, and unless they are used in time, the kitten may lose one or both eyes.

The Ear of the Cat. Intricately and delicately made, the cat's ear is not only one of the most expressive parts of his body, it is an essential in his front line of defense. Much has been made of the dog's acute sound perceptions, the high-frequency sound waves that are registered by his keen hearing apparatus. The cat's ear is almost equally keen, but since the cat is not considered a "working" animal, one who uses his sound perception for your good and mine, his ear sensitivity is often overlooked.

Take an hour someday and watch your cat's ears. The outer ear, called the "pinna," swings, moves, flattens, points as it scoops up a myriad of tiny sounds that never reach you even if you have the remarkable hearing ability of the great music composers and maestros. I can only guess, but I am sure that little noises to me are big noises, alarming noises, to my cat family. Pets finally adjust to the sickening noises of the city, but come one unfamiliar frequency, and they will alert instantly out of peaceful sleep. If you want to know what's going on around your house, watch your cat's ears, and learn to read his signals.

Outer-Ear Injuries. The cat's outer ear is the most easily hurt. In extreme cold, it can be frostbitten. Skin ailments, such as ringworm and mange, can travel to the rim of the ear. In fights, ears are often nicked, scratched, bitten. Some of these wounds and skin difficulties can be treated as you would treat similar damage on other parts of the body. Serious cuts, injuries, and infections are the province of your veterinarian.

Ear Mites. A certain kind of stubborn ear mite seems to prefer the tender lining of the outer ear. Unlike mange mites, they do not burrow but live and feed on the surface, causing inflammation and itching. Country cats who roam are more apt to pick up these annoying parasites. Head shaking and pawing at the ears indicate that they have taken up residence. Let your veterinarian identify the trouble, clean out the ears, and show you how to continue treatment. Unchecked ear mites can cause deafness.

Inner-Ear Problems. These can arise from injuries and infections and also from inexpert probing of the ear with improper instruments. Let this be a warning to you. Let your cat's ears alone. Any ear ailment except the simplest ear nick is strictly out of your hands.

Deafness. As you doubtless have heard, many white, blue-eyed cats are deaf. And some cats, like some people, are deaf to certain sound frequencies. Deafness has been caused by extra-large doses of streptomycin, and veterinarians have been warned about the use of this antibiotic. Deafness is not a common ailment. Indeed, I myself have never known a deaf cat.

D. SKIN AND COAT

Your Cat's Skin. If you have ever stopped to think about skin, you will have realized what a wonderful creation it is. The skin of every living thing—animal, bird, reptile, insect, fish, man—has been especially designed, individually designed to suit each for its own environment.

The cat's skin, including the coat, was planned for an outdoor environ-

The coat of a healthy cat is vibrant and alive, rich in color, soft to the touch. There are no blemishes. The healthy coat is not rough, dirty, or stained. Big Boy has the smooth, thick coat typical of a shorthair in the top of good health. For the longhair the basic coat qualities are the same, the length and the luxury of the hair adding another dimension.

ment. It is a strong barrier against invading disease. It prevents against excessive water loss—most of a cat's sweat glands are in the pads of his feet. It guards against the actinic rays of the sun. It helps to shed water and keep it from penetrating the body. It is a temperature regulator. A double-hair coat, the inner one called the "wool" coat, provides warmth and permits the cat to stand quite extreme cold. And marvelous "tactile" hairs, whiskers and eyebrows, extrasensitive hairs, stretch out beyond the body to warn the cat of danger.

Even the colorings and markings of the cat's skin and coat are a kind of natural camouflage. Spots and stripes blend into sun and shadow, seem one with the patterns of leaves and brush. Try to find your cat someday when he is almost under your feet, and you can test the quality of this camouflage.

Multiple layers make up an outer and inner skin. For example, in the epidermis or outer skin there are four layers all told, including the tough layer on the foot pads. Beneath the epidermis lies the dermis, the inner skin, into which is woven a fine network of muscles, nerves, and blood vessels, the weaving job of a master craftsman. It is the vastly sensitive nerves that let your cat feel beyond your scope of feeling and respond to every faint touch. One set of skin muscles gives the cat the ability to ripple his skin. Another special set of involuntary muscles, all over the body, but with concentration in the tail, was designed to provide the cat with a natural warning signal. These erector muscles stand every hair on end both in fright and fight. Even the tiny kitten, who knows no enemies except by instinct, will suddenly fluff up to twice his tiny size as these erector-protectors go into action.

What Causes Skin Problems? Despite the fine qualities of the cat's skin and coat, he is still vulnerable to skin diseases, due to the invasion of parasites, fungi, and bacteria that account for most of the common skin problems. Age, sex, season, diet, temperature—all influence the kind of skin difficulty your cat can meet. Ringworm, for example, is more common in kittens, eczema more prevalent in older cats. Bald spots appear more frequently in altered males. Fight wounds and their infectious follow-ups are more likely in unaltered males. Warm weather brings flies, fleas, and mites more frequently than cold. Country cats are more likely to have mange. City cats are more prone to dandruff and dry coats. Bad nutrition encourages skin disease, and allergy can spark many confusing signs.

Many skin diseases and irritations are largely superficial and have no serious systemic effects. If the skin surface is injured, bacteria can move in to start infections that can do systemic damage.

Irritated Skin. This is one of those large, nonspecific departments, hard to define. Household chemicals such as disinfectant sprays used for killing flies, roaches, and ants can give your pet great discomfort or even do serious harm, if he gets a heavy dose. Puss may be sensitive to dust and dirt swept in from towering smokestacks, incinerators, or from airplanes and farm machinery laying down fertilizers, insect repellents, and weed killers. Unless the chemicals are toxic to the cat—and do remember that he is far more sensitive to chemicals than many other animals are—these skin irritations will often vanish once the causative agents have been identified and removed from his environment. This is not too difficult, and can be done without interrupting the care pattern for your house, your grounds, and the fields from which come your cash crops.

Dandruff. Cat dandruff looks just like the kind you may have had yourself. Its common causes in cats are heat and humidity conditions in city apartments. However, worms can trigger dandruff, and dandruff may appear as a secondary problem along with some of the serious skin diseases. It is also frequently found on cats fed nearly a total-fish diet.

Eczema. Talking about eczema is somewhat like discussing "the common cold." Both terms are wrongly used to cover a multitude of ailments that defy definition.

Traditionally, eczema (in cats as in humans) is supposed to define a weepy, itchy skin condition that may scab over, then break out repeatedly, and usually as the result of scratching. There is in humans as well as cats a dry form of so-called eczema. Its cause? Allergy, chemical irritation, parasites, environmental conditions—name it and you can have it. Truly in cats there is probably no such thing as eczema, yet it is a catch-all name that may never vanish from research or the pet owner's vocabulary. "Eczema" can be persistent, even when not defined, and is found usually in cats over four years old. Only a veterinarian, and sometimes not even he, can determine its cause and cure.

Ringworm. Ringworm is also a misnomer, for no worm ever heard of ringworm. This is a fungal infection, so called because of the shape and character of the lesions that appear first as tiny dots. The lesions are round, and grow larger in the same round outlines. The outer edge of the lesion is most involved, and if the skin is broken, bacteria can cause secondary infection. Ringworm may travel all over the body. It can produce bald spots, some of which may remain permanently. Kittens, for some reason, are more prone to ringworm than adult cats. One of the newer drugs called griseofulvin offers a solution and cure to this stubborn and persistent affliction.

Fungal infections such as ringworm are more prevalent in hot, humid environments. But with the traveling public on the increase, ringworm can travel with you and your pet.

Cats are a major "host" for the ringworm fungus. And this they can and do transmit to man. This gives feline ringworm a special public health significance. Conversely, man can transmit ringworm to animals. And remember, too, that weeks and months later, loose hair from a ringworm patient can start the cycle of infection all over again.

Mange. Most pet owners may not be able to distinguish mange from ringworm. Usually the lesions are drier than in ringworm, and the skin has a wrinkled, old look. These sores will scab, and if puss scratches, the door to infection may be opened. A thoroughly unpleasant-looking small mite is the villain. He burrows in and must be dislodged and killed if the disease is to be halted. Mange can appear on any part of the body, including the outer ear. There are two main varieties of mange. One type is much more stubborn and dangerous than the other, but only the doctor will be able to tell which is which. There are a number of mange medications on the market, made by good manufacturers, but best check with your veterinarian before you invest in a nostrum that may not work.

Bald Spots (Alopecia). Fortunately, puss does not agonize about losing his hair as do we vain people. But lose it he often does, and for many reasons. Deep scars from injuries may leave thin hairless lines. The battle-scarred old tom, like the swordsman of the past, wears many such badges of honor. Deep burns can destroy hair follicles and produce bald spots. So can mange and ringworm. Another kind of bald spot, probably related to the human kind, comes with old age or with a change in the endocrine vitality of the cat. Often this is a thinning rather than complete baldness. This same thinning is seen in nursing queens, altered males, and spayed females. Don't worry too much about bald spots, and don't let it change your love and pride in your pet. He may never win a ribbon at a cat show, but what cat cares about ribbons as long as he has the affection of his folks?

Damage from Insect Bites. Fleas are the most common cause of this skin problem. A wide variety of fleas seem to like a wide variety of animals. Dogs and cats can exchange their flea tormentors, and puss may even pick up some from the barnyard animals and any wild ones he consorts with. Animal fleas, by and large, don't enjoy the taste of humans. Of course, there is always an exception. I once had a roommate, in my New York Greenwich Village days, who came up covered with little red spots. Itching little spots. One evening, as I watched, I saw a flock of fleas spring from the rug and settle on her legs. We finally discovered that the house was alive with these pesky insects—introduced by a family of eight cats who had the run of the place.

Human fleas are a totally different breed. They don't usually attack or infest animals.

When an alert cat is around, flies rarely live long enough to injure the skin. The real danger here is that kitty will eat flies and can ingest poisons that you may have used. Dead or alive, flies can also introduce disease organisms that move into the digestive tract. And fly-borne infections can start a series of interrelated ailments.

Occasionally, stinging insects may strike at the cat who will chase anything with wings. As with humans, wasps or bees or hornets can puncture the skin, leave a small surface injury that you may never see, but which may set off an allergic reaction of serious proportions. In my country days I watched a swarm of bees attack a cat, and only swift veterinary treatment saved him.

E. THE RESPIRATORY SYSTEM

When cat people get together, they usually talk about cats and not about people. First will come that interchange of bright stories about the latest antics of Horace, Blue Boy, or Martini. Then, since misery loves company, the dialogue will turn to health problems. Often the focus is on respiratory ailments, since these are so common. Someone is sure to mention "distemper," at which point you can expect the discussion to go off in all directions.

Few words are more used and less understood than distemper. To many people distemper still spells a sneezing, coughing, highly contagious disease which may finally go into pneumonia and be a killer. This is half true, and half false. After years of study, research workers recognize three forms of distemper, each of which primarily injures a different vital system—the respiratory system, the digestive system, or the central nervous system. The enemy in each case is one of a family of viruses, though many experts insist that the only "true" distemper is the dreaded feline enteritis, which does its primary damage in the small intestines.

Infectious viral enteritis can largely be prevented by those "distemper shots" you faithfully give your pet each year. These excellent immunizations provide maximum protection against enteritis, but they offer no protection at all against the virus infections that strike nose, throat, and lungs.

This is something that cat owners must understand, fully understand. The respiratory diseases that some refer to as distemper are more accurately termed "pneumonitis" and "rhinotracheitis." If your cat develops these ailments after having had distemper shots, don't use harsh words to your doctor. To help protect against pneumonitis, another special vaccination is needed. There is as yet no protective vaccine for rhinotracheitis.

The virus that damages the central nervous system is a vicious one.

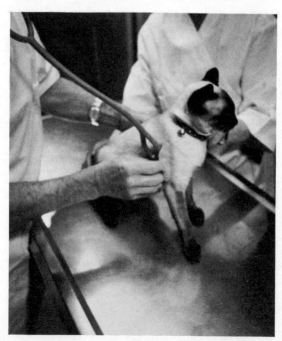

Many of the diseases most feared by cat owners strike the respiratory system. Even in a routine examination your veterinarian will check by stethoscope to catch any telltale signs of trouble.

Dogs are the victims of this form, not cats. The dog who has survived the respiratory form of distemper, who comes home apparently cured, can move into the third and usually fatal stage. Symptoms of stumbling, falling, and body twitching signal the onslaught, which often precedes convulsions. Mercifully, most animals must be put to sleep.

Your cat is susceptible to quite a large number of respiratory disorders that duplicate or parallel your own. The reason is simple. Your pet's breathing apparatus is almost a copy of yours in miniature.

The Cold Complex and Related Infections. Invading bacteria can produce irritations and disease in every part of the breathing apparatus. And these run the gamut from what you would call a simple "head cold" to tuberculosis. Puss can have rhinitis, sinusitis, tracheitis, pleurisy, minor or major pneumonia, and bronchitis because of the host of bacteria or other organisms always around that are always ready to move into an environment which suits them. Bacterial infections are often secondary to a primary viral illness. Some of these "bugs" fly through the air, develop in dirt, come in on your hands and feet. In short, you cannot shut the door or the window and close them out. Some are introduced by chest wounds, and here the fighting tom or accident victim is the most vulnerable. Some enter via improper medication, when the drug gets into the lung, not the stomach, and causes a quick and lethal pneumonia. Only your veterinarian can determine the kind of infection and evaluate its seriousness. Even he may be in doubt, for many of the symptoms of bacterial infection are almost identical with those of the virus diseases, the most frightening of all to those who love cats.

Pneumonitis. This member of the respiratory disease syndrome was finally recognized in 1942. Just like the bacterial infections, this stubborn viral disease usually begins with loss of appetite, sneezing that picks up in tempo, and coughing as the infection moves down the breathing channel. Finally there may be pneumonia. If you have a family of cats, it will be a miracle if any escape. Each recurrent sneeze spreads the organism. Antibiotics, antihistamines, and high-level nutrition plus care will finally halt the attack. But if the veterinarian says "pneumonitis," better prepare yourself for several weeks of nursing, and don't be surprised if a second attack occurs a month or so later. Severe pneumonitis can leave small kittens with a perenially weepy eye, or—as in the case of my Chipper—with a shortness of breath in violent play.

There is a preventive vaccine for pneumonitis. Although it is far from 100 percent effective, it can offer considerable protection.

Rhinotracheitis. Often miscalled "distemper," this critical upper-respiratory disease, virus borne, was finally isolated and named in 1958.

Its onset is frequently somewhat swifter than that of pneumonitis. As the disease escalates, and this it does rapidly, temperature shoots up into the danger zones. Persistent sneezing and usually coughing are early symptoms. Quickly there is a loss of appetite. Discharges from eyes and nostrils may be profuse, and often the nose is completely plugged up. As with pneumonitis, sneezing spreads and perpetuates the attack. You have a very sick cat. Your doctor must use his big guns—antibiotics, vitamin supplementation, intravenous feeding at times—and he must be able to count on you for faithful follow-through if the patient is to live. Mortality is high, especially in young or malnourished cats.

Diaphragmatic Hernia. This results from a breakthrough in the diaphragm, the muscular and tendinous divider between the chest and abdominal cavities. The fibers that make up the diaphragm are parted, much as you would tear a piece of cloth. Through this break, some of the intestinal organs can enter the thorax and disturb the whole respiratory system. This is somewhat like having two people try to live where there is only room for one. Impact accident is probably the major cause of diaphragmatic hernia. I have had a cat hit in a car accident who came up with this difficulty. The intrusion of a loop of the intestines or a tip of the liver into the chest cavity can affect not only breathing and digestion but do damage to the intruding vital organs. Sometimes the diaphragmatic hernia cures itself, but any impact injury calls for an immediate examination to assess this or other serious injury.

Emphysema. This is a word much heard in our time. And although puss does not have the cigarette habit, he may be an emphysema victim. In cats, emphysema is often a corollary to repeated attacks of bronchitis or other low-respiratory ailments. Difficult breathing, which grows more and more labored, finally drags in more air than can be exhaled. The lungs blow up somewhat as does a balloon, and may even rupture. To date, emphysema is not seen too frequently in cats, but the disease may well increase both in people and pets as the air pollution problem grows. Certainly this lung ailment must be considered by your doctor when difficult breathing and persistent low coughing cannot be traced to another cause.

Tuberculosis. This disease has already been mentioned as one of the bacterial infections to which puss is heir. Probably no one knows how much tuberculosis exists in cats. Most of the recognized cases are of bovine origin, so it is the country cat often living in a barn with a herd of cows who is most apt to contract the disease. It is certainly worth mentioning that tuberculosis can be transmitted from cat to human, and very possibly from human to cat, as some of the recent studies indicate. Do not accept this statement as a dictum to rid your home or your farm of cats. Strict tuberculosis control in cows is law in many states, so that the danger of infection, though existent, is small.

Asthma. As with humans, pollens, dusts, drugs, and foods are the common causative agents. If you have ever had an asthma attack, a gasping, choking attack, you can imagine just what a little animal can experience in sheer fright. You probably thought your number was up; and so does he, if he has a seizure. Asthma of the allergy sort is not too common in cats, but asthmalike symptoms frequently appear along with lower-respiratory ailments such as bronchitis and pneumonia. Once again, this is a detection job for the doctor.

Parasite Invasion. Worms sometimes get into the respiratory act. A lungworm widespread in various parts of the United States is fairly common in cats, but often not diagnosed. Your cat may pick up this parasite if he insists on eating rodents, reptiles, and birds. By invading lung tissue, the parasite interferes with breathing and can set off irritations and inflammations that may produce attacks of bronchitis and pneumonia.

Foreign Matter. Cats are sniffing animals. Add to that their natural curiosity, and it is easy to imagine the assortment of things that can enter the nostrils: dust, small particles of dried leaves or grasses, tiny cinders from belching incinerators, chemical powders, and such like. Pete, who insists on smelling and nibbling at anything green and growing, finally got a leaf fragment up his nose and for days worried me with a persistent sneeze. Usually such foreign intruders are dislodged by sneezing. Only occasionally do they demand a doctor's care. Consider them suspect, however, if no other symptoms suggest the more serious respiratory attacks with which sneezing is associated.

Search and Destroy. It must be obvious that the diagnosis of respiratory disease is so complex that even the best-trained veterinarian can be baffled. Since pneumonitis and rhinotracheitis account for a large percent of feline fatalities from the respiratory complex, it is reasonable to assume that medication should be directed first to these ailments, even if diagnosis is not clear cut. Whether the enemy be small or large, a full-scale campaign must be waged.

Digestion begins in the mouth where a very special rough-surfaced tongue and powerful teeth scoop in and chop up food. Strong stomach juices continue this digestion, juices strong enough to get even the small bones of birds and mice under control.

F. DIGESTION

Designing a digestive system to suit a cat must have been a real challenge. The finished product is a major achievement, for although it looks much like the human apparatus in many ways, it performs quite differently and does a really remarkable job of handling the strange collection of things your friend insists on eating.

The things he eats—here is the crux of the matter. Some of those things are the fine foods you have selected for him. But as you tempt your pet with his favorite dishes and worry fondly about his diet, think for a moment of all the other items he seems to relish. Flies and crawly bugs, rodents, birds, the leaves and stems of plants, paper and string, small beads from the broken necklace you forgot to pick up, small hardware like needles and pins. Most cats have a "depraved" appetite for these and many other oddments. I find the edges of my most precious papers raggedly chewed. Pete insists on eating marigolds. And Chip goes for carbon paper and the sticky flaps of envelopes. Miraculously, cats live through most of this—with your protective care of course, but largely because of a remarkable digestive system.

Let's begin where the digestion begins, with the teeth and the tongue. Newborn kittens cut their first teeth about the second and third week. And mother is the first to know as needle-sharp baby teeth nip milk-swollen teats. Permanent teeth come in about the fourth to sixth months, as thirty temporary teeth are replaced by the twenty-six permanents that puss needs for a full set—two less than your quota. Unlike the human baby, the kitten has no teething problems, and unlike you, he infrequently knows the misery of tooth decay. He may never lose a tooth except by accident or if he lives beyond his time.

The cat's tongue is a very special part of his eating equipment. Since his lips can only hold and contain his food, he uses this rough-surfaced tongue like a spoon to deliver the food to a powerful combination of teeth and jaw. When your pet licks you, you must have felt the tongue's rough surface, ideally planned for licking food or cleaning fur.

The cat chews swiftly, much more swiftly than you do, for saliva is not as necessary in his digestive process. He counts on his stomach to do a big job in digestion, for his stomach juices can master even small bones. So well does the stomach function that kitty is spared many of the intestinal ailments known to man. Voluntarily, his stomach rejects some of the things that don't sit well—the nonessential—the teeth and whiskers and skin of rodents, the cold foods you so carelessly asked your pet to eat, hairballs, and some of the idiot things—the beads, the plant leaves, the hardware.

Despite this sturdy and well-made digestive equipment, digestive disturbances are common in cats at all ages. So simple a thing as a sore mouth can stop an eager appetite, halt that smooth rhythmic action of perfect digestion. A small injury, a flea invasion, stress—name any ailment, small, medium, or very large, like the dread gastroenteritis, and the digestive system frequently gets involved to some degree.

Whatever the cause of digestive upset, the symptoms are similar: nausea, depression, loss of appetite, vomiting, diarrhea, or constipation.

Obstructions. Some of the curious items cats eat catch and lodge in teeth and throat. Many actually make it to the stomach or beyond. Obstructions can do damage from tongue and mouth to tail. Most, by some miracle, pass through the digestive tract. Some have to be removed surgically when puss has literally "bitten off more than he can chew." String and threaded needles have often been found trailing down the entire tract, with final injury in the rectum. At any sign of a digestive disorder, a mouth and throat examination is a "must." Often the problem is in plain sight and can be solved before it tracks down deep and confuses diagnosis by simulating the signs of gastritis, colitis, or enteritis.

Every year hundreds of cats die because they have swallowed the wrong kind of food or some foreign material. If you know or suspect your pet has eaten something that could possibly harm him, get him to a veterinarian immediately. It is the untreated cats or those treated too late that most frequently die.

Tartar. Seemingly a small thing, tartar is the source of much discomfort and digestive upset. In this day of soft canned cat foods with no abrasive action, tartar will build up. A yearly cleaning by your veterinarian is best for this. Tartar not only makes eating difficult, but it can lead to gingivitis.

Gingivitis. This tissue inflammation causes bleeding gums, and as the gums recede, there may be other tooth difficulties. Some gingivitis is caused by the organism which gives both man and cat the unpleasant ailment called trench mouth.

Trench Mouth. This is a contagious infection in which the soft tissues of the mouth and gums become inflamed, bleed, and are almost intolerably sensitive. Trench mouth can be treated and controlled with antibiotics by your veterinarian.

Jaw Injuries. A number of digestive system disorders may be set off by a jaw injury. This kind of injury is usually caused by falls or impact from moving vehicles. Jaw fractures are hard to deal with and may require surgery. Without adequate chewing apparatus, and with a painfully sore mouth, the simple process of eating is no longer simple. Even the softest and most inviting of foods will be refused along with that vital liquid, water. The surgeon must move in not only to repair but to use all kinds of supportive medication, vitamin supplementation, and perhaps intravenous feeding until a desire to live and to eat can be reestablished.

Feline Enteritis. The most serious and most deadly of the diseases that invade the digestive tract is viral enteritis (often referred to as distemper), a viral infection of the intestines. This ailment has many names—gastroenteritis, panleucopenia, cat plague, show fever, *maladie du jeune chat, katzenatcurbe*—but by any name it is still devastating, highly contagious, epidemic in proportions, and a killer. Enteritis sweeps across a country, destroying first the little ones and the malnourished. A kitten can be bright and playful in the morning and dead at night. While the organism seeks out the small intestines, the stomach and large intestines are most surely to be involved. The onset is swift. Almost total lack of appetite, vomiting or almost continual retching, high fever that peaks into the disaster zone, and, if the cat lives, diarrhea that continues through the convalescent period as the tender inner lining of the intestines is sloughed off.

My Pink and I lived through one such attack. She brought the enemy with her when she crept in, a stray from the road. She lived in rich health to eighteen, but she was one of the lucky few that survived this disease.

The house or farm that has had an enteritis invasion cannot safely have another cat for as long as a year. Hairs from the infected cat, the blanket he slept on, even briefly, fleas from a sick animal, can pass along the infection. And the animal that survives must have the most tender and loving care. Fortunately, there is an immunization that is most effective. Tiny kittens can be given a serum inoculation, and at about two and a half to three months, full protection must be provided. Because of the stubborn and lethal character of this disease, a booster immunization, once a year, is essential.

Gastritis. As you can easily guess, this is an irritation and inflammation of the stomach, sometimes very painful and acute, sometimes chronic, with the milder attacks much like human indigestion.

Gastritis almost always travels along with enteritis, but it may result from a lot of other things. Foreign materials—the bead, the pin, the string —already mentioned. Laceration by sharp splintery bones—chicken bones —is a common cause. Poison, overdoses of medication, doses of the wrong medications—the list is long. Once again, expect all the classic symptoms from nausea to diarrhea. Let your veterinarian decide the causative factor, since you may not be able to make even an educated guess.

Poisons. In my own opinion, poisons are much less of a cat hazard than they are made out to be. City or country, for more than thirty years, I have never had a poison case.

Because he is the peculiar person he is, puss is less apt to be poisoned than other animals. He is finicky and at the same time satisfied with monotony in diet. He is not a glutton. For contrast, take the dog who will stuff himself on a chuck carcass that smells to high heaven, steal tainted bait from traps, and if allowed, eat around the clock. Not so puss. He turns fastidiously from foods that smell "off," and once he has filled his stomach comfortably, he wants a nap, not more food, however inviting. These admirable traits save him from many an encounter with poisons.

But it is another of his peculiarities that can be his undoing—his natural habit of licking on an all-over pattern. If perchance he walks, hunts, plays, or sleeps in a house or outdoor areas where poisons have been spread, sprayed, or dusted, he can pick up enough poison on fur and feet, and lick off enough, to make him a very sick cat indeed. The job of protecting him against this type of poisoning is completely in your hands.

All poisons are likely to damage the digestive system, at least to some extent, and some also work on the central nervous system. Some do serious harm to liver and kidneys. Some threaten the bloodstream. The pet owner, even the most experienced, is lost on the subject and diagnosis of poison. Symptoms range from anxiety, depression, howling, and salivation, to lack of coordination in movement, unusual body positions, rapid breathing, accelerated heartbeat, collapse, and convulsions. Don't ever try to play doctor if you even faintly suspect poison. Get to a veterinarian—fast!

Drug Reactions. The term "side effects" is now rather well known. You may have met drugs that you yourself cannot take without a variety of discomforts. That sensitive and physically sophisticated creature called "cat" shares with you side effects. Many of these side effects show up in primary or secondary disorders of the digestive system. Your veterinarian knows what drugs to avoid, but since some people dose without direction, you should know that there are problems and sometimes disasters in the use of such things as:

ANTIBIOTICS given over too long a time or one that a certain individual just can't tolerate.

OPIATES AND NARCOTICS to which puss is overly sensitive and which can produce severe stress symptoms or cause him to go absolutely berserk.

TRANQUILIZERS—not as predictable in cats as in humans.

HORMONES—often used to halt the aging symptoms of cats.

VITAMINS—indicated for supplementary use with many diets, but possibly harmful in overdose. This is especially true of vitamins A and D.

HUMAN CONSTIPATION REMEDIES, some of which contain deadly strychnine in dangerous strength.

COAL TAR PRODUCTS—the "phenol" family, often used in insecticide shampoos and ointments.

ASPIRIN, a drug some cats cannot tolerate.

On the converse side, follow your veterinarian's instructions with whatever drugs he gives you. I repeat what has been said before: Many animals fail to get well because their loving owners forget to dose with indicated medications at the right time and in the right amounts. Never forget, either, that occasionally your cat may have a bad reaction to a prescribed medication. Call your veterinarian immediately if your pet seems to be doing badly on a medication and let him decide if this is the case and what should be done.

Anal Sac Impaction. The symptoms of this rectal-area difficulty have already been mentioned—the dragging of the hind quarters, the pulling of the body across the floor, sliding on the tail. Anal sacs lie close to the rectum and contain an oily yellow matter, which is normally expelled with a bowel movement and contributes to smooth elimination. Occasionally these sacs fill up and do not discharge. The oily material becomes packed, evil smelling, and if not expressed, may start infection. Cleaning these sacs needs a practiced hand. It is a job for your veterinarian. Possibly he can show you the technique, if the problem is recurrent.

Intestinal Parasites. These are frequently referred to as "worms," but this description is not fully accurate. The country cat is often more prone to parasites than the city pet, but parasites are rather common in all cats and at all ages. Four types of intestinal parasites are the prime invaders of the digestive system—roundworms, tapeworms, hookworms, and coccidia.

Of the four, roundworms are the most familiar. Some cats live for years with roundworms, and show few signs of damage. Others, especially the poorly fed, grow thin, inactive, tend to be pot-bellied, and have a dull, dandruffy coat. Both kittens and older cats sometimes vomit the worms or eliminate them in bowel movements, and so the invasion may end. Don't count on this as a solution, however, because usually only a portion of the parasites inside a pet are eliminated this way. The remainder stay inside and propagate the infection. Best have your pet dewormed. Usually this treatment should be done by a veterinarian for there are sometimes side effects with which the pet owner cannot safely deal.

Hookworms, less common than roundworms, not only drain the cat's vital reserves by feeding on blood and tissues, but can set off chronic cases of gastritis and enteritis that seem to defy treatment. Under the right conditions, any of the intestinal parasites can cause similar disturbances. The danger from hookworms is less in cold climates, greater where temperatures stay high. However, the hookworm belongs to a large, thriving, and international family. Cats usually pick up hookworms by eating rodents, rabbits, or other animal life (sometimes fish) that are infested.

Tapeworms. These parasites are most likely to indicate their presence by causing periodic digestive disturbances or crawling out of the anus onto the fur around the rear parts, or by passing out with a bowel movement. They frequently look like grains of rice, flattened from top to bottom, and move along by vigorous contracting and expanding movements. It is an old wives' tale that an individual with tapeworms is always very thin and eats incessantly. If your pet is well nourished, the chances are that he would not show either of these signs.

Coccidia. These are tiny parasites, protozoa, that can be seen only with a high-powered microscope. They infest the cell linings of the small intestines. In their reproduction cycle, thousands of oocysts or eggs are created by the parent organism. When this happens, the intestinal wall is ruptured, and this damage causes a bloody diarrhea. Most people think of coccidiosis as a disease of chickens, and so it has been for many years, a dread disease which in the case of poultry has largely been brought under control. More recently coccidiosis has been appearing in city cats who feed on filthy food or in some way come in contact with the feces of infected cats. Very quick diagnosis and prompt treatment are essential. If there are other cats in the family, the coccidiosis cat must be put into an isolation ward. The litter box of the sick animal must be cleaned many times a day, after every elimination, or your pet can quickly reinfect himself.

Sources of Parasite Infection. As already mentioned, rodents, rabbits, and sometimes fish are hosts for parasites of various kinds. Flies, roaches, birds, reptiles—all may be infected with some type of parasite or be a transfer host. If your pet insists on eating any of these things, he can pick up an infection. Even unborn kittens are not immune to the danger since they can be infected by an infected queen. Whatever the parasite, it can be transferred from cat to cat via the litter box. If one cat in your family has worms, the chances are that all the rest will soon share the same ailment.

From Cat to Man—and Man to Cat. Never forget that, under certain circumstances, the cat can transfer his parasites to man, and man in turn can infect cats. This possible interchange should not be discounted, especially in homes with children.

Parasitism is no field for the amateur. If it is suspected, examination of a sample of feces will pinpoint the kind of parasite and it can then be treated with the specific medication that best eliminates it. Many "wormers" you may buy in retail pet departments may not be specific enough or strong enough for your cat's particular parasite.

G. THE NERVOUS SYSTEM

You may well envy your cat his nervous system. It is both highly sensitive and very sophisticated. You can see for yourself how this central control system works. In the smooth, quick, accurate movements of a lithe body. In an instant perception of sounds beyond your hearing. In a rapid adaptation of vision from day to night. In the intelligent thinking with which your cat copycats you, or cons you into permissiveness, or plans smartly how to outwit his playmates or his enemies. There is quality in your cat's nervous system and in the signal system that triggers voluntary and involuntary action.

Like you, the cat has a brain cushioned in protective tissue and housed in a bony box called the skull. From this control center flow motor nerve impulses. The back of the brain, the cerebellum, is believed to play a role in much of instinctive and involuntary action. Highly developed in the cat, instinct guides many of his responses. The blind baby kitten, newborn, instinctively crawls to his mother's breast and kneads it to stimulate the flow of milk. Later, instinct makes him crouch and switch his tail as he stalks his natural prey—the bird, the mouse, the flying thing. Instinct warns him of danger and raises each hair on end. Instinct tells the mother cat that birth is approaching and starts her looking for a safe birthing place. Instinct also tells her to gobble up the food, partially predigest it, regurgitate it, and present neat little food piles, one for each kitten.

An intelligent brain and fine network of nerves control the cat's voluntary and involuntary actions. When your cat swirls into play like a dervish, moving smoothly and fluidly, you can make a good guess that his nervous system is in full operation.

Of course, many of the cat's reactions are involuntary, not instinctive. If a thorn pricks your pet's paw, a muscular reflex action makes him withdraw the paw. Even the flow of milk to the mother cat's breast is an involuntary response to her nursing kitten.

The front of the cat's brain, proportionally a much smaller area than yours, is called the cerebrum, and not only contains the sensory areas of vision and hearing, but functions in voluntary muscle control. It is also the thinking section. And don't ever think that the cat does not think. He watches you open a door or a cage, and then quite cleverly finds out how to do it himself. If you have to medicate him, and have done it before, he outthinks you and, as you approach, coaxing, dives under a bed where he cannot be reached.

If your cat is a mother cat, you know well the thoughtful skill with which she trains and disciplines her children, achieving results far better than you can boast.

There are times when instinct and reason team up, and here I have what I believe to be a remarkable story. One of my pregnant cats, in her first pregnancy, was full of anxiety. She cried, wailed, roamed restlessly about the house, got into her prepared box and got out. Started labor and stopped. In desperation, I borrowed a small kitten from another litter—introduced it to my about-to-be new mother—got them together in their nest. Instantly the little one sought for a teat. As she sucked away and drew milk, all the young mother's stress began to vanish. There was an ecstatic purring. Labor began in earnest, and in jig time she presented me with a family of six. Not remarkable, you say, but listen to the sequel.

The next time my queen kittened, she deliberately found and borrowed a kitten. She repeated the process herself. And from this moment on, all the mothers in my cat family, not just the one I had taught, did exactly the same thing as they moved into labor. Through six generations it was standard procedure. Whenever I saw a pregnant cat dragging a youngster across the floor to her box, I knew the moment of birth was at hand. I have often wondered whether a woman in labor would give birth more easily if she had a borrowed baby suckling gently at her breast.

Nervous System Disorders. Less is known about these disorders than about the other health problems of cats. Most veterinarians will deal first with the obvious—a respiratory disease, a broken jaw, skin, eye, and ear problems that can be seen. Indeed, many practitioners fail to recognize nervous disorders, or may discount them altogether.

Whenever your cat has any physical discomfort, however minor, and wherever in the body—ear, eye, tooth, stomach—there is usually a corollary nervous reaction, ranging from what we label "tension" to acute pain.

Damage or disease of the central nervous system is quite different and much more serious, for such damage can interrupt or stop vital body functions—vision, hearing, vocalization, body movement. Since no one can or should give a short course on the cat's nervous system, this section will merely attempt to create an awareness of some rather common causes and signs of nervous system disorders.

Stress. Not long ago, if you used the words "stress" and "trauma" in talking about a sick cat, you might have met amusement. No longer so.

In our human world, stress has magnified in the last hundred and fifty years to staggering proportions. When a Daniel Boone moved west across uncharted prairies, he was under the many stresses of an unknown world that threatened savage attacks by the natural elements, marauding animals, and belligerent Indians. But beneath his feet was solid earth, the air was clean, life, as well as death, was everywhere. The sun, the wind, the rain, all gave promise. Then came what we call "growth and development." Today we and our animal friends are bombarded on every hand by noise, dirt, foul smells, invasions of peace and privacy. "Stress" has been listed as one of the major concerns of our time.

It took economic pressures to throw a new spotlight on animal stress and the need for its control. For example, cattle feeders had long known that calves brought to feedlots lost weight, not just a little, quite a lot. It often took more than a month to bring a calf back to its purchase weight. Every time this happened, some dollars trickled out of the cattleman's pocket. As research people and veterinarians in big beef states bored into the problem, they realized that the cause of this weight loss was stress. Calves torn from their mothers and a familiar pasture, loaded into crowded boxcars or trucks, shipped for thousands of miles, often indifferently fed and watered, and then, as a last indignity, crowded into feedlots with a mass of strangers—these calves suffered from stress that stripped away pounds. It took a revolution in feeding to provide a partial solution to the problem. The formulation of rations was changed. There was massive vitamin supplementation far beyond previous optimum limits. And particular emphasis was placed on vitamin E and the B complex vitamins. With these new rations, stress symptoms began to lessen, even when feedlot environments were very poor. Initial weight loss was slowed, and good weight gain records were finally established.

Just what has this to do with cats? More than may seem obvious. Test cases like the feedlot one intensified attention to the causes and prevention and treatment of stress, not only in cash-crop cattle but in pets.

In cats, the causes of stress are many, and some cannot be avoided. If you have to stuff kitty into a carrying case and haul him by car, bus, or subway to your doctor's office, he is bound to be under stress. Some cats will take this calmly. Others will cry, fight, pant, have a very rapid heartbeat, even run a fever. Even more serious stress results when small animals have to travel by plane or train without the companionship of their folks. Recently when I thought I might have to take my three to California, I had one airline tell me that I might better put my cats to sleep. An exaggeration, of course, but a trip in the bowels of a plane can be traumatic. Teasing children, attacking dogs, getting lost, and serious impact accidents may produce reactions that cross the borderline between stress and shock. Don't ever shrug off stress, even in its mildest forms, and remember that in major intensities, stress can and does kill.

The symptoms of stress have already been mentioned, but do deserve a recap. Restlessness is a most common sign; the cat keeps on the move and seems to find no comfortable place to light. Anxiety is another signal, and this is as easy to see in a cat's eyes as are fear and finally terror. The cat in stress may cry almost continuously. There may be jerky body movements, such as a tail that never stops twitching. Under stress your pet won't eat or may vomit up what he has eaten. In short, he may simulate symptoms of a score of feline diseases.

The cat under stress needs relief from the causes of his tensions plus quiet in a dark room or closet where he is not locked away. Or, in critical cases, he needs sedation and hospitalization. As he comes back to normal, his appetite will return along with his normal good humor, provided the stress he has suffered has not done permanent damage.

Injuries and Tumors. Impact accidents can damage some portion of the central nervous system, and so too can tumorous growth. Depending on the focal point of damage, vision, hearing, locomotion, and other vital functions—one or all can be impaired. Only a veterinarian can assess the point of damage and its possible cure.

Infections. Infections stemming from bites, deep wounds, and cuts can involve some portion of the major nervous system. Never ignore a deep cut or wound. Antiseptic treatment of such a penetrating wound may provide a stopgap measure until an experienced observer can treat and stem the flood of infection.

Poisons. This subject, previously discussed, can cause injury not only to the digestive apparatus but strike at the central nervous system as well. Poisons include strychnine, malathion, chlordane, dieldrin, DDT, lead, a host of chemicals in insecticides, disinfectants, agricultural dusts and sprays, and rodent killers. The signs, whatever the poisons, range from restlessness and anxiety to oversensitivity to touch, high excitement, vomiting, slowdown of muscular activity and paralysis, spasms, and convulsions. So-called fits, except in kittens, may result from any one of many kinds of poisonings, as well as nervous-system disorders. A cat, however small, is dangerous when having a convulsion. Quiet and confinement are the first indicated treatments, until the cause of the fit is identified, if possible.

Drug Damage. This, too, has been defined in digestive disorders. Streptomycin is one of the antibiotics that particularly disturb a part of the central nervous system. Aspirin is another. Forgive me if I repeat the aspirin warning many times. To this day "aspirin" is recommended in many of the quite recent cat books. Aspirin can do more than disturb. It can kill. Never use it unless so ordered by your veterinarian.

So-called simple tranquilizers, used far too offhandedly by people as well as pet owners, may do exactly the opposite of what they are supposed to do: excite rather than quiet. I watched my Big Boy go through twelve hours of anxiety, destructive scratching, and motor imbalance on a "test" dose of tranquilizer designed to discover his tolerance—which was zero—to the test tranquilizer. Often an animal will respond well to one drug and poorly to another, so a test is essential.

Rabies. Known since the days of Aristotle, this disease of madness is caused by the saliva and/or bite of a rabid animal. This viral disease is acute, infectious, and always fatal. The Pasteur experiments in the early 1800s proved the presence of the virus in the nervous system and partially solved immunization. Cats are less prone to rabies than dogs, probably due to less contact with skunks, foxes, and the other natural reservoir hosts of rabies. But a rabid cat is a great danger to man. Strangely enough, he offers little threat to other cats or other animals. Undoubtedly the major reason that more feline rabies is not diagnosed is that a sick cat tends to crawl off and die, whereas most other animals with rabies tend to seek out activity—people or other animals.

Although the danger of rabies from cats may not be great, most health authorities insist that a cat bite be reported by a veterinarian. And that the cat who has bitten be checked within ten days for any warning signs. My Pink bit me as she was being given a routine injection of vitamins. She was not a mad cat, just a tired, old, and sick cat. Before she could be checked, she was gone. But if you have a cat bite, do remember that there is a law, a wise law for disease identification and control. A new drug is now in research that will help to protect veterinarians who in the course of routine care may be bitten frequently by animals.

There are now new rabies vaccines for cats that give a high degree of protection and seldom cause the serious side effects that sometimes occurred with older vaccines. Any cat that has any opportunity whatsoever to run free in the out-of-doors should be vaccinated against rabies.

H. THE URINARY SYSTEM

A great deal has already been said in this health-care section about the urinary system and the serious problems that beset the cat if anything interrupts its full functioning. Any urinary stoppage in cat as well as man can be not only dangerous but deadly. And, unfortunately, urinary ailments are one of the more common feline ailments.

To make this problem completely clear, let us take a close look at the apparatus involved in carrying body wastes through the kidneys, into the bladder, and then through a small tube called the urethra. The urinary system differs slightly from male to female. In the female the urethra is short, elastic, and of good diameter. In the male this tube is considerably longer and somewhat narrower in diameter. In the male the urethra runs down through the penis and so is involved with the genitals. If there is a mistake in the remarkable design of both the human and the animal body, many doctors would agree that here lies the mistake.

The male cat is especially prone to urinary problems that can cause disaster. Every cat owner should be constantly alert to the warning signs of urinary ailments, and this means a constant check on how and how often your pet uses his litter pan.

Urolithiasis. When liquid intake is adequate and body wastes are normal, urine flows freely through this drainage system. For reasons that no one has completely pinpointed, the cat, and especially the male cat, often develops gravelly material that can clog or even totally block the flow of urine. The resulting serious disorder is known as urolithiasis.

Gravel, incorrectly called "kidney stone," is neither formed completely in the kidney nor is it a stone. "Urinary calculi" (uroliths) is the term the veterinarian uses to describe this sandy or gravelly stuff. The calculi lodge in the urethra and behave exactly like a plug. And like the plug in a sewage line, they interfere with or shut off the flow of urine, causing a backup of wastes. Spilling back through the bloodstream and vital organs, these wastes can carry a concentrated and lethal poisoning to create what the doctors call "uremia," or "uremic poisoning."

It is the male cat who is in the most danger. He seems to develop "gravel" much more frequently than the female, and because of the character of the male urethra, the chances of a complete plugging are far greater.

It is the opinion of some veterinarians that castrated males, and especially males that have been castrated young, before the full development of the urogenital system is mature, are the most common victims of this ailment. Others object to this theory with the wise observation that veterinarians rarely see tomcats, or certainly see far less of them than they do of castrated males, and consequently are reaching an erroneous conclusion. One thing is certain, the male cat under four years of age is the most frequent new urolithiasis patient, and a rather alarming number of male cats have this disorder. The female is not exempt, but she can handle the problem better.

Research is now under way in several universities, research aimed at finding what causes the formation of "gravel." Opinions to date include an imbalance of minerals, a calcium-phosphorus imbalance, or an infectious agent. Once this research is tied down, the lethal calculi may well be controlled or cured.

In the meantime, control of urolithiasis is usually possible if the ailment is recognized in time. Symptoms have already been described but are worth repeating. The cat with calculi may quite suddenly show signs of distress. If you can catch him at his litter box, you will see that he strains to eliminate, and goes back to the box again and again. Often pet owners mistake this signal for constipation and administer lubricants or Milk of Magnesia, which does nothing except stir up more trouble. Excessive water-drinking is another sign, and this, too, adds up to more trouble, for the increased liquids that cannot be eliminated increase pressure on the bladder. One other sign is constant licking at the penis, which may be protruding and showing a small mucous plug. Soon there is intense pain, often with high fever, and a cat who cries as he has never cried before. Of course, long before this you should have rushed your cat to the veterinarian. Waiting is disastrous, for calculi can kill within twenty-four hours, or less if the blockage is complete.

If you have not waited until too late, the doctor may be able to manipulate the gravel out, remove the plug, and give the medication that will change the chemical balance of the urine from alkaline to acid. Such medication, if given faithfully every day as long as your pet lives, can often hold the condition under control.

If this all sounds horrendous and frightening, it sounds exactly as it is supposed to sound. Here is one of the ailments that cannot be treated lightly or underestimated.

Cystitis. There is another common urinary ailment of cats—cystitis, or inflammation of the bladder. This can occur with or without calculi. When no calculi are formed, there is no back-up of fluid body wastes, no shut-off in the drainage system. But cystitis alone can be an annoying and stubborn disease, for often infection moves into the inflamed bladder, the walls of the bladder thicken, and the easy functioning of this important part of the waste-disposal system can be interrupted. All too often cystitis and calculi go hand in hand, and whether the disorder is single or double, many of the distress symptoms can be the same. Sometimes cystitis can be cured, sometimes only controlled. Again, proper medication is essential.

Nephritis. Nephritis, inflammation of the kidney, is not too common in younger cats but a frequent ailment of older cats. Infections in other parts of the body can set off a kidney infection—an excellent reason for watching any infection, even what seems to be a simple one in a small scratch. Nephritis is insidious: Rarely can it be detected until it has progressed to the danger point. In old cats it may develop over a long period of time, resulting in a build-up of scar tissue in the kidneys, which may lead into uremic poisoning.

15

How to Grow Old Gracefully

Given the right care, the right food, and people who love him, your cat's life-span can be longer—comparatively speaking—than yours. To equate your ages approximately, just multiply your pet's years by seven. At the age of two he is a teen-ager, the cat equivalent of a fourteen-year-old human. At seven he is middle-aged, has joined the forty-plus club. At twenty he is a feline Methuselah and is pushing toward the one-hundred-and-fifty-year mark.

Heredity, of course, is a factor in your cat's longevity, just as it is in yours. Take my own personal family as an example. Dozens of relatives have lived to be active, healthy ninety-plus-year-olds. I run a good chance of matching their record. So too with my cat family, which comes from a long line of ancestors who averaged fifteen years or better. The odds are in favor of long and good years for Pete and his pals.

How Old Is Old? Your personal doctor has probably discussed with you the difference between actual age and physiological age. And so too will your veterinarian. Whatever the birthday record says, you and your pet will be young as long as you continue to function with the signs of vigor. In your cat, one of the signs of youth is a good coat, hair that is thick, soft, alive. The young-old cat will also have all or most of his teeth and be able to chew easily, even tough foods. In play, the older cat who is not feeling his or her age will romp around like a kid. Indeed the cat

221

In human terms this youthful-looking lady is more than a hundred years old or, in cat birthdays, just past eighteen. She mothered some two hundred kittens, had her last litter at sixteen. Not a miracle, just a combination of good nutrition and the most loving of care.

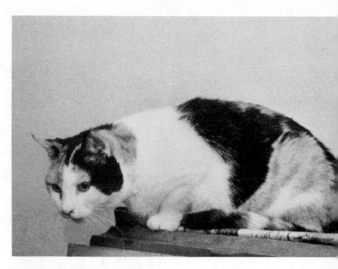

The growing-older cat often needs more frequent feeding. A balanced diet with all the essential nutrients will help to ward off the signs of aging.

who stops playing is giving you a sign that is important. Until two months before she died, Pink played regularly, not with the darting, mad activity of a kitten, but with real enjoyment. When even her favorite toys could not entice her, I knew we were in for trouble. There are many signs of vitality that tell you your pet is younger than his years. Bright eyes, alertness, a pink nose, and quick responses with smooth body movement, all indicate sustained good health.

Special Needs of the Aging Cat. If you were a cat growing older, you would have many of the same special needs as those of people growing older.

High-Level Nutrition. There is no time in the cat's life when optimum nutrition is not essential, but in old age nutrition becomes of paramount importance. Sound feeding in kittenhood is the foundation of longevity. Expert and intelligent feeding in the later years will not only make your pet's life more active and more comfortable, but can add materially to his life-span. The section on "Food and Drink" details the rules of nutrition. In planning the diet for your older cat, follow those rules slavishly. Make sure that your pet gets enough protein, high-quality protein; that the fat content is adequate; that there is a wealth of minerals and vitamins in proper proportion.

With increasing years, cats often lose some of their keen sense of smell and taste. These losses contribute to a lackadaisical appetite. Many old cats literally do not get enough to eat, show a weight loss, and then a train of troubles begins to move swiftly.

Pamper your older pets with snacks of their most favorite foods. And, as you did when they were kittens, feed them three or four times a day; smaller meals, of course, so that they do not put on undesirable pounds. Don't ask the older cat to compete with younger and more rapid eaters who can quickly gobble up the goodies. Provide your old man or old lady with a separate plate, slightly removed from the center of action, where peaceful eating at a slower tempo is possible.

Be very vigilant about liquid intake. If you can't check accurately on water drinking, serve your old friend slightly sloppy foods with juices and sauces that most cats love. A beef or chicken bouillon will often be more tempting than water or milk, and in concentrated form will add taste appeal to even uninteresting foods.

As Pink aged, I often took food to her, rather than asking her to come and get it. And since she seemed to enjoy eating from my hand, I often let her lick tidbits from my fingers. Such little attentions not only help to keep nutrition high but have the added value of expressing the affection and concern that every cat cherishes.

Special Health Care. Regular checkups by your veterinarian are another contribution to growing old gracefully. Usually cat and veterinarian never meet except for protective shots or in case of illness. Periodic examinations to find out if all is well are the least expensive and often the most productive kind of health care.

A complete health history of the older cat is of enormous value to your veterinarian. This important list should always be kept and updated as the years go on. Then you will not have to scurry through a faulty memory for details, and your veterinarian will know at a glance what happened when. Such knowledge may add good years to your cat's life.

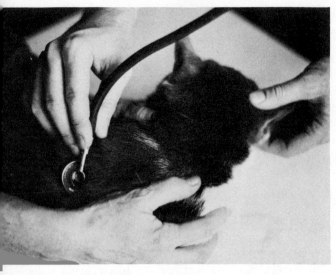

More frequent examinations are indicated for the Senior Citizen. Make it your business to plan check-ups at least twice a year, and more frequently at any sign of trouble, no matter how small.

Extra Affection. No cat can really enjoy life without the sense of being wanted and loved. And for the old cat, love is a breath of life. Indifference and rejection, even the careless unthinking kind, are almost worse than bad food. Spurts of excessive emotion are not the ticket. The older cats needs to be told every day, and many times a day, that he is cherished. He looks for that gentle touch every time you pass, and a quick response to his demand for affection. These are the simple things that sustain his sense of security. Puss has that very human frailty of wishing to be remembered. Remember him constantly, and whatever attention you gave when your cat was young, double it in spades as the years slip away.

Almost all cats are jealous from kittenhood, and they grow more jealous with old age. In a one-cat family your pet may be jealous of your husband or of your child. In a multicat family, cat can be furiously jealous of cat. Take my group as of a year ago. Of my four, one was a teen-ager, one a young adult, one middle-aged, and one a very old lady. The lines of battle had already begun to be drawn. The three younger cats resented Pink and the extra attention she got. Pink resented a threesome that had become a happy little band excluding her. The party of three vied amicably for my hand, sulking a bit if any one seemed the Number One Boy. But to Pink they presented a united and hostile front, and I could not break the deadlock. Finally, Chip, normally the kindest and best-adjusted cat I have ever known, set out deliberately to destroy his mother. And he made his assault in a deadly and frighteningly smart way. He jumped Pink, chased her, and frightened her so badly that she could not go to the litter box or eat her food in comfort. Instinctively he knew that this boss old lady was growing older and less sturdy. If ever I saw a cat try to kill another, this is what I saw happening—a deadly feud between mother Pink and son Chip, fought with tooth and claw.

Disciplining Chip got him exactly what he wanted: extra attention. For months before my old lady went away, I carried her to the litter box twice a day. The day she died, all Chip's jealousy died.

Introducing a young cat to an older cat may introduce jealousy. Often pet owners decide to add a kitten to the family. As your long-time companion watches you spend hours enjoying the new little one, he may well feel completely rejected and left out. Don't put your old friend through this stressful experience. Or if you try to blend the old and the young, make sure that your older cat gets more than equal attention.

Sleep and Warmth. Many of our senior citizens trek to Florida or Southern California, seeking the warmth of the sun. And many of us relish the chance for an extra hour or two of sleep in the morning and a snooze in midday. Again, like you, your growing-older cat enjoys extra hours of sleep and is more anxious to find a place in the sun or tries to hug the radiator.

Children in your family may not understand an aging cat anymore than they understand you or your spouse, when you ask to sleep late without disturbance, or elect a sunny beach instead of a ski slope.

Ailments of the Older Cat. The older cat is prone to most of the ills, ailments, and diseases of the younger cat as well as health problems that intensify with age. As with you, even minor illnesses, which would never have put you down at twenty, may send you to bed at sixty. All body functions slow as we all, pets and people, grow older.

Constipation. Man or cat, one of the most insidious ailments of old age is constipation. It goes along with less exercise, less interest in food, and, certainly in the cat's case, with a lower intake of fluids. When not enough fluids are taken in, water is extracted from body tissues. Even so, the fecal mass moving through the intestines can grow hard, and hard to pass. Hairballs often add to the problem. The result: constipation which must be fought with diet, Vaseline or other lubricants, and often with medications that add bulk and softness to the stools. Constipation in the older cat can contribute to the seriousness of any other ailment, even a small one. It must be watched for and kept in check at all costs.

Mouth and Teeth Problems. Even young cats can suffer from a sore mouth, bad teeth, or gingivitis. In the older cat, such ailments can be serious. Loss of teeth makes chewing more difficult and discourages eating. Gum and tooth infections can set off a whole chain of infections all through the body. When you take your old friend in for a periodic physical examination, make sure that a complete check is made of the chewing apparatus.

Tumors. Growths, some of them malignant, are more common in the older cat. The mother of many who has finally started to deliver weak or dead kittens and who develops mastitis may be showing the warnings of uterine or ovarian tumors.

Diabetes Mellitus. As in man, a dysfunction of the pancreas may be responsible for blood sugar. This disease is more common in the castrated, overfat male cat. A change in diet to include things like macaroni and cheese, cottage cheese, and egg yolks can help to control the disease.

Skin Diseases. Older cats more often show signs of eczema, that umbrella ailment that covers a lot of skin irritations. Watch out for small crusty scabs that can infect, or for dry and thinning hair areas. Skin problems that seem so minor are often the most stubborn to control—especially in older animals.

Heart Failure. As already indicated, the cat has few major heart problems, except in old age. There comes a time when that strong, faithful heart can give out. Your veterinarian, who knows your old cat, may want to take a blood sample from time to time, and this will help him to gauge the condition of heart and circulatory system.

Anemia. This, too, has been detailed under "Heart and Blood" in Chapter 14. Anemia occurs much more frequently in the old cat than in the young one. Once again, diet and medication can often hold the line.

In protecting your old friend, you come back, over and over again, to good diet and regular physical examination. With a high level of nutrition, even very serious illnesses can be fought and conquered or held in check. With regular medical examinations, trouble areas can be spotted before they flare up into bonfire disaster.

Aging can be the natural letdown in all body functions, a letdown that is in balance—a slowing tempo, rather than the quick beat of youth. It is when one part of the physical apparatus suffers real damage that there is cause for alarm. A major dysfunction in one body system can upset the whole rhythm and escalate the normal aging process.

If you and your pet age together, you will have much greater understanding of each other. You will not only respect your pet's special diet needs, but you will be alert to the medical discoveries that help to ward off aging. Vitamin and mineral preparations, hormones, cortisone, antibiotics, and vaccines are just some of the weapons your personal physician and your veterinarian both employ to add vital years to your life, and to the life of your pet.

16

There's No Place
Like Home
for Cat Accidents

More cats are killed at home than in the streets and highways, or by cat-hating cranks, or by animal research workers against whom humanitarians cry out so loudly. Even responsible and loving pet people fail to recognize the dangers carelessly allowed to exist in a house and its surrounding grounds. So let's have a look at the long list.

Playtoys. String—often with a piece of paper tied to the end—has long been the favorite of all homemade playtoys. This simple device enchants kittens and cats alike. Either swinging from your hands or hung in a doorway for self-play, it becomes a flying thing—a bird, a butterfly, an insect—that demands chase and catch. All very well until the paper comes off and your cat attacks the string, chewing at first and finally swallowing inches of this treacherous stuff. With luck, the digestive system may work the string through without injury occurring. Or the string can win, lodging in and plugging or lacerating some part of the digestive system.

Little balls or beads that are small enough to swallow can quickly and easily choke a cat. And even the *catnip mouse* presents problems. Dyed some brilliant hue to attract the buyer, not the cat, the felty coat is ripped off and swallowed in a matter of hours. Modern dyes are probably safe, but they stain mouth and coat, and a lump of felt in the stomach makes no contribution to easy digestion.

Find me a cat who does not love a *bag* and I will say you have a sick cat. Bags provide great hidey-holes. If I leave a good-sized bag on the floor, I make sure never to kick it accidentally or step on it, for the chances are good that inside there will be a cat asleep. The bags that spell danger are the shopping bags with handles and the plastic shrouds from the dry cleaner. In play, the handles of the ever-present shopping bag can fasten around the cat's neck. Perhaps he can shake himself free, but if he tries to dive under a piece of furniture or through a half-shut door, he can well-nigh strangle himself. I make sure all the handles are torn off before my gang gets into action.

The plastic horrors are even worse. Like to spend an hour encased in nonbreathing plastic? Like children, cats will crawl into anything that can be crawled into. Don't put this dangerous temptation in their way.

Equipment for Household Chores. This is a fairly large department. It includes sewing equipment—thread, needles and pins, buttons, skeins of mending wool, hooks and eyes and other small clasps, all the junk you would find in the bottom of your sewing basket if you turned it upside down. Then there is the collection of tacks and small nails used in home upholstery, or the little hardware that cats insistently claw out of your chairs and divan. And bits of Scotch tape, discarded typewriter ribbons, wood shavings from home workshops, wrappers from cigarette packages, just to mention a few, and you will begin to get the picture. It takes constant policing to clear away such debris. I woke up one night just in time to keep Chip from swallowing several yards of carbon ribbon from my electric typewriter which he had dragged out of a wastebasket.

Needles and pins are the most dangerous. These can scratch and cut and puncture sensitive and vital internal organs. Make it a rule to vacuum work areas as soon as you finish working.

Decorative Plants. Some cats are plant-eaters—Pete among them —and certain of the decorative household plants can do damage. Large-leafed ivies are on the list. So is philodendron and mountain laurel. Other plants not poisonous may have dangerous barbs, like barberry, a standard decorative hedge in many home plantings. These barbs can protect a cat against its natural enemies, but they can also scratch and wound and start infections.

Household and Garden Chemicals. Now we are in the big danger zone. Many of the household and garden or farm chemicals are poisonous to cats. Although the following list is not complete, it pinpoints the dangerous chemicals. Since trade names change and vary, put on your glasses and read the labels.

Police your home work areas—where you sew or have a workshop or keep the paraphernalia that an artist must use. That delightful skein of wool, thread and needles, buttons, tacks, pencil shavings, all kinds of oddments, can go down a throat and cause deep trouble.

Many cats are plant-eaters, and a number of plants are dangerous to cats. The favorite big ivy, the philodendron, the mountain laurel are considered poisonous, and even such simple things as marigolds or lilies can cause respiratory and digestive upsets.

RODENTICIDES

Thallium sulfate, commonly used by professional exterminators.

Antu, once very popular rat poison and sold erroneously as safe for pets.

Warfarin, widely used rat poison that kills by causing internal bleeding.

Sodium Fluoroacetate (1080), a poison that attacks the heart and central nervous system.

Strychnine, little used today except by pet poisoners. Swift and deadly, it strikes the nervous system.

Squill, a widely sold rat poison that produces violent vomiting.

Lead used in paints and in smelter ash spread on driveways. Poison is picked up by walking or lying on treated surfaces.

NOTE: Even fumes from paint can make a cat sick.

INSECTICIDES

BHC
Chlordane
Dieldrin
DDT
TDE
} chlorinated hydrocarbons, used as dusting powders, dips, sprays, and in paints to destroy insects and mites.

Any insectide including *arsenic* should be avoided.

ANTIFREEZE

Ethylene Glycol, almost the only poison cats like to take—they enjoy the taste.

HERBICIDES

Malathion
Parathion
} organic phosphates used as agricultural sprays.

Arsenic herbicides should be avoided.

HOUSEHOLD CHEMICALS

Bleaches used in laundry.

Grooming shampoos containing coal-tar products. Usually insecticidal shampoos.

Just make a clothesbasket convenient and you will find it filled with a cat. But don't expose your pet to laundry chemicals that can give him serious digestive upsets or actually be lethal.

Deodorizing and disinfecting sprays of the Lysol type.

Roach, ant, and fly sprays, some of which include arsenic.

NOTE: Any strong acid or strong-base chemicals should be used with caution.

FUMIGANTS

Fumigants often containing cyanide, which is deadly.

Traps. Set a mousetrap, or set a trap for wild marauding animals, and you may catch a cat. Normally, the cat is completely disinterested in trap bait. He could not care less about that hunk of cheese when he has more tasty things to eat. And unlike the dog, he will not steal bait from a trap, because it smells bad. But because of his curiosity, he can get caught in a trap. That inquiring paw plays with the thing, and there he is, caught, and often maimed if he manages to struggle free.

Excavations, Alleyways, Cellarways. City or country, there are all kinds of excavations or areaways into which inquiring cats can and do fall. In the most familiar of these—the cellar—thousands of cats have been trapped. In the country, I have had cats fall into foundation diggings, and in the city, I have bailed them out of alleyways and those slots down to the engine room. In your own home and on your own grounds you can see to it that excavations and diggings are covered; that cellarways are not blocked off; that outside buildings are not shut until it is determined that no cat has hidden away in the tool shed, the garage, the barn, hidden away without some access that any smart cat will find.

Windows, Fire Escapes, Terraces. These are city hazards, big ones. Even the smartest cats will occasionally make an impossible jump. Dropping from a barn haymow into a pile of soft hay beneath is done every day by the country cat—and usually with safety. Dropping the same distance from a concrete ledge to the floor of a cement alleyway is quite different. Both Chip and Big Boy have made such uncalculated leaps—whether jump or fall, I do not know—and lived to tell the tale, lived with

Inviting your pet to examine the delights that wait just outside an apartment window is rather stupid. In city dwellings the incidence of disastrous falls resulting in jaw and other major body injuries is alarming.

Cat on a hot and dangerous tin roof. You may find it amusing, until that day when puss takes a leap.

The roaming cat enjoys pleasures unknown to his house-captive brethren. If dangers untold lurk outside the screened door, your cat may have to adjust to indoor living.

no injury at all. Not all cats are so lucky. Pet people who think it is amusing to let the cat dance on a windowsill, run up and down a fire escape, or take a walk on the terrace railing are irresponsible. City veterinarians are constantly faced with the problem of putting the cat to sleep or back together again.

Streets and Roads. "To roam or not to roam . . ." that is the eternal question argued by cat owners. If dangerous streets and roads run close to your home, you may elect to keep your cat a house captive. Doubtless he will be safer indoors, but he will miss half the fun of life. In all the years that I lived right on a busy country crossroad, I lost only a very few of my free-running cats, one to a drunker driver, one to an idiot group of motorcyclists who chose my corner for a relay race. The smart cat who lives close to traffic lanes grows exceedingly competent. With a few assists from you, he may never have an accident. Make it a rule never to let your cats out any door that faces road or street. Feed them and play with them at the back of the house, and put in a cat hole or cat gate on the back porch or garage or whatever portion of the building faces a garden, however small. Cats, being creatures of habit, consistently follow the small pathways. In the backyard of my country home there was a tiny diagonal roadway running from the grape arbor to the enclosed back porch. This faint but quite distinct path had been beaten into the grassy lawn by hundreds of little feet, crossing it many times a day. Even tiny kittens were soon taught by attentive mothers to use this "great highway" as an access route to the interesting world of garden, orchard, and cow barn. It would be ridiculous to suggest that you will ever completely control your cat's wandering, but you can help him to develop habit patterns in safe areas.

Curious kitty will some-
times outdo his ability.
Cellarways, excavations,
foundations, cellars,
should be cat-proofed
unless you want to
search frantically for a
missing cat and some-
times not find him.

Photo by Sue Meyers

Plants around your
home will give your cat
protection. A thorny
tree, barberry, even a
rose garden, will pro-
vide important areas
where all is safe and
camouflage good.

To a cat, a dangling electric cord is just another plaything. Electric shock and resultant burns are common in homes where live wires are left within reach of investigating claws and teeth.

Electric Wiring. Faulty or careless electric wiring has been the cause of many cat accidents. Extension wires that trail invitingly across the floor look much like the cords and string you have encouraged your pet to accept as playtoys. Both kittens and older cats who should know better will bite at electric cords or dig into them with sharp claws. The result—burns, sometimes quite serious, and, often, electric shock. It is simple to eliminate this hazard, a hazard not only to your cat but to the unwary person who tries to separate cat and wire. Take the time to fasten extension cords neatly along the baseboards, and tauten or shorten the cords hanging down from lamps so that they do not drape in easy-to-hook loops.

Gas Equipment. I am sure that you do not train your cats to jump up on furniture or equipment, but try to keep them from doing it. Most of the time only the furniture suffers, but in the case of gas stoves, not only your cat but the whole family can be hurt. I was awakened one morning by my landlord frantically pounding at my door. The hallways were filled with gas, and it was coming from my apartment. It took only a minute to discover that one burner was turned on full, and a second partially turned. Footprints on the top of the stove pointed a finger at the culprit. I saw to it that the episode did not recur by having a simple lock put on the burner knobs. If you have a persistent and agile jumper in your house, I suggest that you do the same, and sleep safely.

Loneliness. The greatest health hazard in your house is not poison or a trap or bad playtoys, but a simple and not-so-simple thing called loneliness. Cats, like people, have to be wanted and loved, and they need their people around. If they feel deserted, they may refuse to eat, or run away, or get into strange and dangerous mischief never attempted when you were there. Or in an odd way they may commit suicide. In my years of giving cats for adoption I have made two tragic mistakes that illustrate my point. I gave a kitten to a young and lonely college student whose love for animals was evident. He tried to spend time with his new pet, really tried, but he was also trying to get a law degree. He came home one night to find that the kitten in loneliness had eaten the box litter. The kitten died in his arms, and he had the decency to call me and tell me that this was his fault.

A second kitten I gave to a family that seemed to be right: a house in the city, children who wanted a pet, a backyard for outdoor play. What I did not learn until later was that the children of this broken home had been feeling rejected—one was under psychiatric care—and the mother, an intelligent and successful businesswoman, thought a cat might help solve her children's problems. The cat wisely identified with mother, not with the children. But then came the day when mother wished to take a holiday. She called me to say that she hoped the cat would live through this. He had learned to go up and down a wall from the garden into a second-story bedroom. She would leave him food and ask a neighbor to look in. Live through it indeed. Live-it-up would be more accurate! In her absence Teeger taught a group of alley cats how to climb into the second-story bedroom. When the family returned from vacation the house was a shambles.

People and pets can live long and happily without a lot of money, with major health problems, and through great adversity as long as they have a sense of security. When they, people and pets, give up emotionally, they can easily throw in the towel and give up physically, not care to live.

17

Discipline

Any chapter on cat discipline can be a short one. Not because discipline is impossible, but because it is really so simple. Essentially discipline of your pet means teaching good manners. And depending on what are good manners in your home, you can share your discipline with your cat.

Table Manners. In my house, eating at the table with the family is not good cat manners. Some pet owners find it fun, for a time, to share with a pet the steak or chicken or whatever is for dinner. I have friends who even set a place at the table for the cat. And then there are those who offer tidbits under the table. You may enjoy this, but how about your guests? Or your children whose table manners, along with other manners, you are trying to develop?

Begging, constant begging, can be a combined problem of manners and nutrition. How cutely your cat begs makes a good story for your friends until the amusement of the story runs thin, your patience runs out, and your pet grows fat and lazy. My cats know exactly when and where they will be fed. They know they can get occasional snacks, but since begging is firmly discouraged, they have learned not to press this point. If you have a sick or old cat, throw all of the rules away. Be as coaxing or permissive as you wish when the major problem is to get food, some food, eaten naturally.

Mischief. There are very few bad cats, but there are thousands of mischievous cats. They really don't intend to get into mischief. They just must investigate everything, and in so doing they can disrupt the order of your house. I don't happen to believe in putting an animal in "his place." My cats have complete run of my house. There is no closed-door policy. When they are not shut out or restricted to some area, I find there is very little mischief. Oh, yes, occasionally they roll a small rug into a ball or overturn a chair in violent play, or knock something down and break it. And scratch they will, since sharpening their claws is as natural as breathing. If your upholstery and household belongings are more important than your pet, don't have a cat. I know of one breeder who swears he can teach a cat to scratch on only one scratching post, a special one sold by the breeder. He may have found the secret, but this I cannot validate.

You may find it hard to believe, but most cats come to respect the things you respect and from which you do not ban them.

Punishment. Physical punishment of a cat gets you exactly nowhere. Or perhaps I should temper this by saying that only once did I resort to what I call serious physical punishment. In the country, where we always had spring baby chicks, I had one cat that thought them birds and so fair game. When I caught him with a dead chick, I did not beat the tar out of him but I did tie the dead chick around his neck. This form of punishment he understood, and never again did he trespass. Clap your hands at a misdemeanor rather than slapping the cat. And don't do this constantly, just often enough to make it clear what you mean. Remember that you are dealing with an intelligent individual who wants your love and trust.

Even if your cat scratches you, don't whip him. Sit down and figure out whether you invited the scratch. If you did, don't repeat the invitation. I was scratched yesterday when I picked up Big Boy and somehow hurt him. Before I cleaned up the scratch and medicated it, I petted Big Boy and told him I knew he meant no harm.

The Dirty Cat. This is another problem, and, as I have said before, few cats are naturally dirty. Some that have not been well box-trained will hunt for corners and use them. Kittens are major offenders. Cats left alone or left with dirty litter may also misbehave—and with good cause. If you catch the cat in the middle of the act, fall back on an old technique. Rub his nose in the mess before you clean up. Show him firmly where his litter box is located, a clean litter box. Disinfect the area he has fouled so that no scent may draw him back. The chances are that you may never have to repeat the process.

18

Play and Playtoys

Play is as natural to a cat as breathing. Almost as soon as his eyes are open, the tiny kitten begins to roll and tumble with his littermates. As a senior and somewhat more sedate citizen, he still plays like a kitten, but in short spurts, not hours on end. Indeed, when your cat does not show any interest in play you can be almost certain that there is something seriously wrong with him.

Play is for fun, for exercise, and to satisfy that ancient hunting instinct which has taught the cat to stalk, pounce on, and catch anything that moves. Best of all your cat likes to play with you. Next comes his cat friends or other animal and bird companions. If you want your cat to live the good life, take some time every day, even a busy day, to play hide-and-seek, catch, and retrieve. Pets, like children, love these simple nonsense games.

Every family of cats invents its own games. My three delight in a kind of polo game played violently with a ping-pong ball. And each morning and night they run a frantic race from room to room, dashing through doors and windows, hurdling small pieces of furniture.

Playtoys. A cat's toy can be anything. Don't bother to buy the so-called cat toys made by manufacturers who obviously don't know cats. Your house is already full of all sorts of things that make popular, safe, and wonderful toys. Chip's favorite is a newspaper under which he can

Often the constant play of a family of cats takes on some of the aspects
of a mock battle. It may begin rather mildly . . .

. . . but as battle line moves, the opponents warm up . . .

. . . until finally, in the best judo technique, these gentlemen wrestlers take their stance.

Fifteen minutes later these great good friends are fast asleep in each other's arms.

hide, concealed, he thinks, or carry around on his back, inviting chase. Pete prefers a bouncy bead to be chased around the bathtub. Since this bead is small enough to be swallowed, I serve in the dual capacity of outfielder and umpire, carefully hiding the bead away at the end of the game. Big Boy dotes on belts and pieces of stout clothesline which swing constantly from drawer pulls. Other favorites are a rabbit's foot to which I have fastened a small bell, a small and tinking film reel from my camera, a clothespin, an empty tissue box, or an old shoe with a small ball inside which must be fished out. All provide endless hours of amusement.

Like children, cats stash their playtoys away and refind them when the spirit moves. At least once a week I put on a search for the missing collection. And this does me far more good than some dull setting-up exercises, for I have to crawl under things, poke into corners, dig through closets, and stretch muscles that would never otherwise be stretched. Since play simply cannot be visualized in words, I have tried to capture some of the fun in pictures.

No need to buy playtoys. Any house is full of things that will intrigue any cat. An empty tissue box with a ball inside gives hours of pleasure as the ball is fished out and dropped in by a handy player who knows how to keep the game going.

Swinging a stout cord—clothesline or belt from any drawer or doorknob, and you have created a perpetual and interesting plaything. A dozen times a day Big Boy does a daily dozen with this simple device.

A bouncy bead in a bathtub is Pete's most favorite of all sports. This builds to a frantic game as the bead ricochets from side to side. I act as umpire and outfielder, carefully watching at all times, for this playtoy is small enough to be swallowed.

Running water fascinates cats. A drip or a tiny stream seems something alive that must be caught. And there is nothing simpler or safer than to let your cat play in the bathroom wash basin.

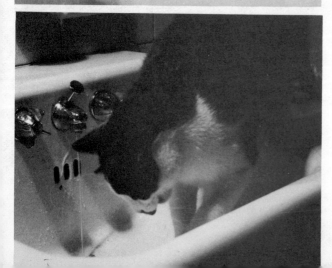

Chip dotes on newspapers. The game begins as he hides, completely concealed, so he thinks.

And it carries on as he dashes around the room, paper on back . . .

. . . inviting attention and participation.

Best of all, a cat loves to play with his folks. Shu Shan and his mistress have worked out a high-jump routine that is worth a price of admission.

From a low stand or often from the floor, the cat jumps straight up . . .

Photos by Frank Bear

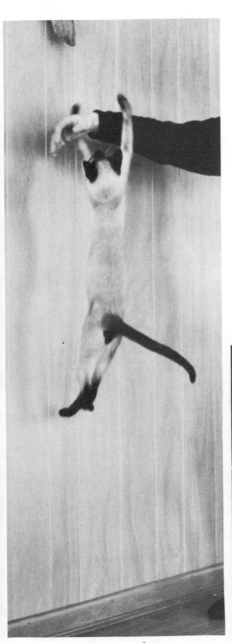

The ping-pong ball is one of the greatest playthings. A family of cats plus a ball equals an exciting polo match. As a note to owners, this is one toy that is easy to find even when it has been stashed away.

. . . to swing from an outstretched arm. Scratched hands? No. This aerialist is an expert.

19

ESP and IQ

There is a constant and unending argument between cat people and non-cat people, first about feline intelligence, and next about that strange psychic quality that we label ESP. No one who has lived closely with a cat, lovingly as well as closely, can doubt his smartness. And a few—I among them—have been privileged to watch and share some moments of extraordinary perception.

There are, of course, degrees of smartness. While I have never known a stupid cat, I have known a number who certainly did not belong to the brain trust. They were less responsive, less quick in decisions, less inventive in play, slower to learn to eat and drink as kittens, a bit harder to box-train, but all in all very pleasant and agreeable pets. It is my personal opinion that a cat's intelligence often depends on his people. In a society where he is encouraged to be free and unafraid, where people never think of him as a playtoy or an animal to be "kept in his place," where he is treated as an individual, even a not-so-smart cat will develop. Not just charm and personality, but an optimum mental stature—optimum for him.

Don't confuse cute and amusing tricks with real intelligence. All cats will wind around your feet to invite attention or snuggle close to demonstrate that they want to be near you. All cats will learn their names and come to a voice call. Tumbling, running, darting kittens who dance stiff-legged like little horses are doing exactly what happy kittens have done for centuries. This is normal, but then there are those special occasions and special cats with ability to plan, organize, and make judgments.

I remember well a black female called Sissy who lived for years with me in the country. As neighbors moved in and a rural corner began to look like a real-estate development, she grew shy and wary. She was heavy with kitten, and suddenly she disappeared. I searched house, barn, fields, but no Sissy. One day when I had given up hope, she appeared on my back step—thin and not in too good shape, full of breast, which meant she had had her kittens. But where? We fed her, welcomed her, and petted her, but she had obviously come on a mission and was in a hurry to get at it. As she took off across my lawn, she kept turning back to see if I would follow, and follow I did. It was more of a trip than I bargained for. We crossed the road into the east pasture. She crawled under fences while I climbed over them. We were headed in the general direction of an empty house, a summer home used only occasionally by the owner. As I hauled myself over the last barbed wire fence, Sissy sat in the middle of a woods lane and waited for me. Each time my clumsiness delayed me, she made allowances, slowed down. The lane led to the garage of the deserted house. I made the last fifty feet on a run just in time to see her squirm through a slit in the garage door. For the first time Sissy cried. Between us was a padlocked door, so I did what even in retrospect seems impossible—forced an entry into my neighbor's outbuilding. The garage was full of things over which I stumbled, but Sissy was still crying and leading me by voice up a precarious ladder and into the eaves of the shed. There, stowed away on a heap of rubbish were her kittens, a litter of six.

Once she was assured of my understanding, she settled down to nurse and wait until I could get back to the farm, organize a rescue crew, and carry her and her family back home.

Pete, the youngest in my current cat family, is unquestionably one of the smartest cats I have ever had. Not only is he a highly entertaining cat with a built-in sense of the ridiculous, but he has great sensitivity to people he loves. Given his choice, he would never be far away from me. Although he is not a lap cat, he has a remarkable understanding of personal contact. He likes best to lie on a chair right next to mine, or at my desk on some of my working papers. In this closeness, which is also separation, he will reach out a paw—and it is a big paw—and lay it gently on my knee or arm. Just this, no more, a kind of sophisticated affection that has the same sharp meaning as the quick and gentle touch of a hand.

This strange and delightful little cat has what both I and my veterinarian recognize as attacks of "nerves." Whether the cause of nerves is Pete's "under-control" urinary problem, we cannot figure out. When the nerves get raw, Pete has twitching ears, a rippling skin, and fear evinced by a rapidly beating heart and accelerated respiration. Recognizing his discomfort and not knowing how to handle it, I did what I would have done to an overwrought child. I put Pete to bed, under the counterpane of my bed, which to him is a haven of safety, and kept my hands on him until heartbeat and breathing slowed. The nervous upsets have lessened, but when he feels one coming on, he no longer hides in some dark corner. He deliberately comes to my bed and puts himself to bed, under the counterpane. With a few hours in security, he is once again his own gay, rollicking self.

Most of the smart cat stories are told of females, but there is a special one about a male, an outcast tom, which I find expectional. This tom, who never had a loving family, found a life for himself in the rocky caves of an island off the shores of Tuscany. Then one day he met the lady of his choice, a summer visitor to a nearby villa. Carolina, the queen, was one of those rare female cats, a frigid lady who refused all suitors. It took the caveman cat to woo her and win her. It happened this way.

Every year Carolina's family left their home in Rome and vacationed on the island of Giglio. Like others in the small village, they knew of the vagabond tom, had fed him from time to time, and even given him a name—Nicolino. Theirs was a courteous, pleasant, but uninvolved relationship. Nicolino always announced his presence with a polite cough, a gentlemanly "ahem." Fed tidbits, he ate fastidiously. Often he vanished for weeks.

One summer Carolina's mistress decided to take her pet with her, despite the cat's fear of travel. Immediately on reaching the island cottage, Carolina was released from her carrying case, and to the dismay of her mistress, leaped a garden wall and fled up into the fig orchard on the rocky hills. Nothing could lure her back, neither loving calls nor tempting food. The family caught distant glimpses of their back-to-nature pet, and occasionally, as they walked in the orchard, saw brilliant blue eyes staring down through the leaves of the fig trees. Sorrowfully, at the end of the summer, the return home to Rome was made minus Carolina.

A year passed and another summer came. Once again the Roman family sailed to their island home. Busy with the pleasant business of unpacking, they suddenly heard a familiar sound, a polite cough, and "ahem." Yes, it was Nicolino, but with him came three small strangers, three tabby-and-white kittens with brilliant blue eyes.

On each succeeding summer day the episode repeated itself. Down from the rocks and onto the terrace Nicolino herded his charges. When they were full fed, he led them back to the hills. With no sign of Carolina, it was soon apparent that she had met with an accident after giving birth to a litter sired by the intriguing tramp. Realizing his inability to feed the kittens properly, Nicolino had sought help in the place he knew he would find it. And for a summer he gave up his roving ways as he accepted the responsibility of a family.

As the little ones grew big and strong, they also grew more wary. While the summer waned, they drifted away to the wild life of the hills. And according to the island folk, there is still a tribe of blue-eyed tabbies who hunt and play in the fig orchards.

Where IQ ends and ESP takes over is hard to judge. A photographer friend of mine who had an unusual identification with cats tells a tale with strange overtones. He and a group of friends bought a house in Bucks County, Pennsylvania. A cat was a part of the establishment, a cat named Gertrude, who had very curious and unusual markings. One weekend, fire from a source never identified swept the house. The guests got out and just barely got out alive. When a search was mounted to find their cat, no cat could be found. There was no trace of the cat in the charred building, nor was she seen again in the neighborhood. Two years went by, and the house was rebuilt. To celebrate the reopening of the reconstructed home, everyone, including my cameraman friend went down for a weekend. While dinner was in progress, my friend heard a cat cry. He opened the door, and in marched a cat with tail flying, a cat whose color and markings exactly matched those of the missing Gertrude. To his lap she jumped, purring loudly. She ate an ample portion of the house-warming dinner, then warmed herself on the hearth, completely at home. Was this the cat lost in the fire? Could there be an identical twin? No one has ever known. There was just one difference between the two cats, the "new" Gertrude was younger than the "old" Gertrude had been at the time of the fire.

I have one other very strange story, authenticated by an educator who spends every summer in Bombay, representing both the Indian and Canadian governments. For years, Jim and his wife had a pair of Siamese who were devoted to each other. In Jim's Bombay apartment there was a terrace edged by a precarious railing. The Siamese pair loved to balance on this railing and seemed so sure-footed that my friends allowed the dangerous pastime. One summer the female Siamese came down with a serious intestinal disease and was rushed to the veterinarian. As the days passed, the male's anxiety and distress grew. He spent more and more time on the dangerous railing. One morning the phone on Jim's desk rang, and as he answered it, he heard two frightening sounds, the scream of a cat and the crying voice of his wife. The Bombay veterinarian was on the phone to say that Sechuri, the female Siamese, had just died. And as he turned from the phone, Jim met the news that Senu, the male, had just jumped to his death from the railing—jumped, not fallen.

Among my friends are a number who lived through the bombing of Britain and the Berlin holocaust. They tell me that hours before the bombers roared overhead, the cat population began to take shelter. With some sixth sense, these wise ones knew that disaster was approaching. Often, so I am told, it was the family cat and even the street cats who led the way to underground shelters.

Way-out stories? Not at all. Similar well-documented reports come from all over the world.

20

The Animal Kingdom

I have often wondered about the ship's cats on Noah's Ark. Unquestionably they must have been aboard, and if I know cats, they functioned as activities' directors, for the normal and intelligent cat is a first-class fraternizer. Unless he is hunting or being hunted, the family cat is both a friendly and a fearless soul and gets along amicably with other four-footed ones, both tame and wild. I have watched some strange relationships flower and flourish between baby pigs and barn kittens, between an ornery old red cow and her favorite tabby, between a brilliant and cocky little banty rooster and a cat family who took up residence in the brooder house. So forgive me if I yearn a bit about those good old days down on the farm.

I remember one blizzardy December day when I saw a small creamy-brown animal cowering under a rain pipe. On closer look I knew I had an opossum visitor. He was a little fellow, frightened and cold, so I invited him in. Two hours later I found that he had accepted the invitation, crawled in through the porch cat hole and taken refuge under a cabinet. Since I did not know what opossums ate, I offered him some of the dinner my cats were enjoying. The quickly emptied plate told me that I had a hungry one. To cut a long story short, Mike, as I named my visitor, spent the winter with me. He and my cats soon made friends, and often I saw them all eating together from the same plate, with the opossum hissing softly. Come spring, he was gone, and I never expected to see him again.

A year passed. The first heavy snowfall of the winter moved in. Then one night as I walked out on the back porch, I thought I was seeing double. There were two opossums, not one. My original guest had found a mate, and in the manner of men, had promised her a fine and comfortable home. Mike and Ike were with us for three winters, always coming back when the weather got inclement. Increasingly bolder, they moved into the kitchen and built a leaf-lined nest in the bottom of the coal-gas stove. They ventured into the living room and warmed themselves by the fireplace. They even allowed me to pet them. Strangely enough, no one but me ever saw the opossum twosome. My farm tenants swore that I was putting them on. But every Friday night as I drove in from the city, my wild friends were waiting and in comfortable communication with my cats. The fourth winter rolled around. Mike and Ike were back again, and the constant rustling of the leaf nest told me that we had a new family on the way. Then one weekend came the disaster news. A female opossum had been found dead in the road, hit by a car. I never saw Mike again, and I don't know the end of the story. Opossums, so country folks believe, are monogamous. They never mate a second time, I am told.

There is another country night I remember well. My husband and I were talking in the living room when we heard a strange knocking on the stone front porch. I investigated and found a small black-and-white animal with his head caught in a mayonnaise jar, hitting the jar against the stones. One of my cats, I thought instantly. But with a second look I saw that the white was a white stripe down the back. My visitor was a skunk and asking for help. Without stopping to evaluate the consequences, I picked up the terrified animal, and with a quick twist, pulled off the jar. The skunk was just a baby. We eyed each other briefly, and then as I put him down, he slid smoothly off the porch into the sheltering hedge. I say, "he," but perhaps my caller was a she, for eight months later a lady skunk turned up on my back porch, a very pregnant lady. Like the original visitor, this lady minded her manners. She, like the opossums, ate with my cats, and was with us until she knew her time had come.

For years writers and cartoonist have made merry with the cat-and-dog myth. Truth to tell, most cats get along with most dogs if they are properly introduced. Puppy-kitten relationships establish themselves. With older animals the development of harmony depends on you.

My fine police dog, Von, provided a perfect example. Von came to me when she was four years old, just released from the Army. She had never known a cat, and when she saw my cat family, she instinctively gave chase. The situation had to be resolved immediately. I tied Von to a tree and persuaded one of my cats to approach. While I petted the cat, I talked to Von, telling her that we loved cats and that she must never do them any harm. She watched my every move with her intelligent eyes, cocking her head on the side as if to catch each word. Then I untied her and waited. For a moment the two confronted each other, then both turned and walked away as if in indifference.

Von never learned to like cats, but she never touched one in the many years she lived with me. In time she permitted small kittens to crawl up on her back and go to sleep. When Von's pups played with the cats, she watched carefully but unconcernedly. Cats and dogs—I had five dogs at the time—lived together in mutual respect, something most human families never achieve.

Animal hostilities are often man-made. Commands like, "Scat!" "Go get 'em!" "Sic 'em!" lie at the root of much animal warfare. Take any kind of an animal or a bird into a home where a cat lives, make the proper introductions, let nature take its course, and you are in for some remarkable and revealing experiences.

Forget the cat-and-dog myth. Most dogs like most cats if they are properly introduced and brought up together.

Photos by Henry Briggs

Even when so precious a thing as a kitten is involved, the inquiring attention of a playful pup never alarms a wise mother cat.

In a country environment strange friendships flourish and flower. This teasing paw with claws carefully sheathed means no harm . . .

Photos by Henry Briggs

. . . to an understanding companion who expects and gets a most loving reward.

And as for games—well, you are in for a real experience as your cat and your dog invent every known kind of play activity. This is the first step of a frolic.

Photos by Henry Briggs

Young animals of whatever species almost always accept each other and form warm alliances. Instead of the proverbial lion and lamb we have here a young goat, two small pigs, and a pair of kittens ready to bed down for the night.

21

Traveling with Your Cat

On foot and unrestrained in his own home environment, a cat moves easily, happily, and competently. Even in strange and precarious locations far from home port, he retains his competence, blends it with caution, and does amazingly well as long as he is solidly planted on his own four feet. If you have read S. E. Burnford's *The Incredible Journey*, that fascinating story of a Siamese cat who led two dogs through a Canadian wilderness, you will understand something of the drive, courage, and instinct that can carry a cat over unknown miles to the place and especially the people he loves.

Cage puss in a carrying case, a shipping box, the back of a car. Ship him by train, bus, plane, and his assurance is shattered. Yet travel he must today, and by every known form of transportation. Just how can you adjust him to being moved, make a trip less traumatic? And what do the common carriers and the hotels, motels—those so-called homes away from home—have to say about a cat passenger or guest of the house?

Traveling Stress. To the cat there is perhaps no greater stress than the stress of traveling. And many owners underestimate the health problems that may come as an aftermath. Just a simple trip across town to the veterinarian turns fearless Chip into a shaking, panting creature who cowers in his case or crawls up from an examining table to burrow under my coat. A similar trip for Big Boy proved so disturbing that he developed a bad respiratory ailment—an ailment he would doubtless have escaped had the excitement of the small trip not made him vulnerable to a virus that is always lurking. When I moved from one apartment to another—a twenty-minute trip by taxicab—all three of my pets crawled under a couch in the new place and refused food or water for the best part of a day.

The signs of traveling stress vary. A pleasant, gentle cat can turn into a biting, clawing tiger. A clean, fastidious cat can vomit or defecate in his carrying case. Trembling, drooling, crying—from the level of a plaintive miaow to a strident scream—one or all can make traveling a kind of nightmare for the cat and his concerned owner.

Travel with Your Cat. If at all possible, travel with your cat. You will make his experience much more bearable if you are close at hand, can touch him occasionally, and talk to him in familiar language. Without you he feels completely alone and deserted. Whatever your method of transportation may be—on foot, by car, bus, train, or plane, try to be there in person. Never ship your cat off into the blue, in a baggage compartment, unless this has to be done. In his own case and in your lap, on the seat next to you, or tucked under your feet, he has some sense of security, which he cannot achieve mixed in with other carrying cases, kennels, and luggage. If you are moving by plane or train, try to book a nonstop trip. The faster you get there, and the smaller the number of changes, the better for both of you.

You will find all the personnel handling common carrier service immensely interested and helpful when you talk about a cat passenger. They will go to endless trouble, try to eliminate as many of your problems as possible. Even on a telephone, voices grow warm when you say, "I'm taking my cat with me."

Feeding When Traveling. The problem of travel feeding falls into three parts. Feeding before a trip—feeding during a trip—feeding after a trip. Long trip or short, and by any means of transportation, allow four to five hours between feeding and traveling, and make sure that the pretravel meal is a light one. Start this feeding-watering early in the morning, and condition your cat to the pattern by going through the whole routine, and on the same time schedule, for at least a week in advance of your trip. With a four- to five-hour interval after a morning feeding, puss can function normally, use his litter box, sleep, play, and groom himself. Now he will be able to stand a stretch of time in which his whole pattern will disrupt.

Feeding during travel must be kept at a bare minimum. Unless the trip is a long one and broken by intervals of rest, all your cat really needs is water. If he has any wish for food, which is doubtful, the dry pelleted foods are indicated. Even on a long trip, the primary need is for water. A cat can go for several days without solid food, and without harm, if he gets liquids.

At the end of the line, liquids come first. And then slowly, and not as lavishly as you might wish to feed, small quantities of tempting favorites, followed by small quantities of a well-balanced ration. Carry these food supplies with you, even if you have to leave behind some of your personal possessions. Familiar food from a familiar hand has a great soothing effect. Before I planned a trip to California with my pets, I also made sure that the same foods, the same brands of foods, would be waiting on the West Coast.

Sedation for the Traveling Cat. Our much used and often over-used tranquilizers come first to mind. If you have read the health-care sections of this book, you will know by now that cats react differently to tranquilizers and to different tranquilizers. Do not give your cat a tranquilizer unless you have tested his reaction. Your veterinarian will cooperate by giving you several kinds of pills. A simple tryout while you are still in home quarters will tell you what you need to know. With some tranquilizers, some cats go peacefully to sleep, a drowsy, pleasant sleep. Some show anxiety and disturbance on any tranquilizer. If you get this reverse reaction from your tests, forget tranquilizers.

One of my veterinary consultants has recommended light anesthesia, sufficient to put a cat to sleep for a rather long journey. He gave this sort of sedation to some animals traveling with his doctor son, a man completely competent to deal with adverse reactions. Anesthesia is not to be used lightly. It could be lethal to older cats, kittens, sick cats, or those with odd stress reactions.

Probably the best sedation is a combination of an empty stomach, the most comfortable carrier possible, and a water bowl. The loss of a pound or two will hurt your pet less than drugs with a questionable effect.

A. TRAVELING EQUIPMENT

Container, Collar, and Leash. Everyone who has a cat needs these three things. Unless you are a Siamese person who walks a pet in the park, the collar and leash may see little use. But it is wise to invest in the combination, for there may be a time when you will need such restraining equipment.

A container—a stout container—is a "must." That container may be a corrugated box from the supermarket, a wicker basket with a tight lid, a canvas airplane bag, or one of those specially made cat-carrying cases. Avoid flimsy equipment, boxes and bags that come apart or cannot be tightly fastened. The frightened traveling cat has a phenomenal strength and can rip apart even sturdy-looking containers.

A prime requisite for a carrying container is good ventilation. Under stress the need for air, and lots of it, increases. My veterinarian has told me about dozens of animals who have reached his office dead—not from the illness they had, but from suffocation. The old-fashioned pillowcase container does not admit sufficient air. Even the good carrying case is no good if the window cover is fastened down by some well-meaning person who wants to keep her cat warm.

The Carrying Case. You will never regret the purchase of a carrying case. A good, safe, and comfortable carrying case need not cost more than ten dollars unless you want to turn it into a status symbol. Buy one when you get even the smallest kitten. Buy it big enough to make that kitten comfortable when he grows to be a sizable cat. Don't try to borrow a case from your friends or the people who give you an adoption cat. Indeed a carrying case will win interest from families who are placing kittens for adoption and from your veterinarian, who does not relish animals running loose in his waiting room.

The carrying case is essential for trips longer than the one down the street to the doctor's. It finds its place in the back of the car, on a train or bus, and may even be accepted by the airlines. And without a carrying case, don't expect to walk in and be welcomed by a hotel or motel. The hosts of the nation are far less genial when they meet you with a roughly tied box under your arm and a yowling cat inside. Rightly, at this point, they doubt who controls whom.

Let your cat get accustomed to carrying equipment at times when you do not plan to carry him. Frequently I put my carrying case on the floor, and frequently I find it filled with a cat, peacefully asleep. The less strange the carrying case, the less frightening to your pet when he must be locked in and taken away from home. Get him accustomed to a closed case, and practice opening and shutting the latches, for you may have to snap them in a hurry.

B. TRAVEL BY CAR

It is not difficult to teach a cat to travel by car. Just start him off young. If the cat learns the routine as a baby, he will take it in his stride. If he

Add a collar and a leash to your essential cat equipment. Only the Siamese likes to walk at the end of a leash, but there will come a time when you need these restraining devices for any cat of any breed.

makes his first car trip as an adult, he will cry, be miserable, and often get sick.

Begin with small trips—to the shopping center, to grandfather's house— so that little cat gets the sense of car movement, understands that the engine is not roaring at him, and even learns a kind of delight in watching the view go by. Never, but never, take your cat in a car without carrying case and/or a collar and leash firmly fastened and tethered, so that your pet cannot decide to take an exploratory jump. Road accidents caused by car-traveling animals run into alarming figures.

I have friends who take their cats on motoring vacations. There is a litter box on the floor of the back seat area. Small water and dry food containers are in easy reach at the end of a leash, and soft sleeping spots are carefully arranged.

Another family I know well has traveled their cat and dog coast to coast by mobile home, or camper, or whatever it is you hitch behind your car. These seasoned animal travelers have a ball. The pets are fed when

The see-through top, so the experts say, gives the cat more confidence. I question this, for if you see something frightening, where does the confidence go?

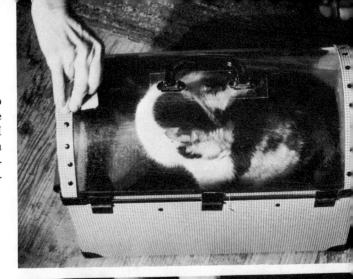

A carrying case is a "must" for any cat owner. Kitty may not like it but it will take him safely and most conveniently to the animal hospital, get him aboard a plane in first-class compartments, make him an acceptable guest in hotel and motel. Check the operation of catches, so that you can close them in a hurry.

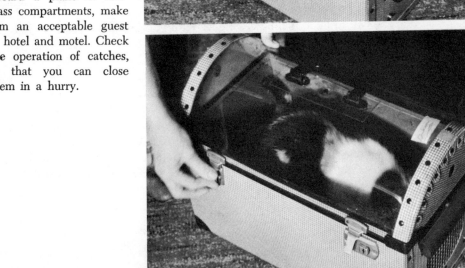

their family eats and allowed to investigate the new location whenever the camper comes to rest for an overnight or overday stop. Strollers are always under surveillance and control so that they do not decide to take off on a jaunt of their own.

C. BUSES AND SUBWAYS

Because of economy reasons, many cats have to travel on buses and subways. For the protection of the cat and the other passengers, a carrying container is necessary. Some bus drivers will permit a leashed cat on board, but many people will not sit close to a cat who may try to get friendly, even though restrained by the owner. If only for courtesy's sake, do use a container for bus travel. Incidentally, no pets can be carried on interstate bus lines.

Recently I saw an ingenious device designed by a woman who obviously had few dollars to spare. She had turned a shopping cart into a convenient carryall. A stout laundry bag with a tie cord was fitted into the bottom of the cart. This held litter in a small box, canned cat food, evaporated milk, eating bowls, and small medical supplies, plus a cushion for kitty and a blanket. The cat, in a strong, well-ventilated corrugated box, was strapped firmly into the baby-seat shelf of the cart. Even an old woman could wheel this conveyance down the street, down subway stairs, and onto a train. "There's always someone who helps me up and down," she told me.

D. TRAVEL BY TRAIN

I cannot honestly recommend this transit method unless the trip is short and the cat, in his traveling case, goes with you into the coach. On longer trips, across country, the railroads permit you to travel with your pet—and at no charge for the cat—only if you purchase compartment space. This may sound like an easy solution to the travel problem, but unless your cat can take train motion and noise, you both can have a rough time. If your pet must be relegated to a baggage compartment, leave him at home or find another way of travel. There have been some rather dire stories about cats shipped by train, animals that have arrived late, often long overdue, and in bad physical condition. The apparent economy of train travel may prove very false if you consider the possible cost to your cat's health.

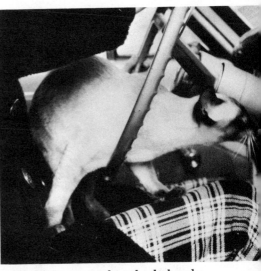

This is a no-no, a warning to cat owners who have never learned what a loose cat in a car can do.

Could you turn the wheel sharply and in time, with a cat in this position?

Suki's favorite traveling compartment is a baby carriage which he frequently shares with his young master. If your cat is healthy and gentle, such intimacy is safe.

Photo by Frank Bear

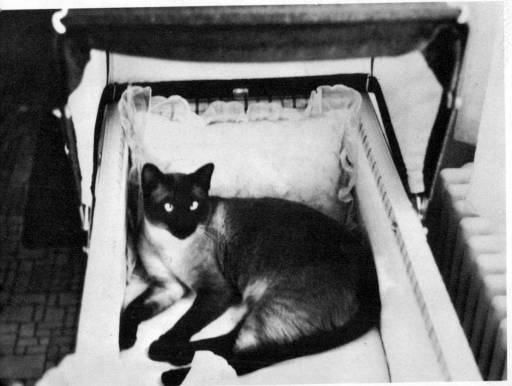

E. TRAVEL BY PLANE

Today more and more pets travel by plane because that is how their people travel. In checking the airlines, you will find that flight personnel thoroughly understand the people-pet travel problem. Regulations differ slightly from line to line, so be sure to check with the carrier you choose. A sturdy case of your own is quite acceptable. If you lack one, almost all the airlines now have a collapsible carrying case which can be purchased at under two dollars. These collapsibles come in varying sizes, depending on the size of the cat: 23 by 15 by 15 inches, 18 by 12 by 9 inches, and 18 by 18 by 12 inches. The collapsible cases can be secured in advance of flight so that you do not have to shift your cat from one container to another in the middle of a busy air terminal. On first-class flights and on some tourist flights, one cat, *one,* can be carried aboard with you, and depending on available space, can be stowed on the seat next to you or under your feet. Some airlines permit removal of the pet from the case at takeoff and again at arrival. I would argue against this procedure, since any extra movement of your pet may increase his fear. Far better just to open the case a little and put in a comforting hand.

The real problem of air travel begins when you have more than one cat. Since only one may go with you in the passenger area, the rest, no matter how small or large the number, go into a baggage compartment. You must make the difficult decision. Which cat of a multiple-cat family must have you close at hand? Which can take it, downstairs? This is often a hard decision to make.

There is also another important decision to be made on cases and/or kennels. A collapsible case or your own carrying box may be great in a passenger compartment, but it is no good down where baggage shifts around. Small and well-made kennels are sold by most of the airlines. These are usually of plywood and can be sturdily fastened together with clasps and screws so that they can't break open, but can be simply and quickly opened. Ventilation is again a prime problem, especially in kennels that may be pushed tight against other kennels and luggage. A screened window and a number of airholes on the other three sides are essential. See-through tops are not good here. Not only do such tops crush more readily than plywood, but the greater the privacy the cat has, the less his fear. Collapsed kennels can be purchased well in advance of flight, from ten dollars up, depending on their size. Some have small sliding doors through which food and water bowls can be put in.

If you must ship some of your pets in kennels in baggage compartments, do not try to put two animals in one kennel. Instinctively, you may say, my pets will do better if they have each other's company. Now you are thinking emotionally. In a storm or just simple rough weather, everybody gets tossed about. Under such conditions two friendly cats might, in fear, grow unfriendly. Also, a kennel built for two might have sufficient headroom so that animals could be bounced up and battered around. One container per cat, please, whether with you or without you.

The cost of traveling pets can be considerable, if you have a large animal family and always take them along. To the cost of containers add the excess baggage charges for your cat. My twenty-pound Chip, complete with plywood case, weighed in at twenty-three and a half pounds, and the bill from New York to Los Angeles came to $10.00.

A recent telecast told of a pet-minded lady, a breeder of poodles and a befriender of stray cats. When she left for South America, she could not bear to leave a single one of her crew behind, and so some sixty or more animals traveled with her at a cost of better than $2,000!

If puss must go down into the bowels of a plane, check your airlines and get their recommendations on traveling cases of strong plywood with plenty of ventilation holes and screens. Even on a trip to the animal hospital, animals can arrive dead unless ventilation is adequate. Under stress, more than the usual amount of air is essential.

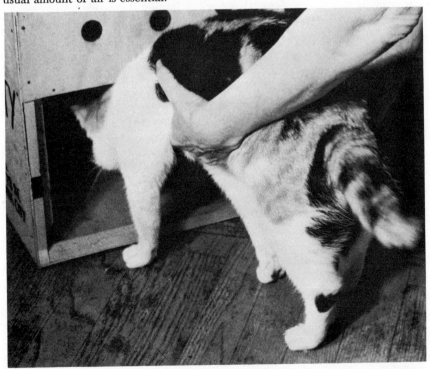

F. TRAVEL BY BOAT

The cat, a notoriously good sailor, is welcome aboard most of the trans-oceanic lines. However, the cruise ships say firmly, "No." As a seagoing mariner, your pet will usually be confined to a kennel and kept below-stairs in a baggage department. You can, however, see him regularly and supervise care and feeding. The shipping cost per cat begins at about ten dollars, and a kennel, which is much like the one available through the airlines—a sturdy, well-ventilated plywood box—is about the same price. Best check the steamship line of your choice to make sure of their latest rules.

G. HOTELS AND MOTELS

Lodging places usually have distinct rules about accepting pets. Don't try to sneak a cat into a hotel or motel. Find out in advance whether your pet is welcome, and under what terms. These vary from chain to chain and often from state to state. There are some rather sound reasons why the nation's innkeepers are not fascinated with cats, anymore than they are fascinated with some of the traveling public. Humans adopt towels, blankets, small room-equipment, and spill food, liquor, cigarette ashes, and cosmetics over rugs, bedspreads, and furniture tops. This spoilage is taken into consideration as the price for a night's loding is determined. But add a cat, even a polite cat, who is turned loose in a strange room, and the end result can be disaster. If you are permitted to carry your pet into a motel or hotel, take with you litter, food, small water and food containers, and a can opener. Confine your pet to a bathroom, which is easily cleaned, and you will rate as that rare person known as a "welcome guest."

22

How to Photograph
Your Cat

As I plunge into this chapter, let me hasten to tell you that as a photographer, most professionals would rate me a rank amateur. Although much of my business life has been enmeshed with photography, both motion and still, I have rather consistently left the business of picture taking to those superior beings known as cameramen. It was only a few years ago that I had the temerity to pick up a camera and use it, and instead of tackling something simple, I took a broad jump into one of the most difficult and exacting of all film work—animal photography. There are a number of world-famous photographers in this field, as doubtless you know. These experts have forgotten more than I will ever learn. But from where I sit, still learning by the trial-and-error method, perhaps I can offer some suggestions that will help you have as much fun as I have photographing my pets and those of my friends.

Animal Know-How. Of one thing I am completely sure. A deep understanding and love of animals and an intuitive knowledge of how they think and behave are the real secrets of animal photography. The best cameraman with every technical skill fully developed can turn out fine but often routine pictures. It takes more than a knowledge of film stock, *f*-stops, and exposure meters to capture the personality of a cat, his beauty and mystery, his amazingly human qualities.

If you have this understanding, coupled with the immense patience it takes to get meaningful pictures, then you can take a first giant step into animal photography, even if you have never before operated a camera.

I have a large number of photographer friends who have offered to spend a day doing hundreds of pictures of my cat family. I find it difficult to explain to them that cats do not pose, cannot be persuaded beyond a point to perform, and sleep quietly and peacefully for many hours of the day. My cats play frantically at five A.M. and often at midnight when I come home late, so these are my best shooting hours. Unless you are ready to work on your pet's schedule, not on yours, you may end up with a lot of pleasant, unexciting results. It will take months, not a day, to assemble a small set of pictures you can be enthusiastic about. I have lived for a year with a camera draped around my neck, so that at a moment's notice I can catch something that may never be duplicated.

Plot a Movement Pattern. Since cats are creatures of habit, they follow a definite movement pattern: Whether you and your pets live in a small apartment or an ample suburban or country home, you will discover with watching how exact this pattern is. Every day your cat goes through the same doors the same way, many times. He has favorite jumping places, resting places, playing areas. He sleeps in chosen spots, eats and drinks where you have taught him to eat and drink. Begin your adventure in cat photography by spotting these areas and patterns of movement, for it is in these constantly used locations that you may get your best photographs. Don't be silly enough to imagine you can pick up puss, set him down in front of your camera, and ask him to do his most charming tricks or to give you those personality expressions you boast about to your friends.

Study your cat closely, both in motion and at rest. Then decide what activity or characteristic pose you want most to photograph. Is it the way he sleeps? The way he talks? The way he walks? Is it the expression in his eyes, the movement of his tail, the beautiful way he jumps? Are you most interested in getting pictures of your children and your cat as they play some favorite game? Make yourself a good solid list of shots you would like to take, then catch them when you can. Don't make a production of this, just have fun, and coldly throw away the nearly good pictures, striving for the ones that have real quality.

Helping Your Cat to Pose. There are those occasional cats who will work with you in your photographic efforts. My Pete is one. With encouragement he will play his special games and keep on playing, sometimes for hours. This is not usual. A cat's interest and attention span, like that of a child, is limited. This span of attention can be lengthened a bit. Favorite foods will lure even a camera-shy cat out of hiding and keep him on-camera for a reasonable period of time. Participation in his games, your personal participation or that of your child, will intensify the game, get the action going, give you a chance to take the multiple shots that are often necessary to get a single good take of one activity. Introducing new elements into the cat's environment will also trigger reactions that make good pictures. Recently I brought home a squeaky toy. My cats eyed it warily and ran away. It sounded alive and somewhat dangerous. As they grew more accustomed to the thing they began to enjoy it, and from this came a series of amusing pictures. Bring a new anything into your house —a package, a chair, a stepladder—and you have set the stage for a whole new set of unusual action pictures. Or still better, add a new pet—cat, puppy, bird—and then make a camera record of the remarkable things that are bound to go on.

People-pet pictures should certainly be on your list. Here you may have to enlist the help of photographer friends. Rarely does a cat perform with strangers as he does with his favorite people. And even with you also in the picture, puss may not trot out his bag of tricks and affectionate gestures. A cophotographer who is a frequent and familiar guest in your home will finally be accepted by a relaxed and at-ease cat, who will move naturally and charmingly into all his expressive routines. By all means look at the cat picture-books done by the experts. They are full of ideas you can try to copy.

What Camera? Use the camera of your choice, the one that gives you a sense of competency and gets the results you want. This can be one of the cartridge loading cameras, which calls for little more than good focusing ability, or it can be a very professional piece of equipment, which demands skill. The more professional your camera, the more you must learn about the fine techniques of light and exposure. If the fun goes out as technique moves in, stick with the equipment that gives you enjoyment and still gets you enough of the pictures you want.

If you have invested some thought and money in any camera, do that really sensible thing, read the information booklet included with the equipment. I personally wasted a lot of time, film, and money before I went back to my little book and discovered a special setting on my camera that made the difference between no picture at all, a fair picture, and a really good picture.

Read a Book. Some home-style photographers pride themselves on never reading a book of instructions. Not even a basic book that defines such simple things as good picture composition, interesting shooting angles, and how to straighten lines so that the picture does not have a strange topsy-turvy look. By all means, buy a book you can understand and consult it constantly.

Lighting may be one of the toughest things to handle or even understand. For outdoor shooting, that little roll of instructions that comes with your film will give you excellent directions for shooting under different light conditions. Indoor shooting is something much more complex. If you choose to work with available light, you must have a light meter and must learn to read it intelligently. Entire books have been written on photography with available light. I could not even attempt to guide you in this area, except to say that learning to work with available light is worth the effort, an enormous effort. Available light pictures have a kind of realism not possible under any other circumstances.

For indoor shooting I have used both flash and photofloods, and personally I do not like either. With flash, the eyes of the cat become pools of light, usually lacking the pupil, so that sensitive eye expressions are lost. Flash frightens many cats, and in fright animals are not themselves. I am sure that photoflood properly used can be excellent, but just who can quickly turn on the right amount of photoflood in exactly the right action spot? I used to hang photofloods on the backs of chairs well distributed in all of the traffic lanes of my apartment. But rarely were they precisely placed, and by the time they were relocated, the action was long gone. Remember, too, that unless the light of the photoflood can be properly bounced from good reflecting surfaces—such as a light-colored wall with a flat finish—the picture will be full of annoying back glares or strange and pictorially bad shadows.

A strobe unit, which can be easily hitched to my camera, has given me the best results. Strobe, electronic flash, does not disturb animals. True, the lighting is flat, but irritating shadows are eliminated, details of eyes are not lost, and with the right strobe unit suited to your camera, you can shoot to advantage indoors and out and at the speeds essential for animal photography.

Speed is the essence of animal photography. A cat is completely motionless only when he is dead. Even in deep sleep he will move, roll, speak, twitch, open a lazy eye. To capture motion, you need high-speed film, a camera that can be set to operate at 1/250 or better. Until you have tried to film and stop action, you will never know how swiftly a cat moves. At exposure settings of 1/125 or less, it is impossible to avoid blurs. The end result will be a completely or partially fuzzy picture which you may misinterpret as being an out-of-focus shot.

Motion stopped by swift, well-lit exposures will suddenly show you things your eyes have never seen before. Just exactly how does the cat walk? What is the position of the front paws in a pounce? How does he move his mouth and tongue as he talks, yawns, eats, grooms himself?

Focusing for motion-in-still presents new problems to the untrained photographer. Your focus is sharp and clear as your pet starts to run to you or leaps to tumble in a mock fight. You must anticipate just where the exciting action will occur, focus on the spot your cat will reach when you want to shoot, not on his takeoff point. Don't be amazed if you miss this many times. Just keep on trying. To help you focus, throw some small and familiar object, such as a playtoy, at the point where you want sharp focus and try to bring your pet to that point. Some of the captioned pictures in this chapter will illustrate what I am talking about.

Backgrounds. Obviously you are not going to redecorate your house just to get good cat pictures, but depending on the color of your cat, backgrounds will make a vast difference in the quality of indoor pictures. Charcoal-gray-and-white Chip, whose gray is almost black, stands out best against light, simple backgrounds. His body contours are completely lost against dark wood tones or deep-toned fabrics. Golden-red Big Boy, with his well-defined tabby markings, needs plain or textured sharp-colored backgrounds to show him off at his best. Patterns in rug, drapery, and upholstery distract the eye from distinctive coat markings. An inexpensive collection of yard-goods lengths in a variety of colors will solve the background problem in portrait shots, but, of course, are of limited value in action pictures which must be shot where the action is. Probably the most difficult cat to photograph, indoor or out, is the black cat. Certainly he is hopelessly lost against monotone grays or any of the dark "jewel" shades often employed by interior decorators. Factors in background color, texture, and pattern are quite as important in black and white as they are in color, for in black and white, colors are simply translated into gray tones ranging from near-white to almost dead-black. Many of the good photographic instruction books carry a gray scale guide which shows you the tonal gray values you can expect from red, green, orange, and so on.

As you choose backgrounds for color photography, lean on everything you can discover about color harmonies. A red cat, like a red-haired woman, is simply great against sharp blues and greens. Icy blues make white cats look whiter, and at last you can make that black cat stand out against yellows and yellow greens, for example.

Many new photographers find themselves disappointed with the color quality of their indoor color shots. If you have this experience, take yourself and your camera and the pictures you don't like to a skilled camera friend or to the expert who works in most good camera stores and find out how to get the very best out of the equipment you own. Color photography is considerably more expensive than black and white, and there is little to be gained in wasting time and money if some simple corrections in techniques will help you to capture the true color beauty of your pet.

Keep a Record of What You Do. A record of the light conditions under which you have shot, the exposure times, and *f*-stop settings will be of enormous value in correcting mistakes. This is a bit of a chore and you will at times curse yourself for failure to remember the details. If you keep a fairly consistent record, you will note a growing improvement in your pictures. Even with considerable knowledge, don't expect to get twelve good shots from twelve exposures. Remember, you are not doing a photographic study of a bowl of violets. That actively moving, smart-thinking, mischievous critter in front of you can, by the turn of a whisker or paw or flirting tail, make or break your best efforts. If you emerge with one top shot to a roll of film, be immensely happy. When you begin to get twenty to thirty percent of good takes, you have graduated into the semipro class.

Prints. Find the best local source for developing and printing. There is a variance in quality that you will finally learn to recognize. Don't spend a lot of money having everything enlarged. Get someone who knows how, to help you in cropping on a contact print, so that the best possible enlargement of the best section of the negative can be made.

Don't bore your friends with your cat pictures. If you travel with cat people, they will be interested in your poorest efforts, your utter failures. Even film buffs with their own special film interests will be polite but disinterested in cat pictures that turn you on. Enjoy your own pictures and their increasing skills, which will increase if you want to get results and if these results are a source of real satisfaction.

As a hobby for the young at heart from nine to ninety, I can think of nothing more exciting than pet photography. It has given me kicks I get from nothing else. My camera store recognizes me as that nuisance customer who is always hovering and waiting for prints to come back. May this same keen pleasure be yours.

Has your cat a special pose that you find most endearing? Chip's frog-legged relaxation with feet poised daintily in air always breaks me up. I have filmed this a dozen times, always in hopes of bettering my shot.

Unless you still like still pictures, set your camera for action. It may not be truly professional, but I leave shutter speed at 250 for I have learned that only with this setting can I hope to get the in-motion pictures I want. Never underestimate the speed with which your pet moves.

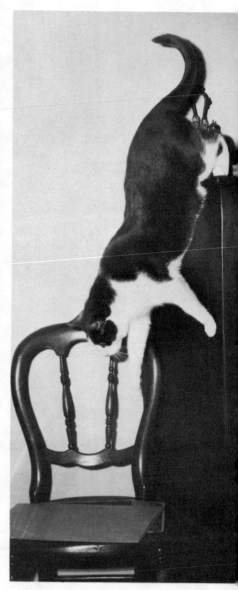

If you really want to know how your cat moves, reach for pictures that stop motion. The strobe attachment for my camera caught this jump in midair. Light walls acted as reflectors. When using strobe, regardless of written instructions, make tests on exposure times and light stops, record each shot, and determine the right settings for your camera in your shooting situation. Camera setting for these shots, 250/*f*16.

You must learn how to anticipate what your cat is going to do. Here Pete has sighted "prey" of some kind and is ready to jump. If you are ready to shoot when your cat is ready to jump, or run, or play, you will be able to get the action shots you want.

If you have a ham actor in your family, invite his cooperation. My Pete is just such a one. He performs on camera if I set the stage. Your pet may be equally cooperative.

This, I am told by photographers much wiser than I, is an extraordinary picture. Nothing unusual about a cat who likes to preen before a mirror. Unusual in the eye reflection which caught the flash of an electronic flash. This one I cannot tell you how to duplicate.

Hunting pictures are hard to come by, for the cat traditionally hunts alone. If you locate your pet's favorite stalking grounds, you can zero in with a telescopic lens.

Most cat pictures are taken head-on, with the theory that face and eyes are most interesting. I recommend some tail-on shots. Big Boy's tail is one of his greatest charms. Would that I had one so beautiful . . .

Existing light, often called available light, gives you some of the most natural and artistic of photographs. Use the try-and-fail method until you capture the technique, but remember that a light meter is an absolute essential for this kind of indoor shooting. Camera setting, 250/f8.

If you want good portrait shots of your cat, lay something down that you wear regularly. Immediately a cat will move in as Big Boy has on my old sport coat. This is another strobe shot. Notice how the detail of the eyes is retained. Even a shy cat will not wince away from strobe as he does from flash.

INDEX